TORPEDO LEADER
ON MALTA

TORPEDO LEADER
ON MALTA

WING COMMANDER PATRICK GIBBS, DSO, DFC AND BAR

GRUB STREET · LONDON

First published in 1992 in hardback by
Grub Street, The Basement,
10 Chivalry Road, London SW11 1HT

This paperback edition first published 2002
Copyright © 2002 Grub Street, London
Text copyright © Patrick Gibbs

Map by Robert Franks

British Library Cataloguing in Publication Data
Gibbs, Patrick
  Torpedo leader on Malta
  1. Gibbs, Patrick 2. Great Britain. Royal Air Force – History
  3. World War, 1939-1945 4. World War, 1939-1945 – Aerial
  operations, British
  I. Title
  940.5′423′092

ISBN 1-902304-83-7

Edited by John Davies

Typeset by Pearl Graphics, Hemel Hempstead

Printed and bound in Great Britain by
Biddles Ltd, Guildford and King's Lynn

With thanks to Roy Nesbit, Roger Haywood and
especially Norman Franks

CONTENTS

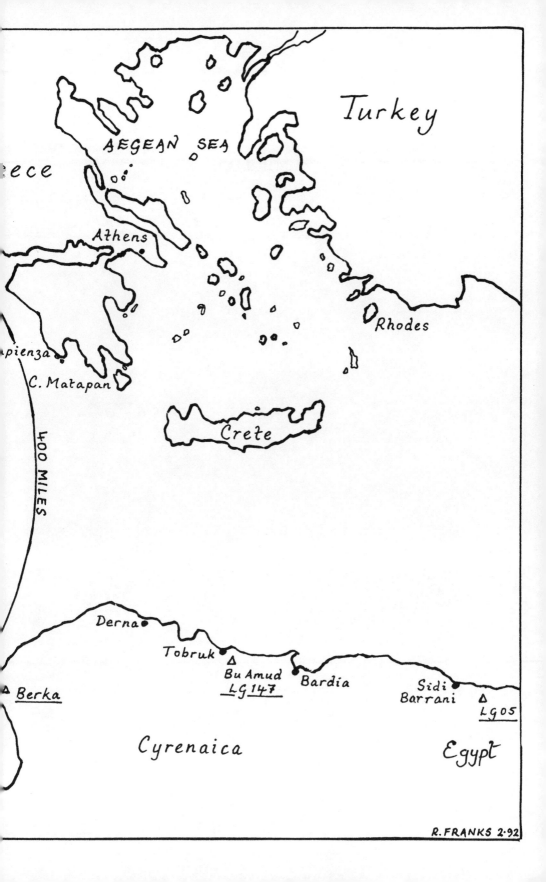

Turkey

AEGEAN SEA

eece

Athens

pienza

C. Matapan

Rhodes

400 MILES

Crete

Derna

Tobruk △

Bu Amud
LG 147

Bardia

Sidi
Barrani

△
LG 05

△ Berka

Cyrenaica

Egypt

R. FRANKS 2·92

FOR JANE

CHAPTER I

LOOKING BACK

THIS is success, that was failure. Such is my verdict on my two tours of operational flying, the first carried out from England, the second from Malta. Success followed failure; that is the order in which I like to see them. History may well ignore completely the desultory operations of the first tour, but it should tell posterity that in the summer of 1942 Malta won a significant battle, a battle which it fought in the air over sea for land; that land was Egypt.

Air operations have a balance sheet, a profit and loss account at the foot of which peace has drawn a concluding line. The columns showing effort expended will be balanced against the effect achieved, and the results subjected to the analysis and cold interpretation of air strategists. Were offensive fighter sweeps justified in that critical third year of war? Should more aircraft have been employed in the anti-submarine campaign or should the policy have been to maintain the 'Thousand' bomber raids just begun? Was it a correct decision to concentrate on a night rather than a day bombing offensive?

Time may answer fully these remote, academic questions, but for the benefit of strategists only; pilots were not concerned. It never occurred to them that an operation which sends an aircraft into the air with a chance of making contact with the enemy was not worthwhile; it always seemed so to them. Squadrons fought little wars of their own, making much of every victory, wishfully forgetting disaster; it was the way to fight and they knew it. In a squadron there was no looking forward into a doubtful future, nor yet any attempt to interpret the past; an active present entirely filled the mind. Success was married curiously to failure, and both lived happily together as life and death. A squadron's missing pilots were never seen as a lengthening

funeral column, a continual reminder of danger and bad luck, but as
a band of friendly ghosts who stood on the tarmac as aircraft took off,
smiling encouragement. They were remembered as living, flying and
fighting, never thought of as dead. They never asked the question "Is
it worthwhile—this time?" as they climbed into their aircraft for the
last flight, nor did their successors; to them the answer was so obvious:
of course it was.

Yet when some operations are viewed with detachment, their worth
is not always apparent; success cannot be judged solely on the damage
wrought, nor failure on the losses sustained. A fighter squadron shoots
down three of the enemy with no loss to itself; a force of night bombers
destroys a factory, losing a single aircraft; a lone Coastal Command
pilot attacks a submarine and returns safely to his base. It needs no
balance sheet to assess the worth of these operations, it is unquestion-
able. But there were many other less publicised activities continuing
steadily but on such a small scale that their effectiveness is not always
apparent. "What did we do?" is the searching question I hardly dare
to ask about the work of my squadron in England, for I feel deep
down in my heart that the answer is a disillusioning negative; for
considerable effort we achieved very, very little.

In the autumn of 1940 and summer of 1941 I was a Flight Commander in No 22 Beaufort Squadron of Coastal Command; the intervening
winter I spent in hospital recovering from injuries, the result of a
careless night flying accident. The Beaufort is a torpedo carrier, and
the squadron's true role was to attack shipping. However, this aircraft
can carry either a load of bombs or a mine as alternatives to the
torpedo, and during my first months in the squadron we were regularly
called upon for such diverse operations as patrols at night over enemy
aerodromes, the night bombing of submarine bases and laying mines
outside enemy harbours. We made attacks on shipping, but were
unable to specialise in them. At this time there was a shortage of
aircraft; the war was hardly a year old, and neither the aircraft industry
nor RAF training had yet started to produce jointly that flow of aircraft and crews which was later to surprise the enemy. There were
many tasks to be accomplished and few squadrons available to under-
take them, so the squadron's versatility was utilised to the full to
supplement operations by Bomber and Fighter Commands.

Later, as more specialised forces became available for these various
tasks, the squadron was able to revert to its true role of attacking ships
with torpedoes. So while the first wartime entries in my flying log book
record such widely differing operations as 'intruders' over Northern
French aerodromes, night attacks on Bremerhaven and Lorient with

bombs, and the day bombing of the harbour at Zeebrugge, later pages contain only accounts of flights on which we searched for, and sometimes attacked, enemy shipping.

Our normal method of operating was to send out small formations in daylight under cover of low cloud, and also aircraft singly on moonlight nights, to search for and attack any torpedo target. These operations, called 'Rovers', were intended to be little more than an offensive reconnaissance of enemy shipping routes. Very occasionally the squadron would be ordered to send out a force of aircraft on a specific mission to attack a single ship, or perhaps a convoy, which had been sighted by an independent reconnaissance aircraft, but usually we combined reconnaissance with the strike, finding and promptly attacking our own targets.

These targets were merchant vessels steaming off the Norwegian, Dutch and Belgian coasts, and in the Channel; they were often in convoy, usually strongly escorted by flak ships, sometimes protected by fighters, and always steaming very close to a friendly shore where fighter squadrons waited on their aerodromes ready to answer a call for protection.

Throughout my year in 22 Squadron the enemy was steadily improving the efficiency of his radiolocation system, and by it receiving more and more reliable warning of aircraft approaching his coast. A Beaufort was, at this time, one of the fastest aircraft outside Fighter Command, but its speed was no match for the enemy's single-seater fighters, nor was the fire power of its twin-gun turret an adequate reply to their cannon. Not only would a Beaufort always be out-fought in an engagement with fighters, but also outnumbered, for the fighter force which protected the enemy coastline was naturally bigger than any we could send at this time solely to attack shipping. So we operated in daylight only when the enemy coast was covered by a layer of low cloud in which our aircraft could seek refuge if chased by fighters. Nevertheless, in spite of careful use of cloud cover, our small formations of two or three Beauforts—operating in daylight—sustained regular losses from fighter attack. If fighters did not intercept the force and claim a victim before the target was found, flak might do their work.

For the enemy did not place implicit trust in his fighter defences alone to protect his shipping from air attack, but armed his merchant ships heavily with multiple quick firing guns of small calibre, and disposed around them flak ships, small vessels mounted with a similar armament. Such a target could put up a formidable barrage of fire which, while not always claiming a hit on one of the attacking aircraft, invariably made the air so hot that a pilot was prevented from concentrating on the careful aim and precision of drop on which success depended.

Flying near the surface of the water to avoid radar detection, and under cover of low cloud, a formation of three Beauforts searches for shipping along an enemy coastline. The sky is watched continually for fighters, the sea for ships. After some minutes of this critical flying within sight and hearing of the enemy, a single merchant vessel, escorted by six flak ships, appears on the horizon ahead. The leader, spreading his formation for the attack, hopes wishfully in the long seconds separating him from the target, that he will achieve surprise, but his hopes are in vain; the attacking aircraft are sighted, tongues of flame belch from gun muzzles, puffs of black smoke fill the sky, and joining them are the intermittent silver lines drawn by tracer shells. The three Beauforts fly together into this thicket of tracer trajectories, steady for an agonising second to take aim, drop their torpedoes at some 60ft over the water, then race out of the white heat of fire into the comparative safety of long range. One aircraft is shot down, one of the torpedoes fails to run, while the white bubbly track of the third is seen to pass harmlessly ahead of its target. Fighters arrive on the scene just when the attacking aircraft might be thought safe and the two survivors climb for cloud or, if it is not within reach, fight a running engagement low over the water, making for home.

Such were our daylight operations, yet we loved them. We never gave a thought as to whether they were worthwhile; they seemed so. If aircraft were continually being lost, ships were occasionally sunk, and the success always obscured the failure.

A similar story can be told about bombing ships, a story of heavy casualties suffered for a doubtful return in success. Only two Beaufort squadrons were engaged in torpedo attacks throughout 1941, and their small scale offensive, directed principally against Norwegian coast and Frisian Island shipping, was insignificant compared with the low level bombing carried out by several Blenheim squadrons of Bomber Command and Hudsons of Coastal, the one operating in daylight, the other on moonlight nights.

A ship offers a small moving target, which is easily defended and difficult to hit either with torpedo or bomb. Just as a short range of drop was the key to the success of a torpedo attack, the result of a low level bombing attack was dependent on the low height at which the bombs were released. It will easily be understood that results, in the form of either a torpedo or bomb hit, were achieved at a considerable cost in casualties, and that inevitably in these operations, success walked hand in hand with failure. When ships were sunk, aircraft were lost, and the pilots of the missing aircraft were invariably the brave and the reckless who pressed home their attack. The reward for achievement might all too easily be death.

The ships which we attacked in these operations were not targets of first importance. Although interior communications in Germany, Holland and Northern France were being increasingly disrupted by air attack, there was no evidence that the enemy was being forced to depend on his shipping routes for transport of war materials; they could never hold for him the importance which our Atlantic lifeline held for us. There is no reason to think that even if the shipping routes along the enemy coasts could have been made unusable by repeated successful attacks from the air, the enemy would at this stage of the war have been seriously inconvenienced; the effort necessary to achieve such a result would have been out of all proportion to its worth, and it was rightly never made.

There was, in fact, at this time no planned offensive against enemy coastal shipping; it was not of sufficient importance to merit such attention when compared with other more urgent requirements. Squadrons equipped with suitable aircraft were allotted to the anti-shipping offensive only when they could be spared from other duties. The Blenheim squadrons, which attacked shipping, were not restricted to this work, but were employed more often in bombing harbours and aerodromes. The Hudsons normally operated against submarines, carried out reconnaissance flights, or escorted our own convoys; to strike at shipping was only an occasional task for them. Only two lonely Beaufort squadrons, Nos 22 and 42, were employed exclusively in operations against shipping, and this was more by accident than design for they were originally intended to operate not against merchant ships, but against naval vessels, for which their torpedoes were ideally suited. However, the enemy's capital ships persisted in remaining safely in harbour, or moved cunningly under cover of a dark night, on which it was impossible to launch a torpedo attack.

The Beaufort squadrons, in these first years of the war, were often ordered to move from their base and assemble at some convenient aerodrome where they would wait, expectantly and not a little nervously, for the news that a battleship was at sea; but it was news which never came. The *Tirpitz* and the *Prince Eugen*, the *Scharnhorst* and the *Gneisenau* sometimes showed signs of restlessness in their harbours, and occasionally changed their hiding place, but never made the expected dash for the Atlantic where they could have been such a menace to our convoys. Undoubtedly the Beaufort squadrons' most effective work was achieved not by their attacks on merchant ships in the face of fierce opposition, but in their unspectacular role of waiting on some convenient aerodrome in readiness to strike with all their weight at some enemy naval unit. The very existence of a menacing torpedo striking force must have been a deterrent to the enemy; at all events he never challenged us, and we won this important naval battle without a gun being fired or a torpedo dropped. In reality it was a significant victory fought against unknown opposition for the safety of our Atlantic convoys, but we did not see it like that; inactivity inspired recklessness, and we grew to hate the continual waiting for a target which never materialised, and to long for steady operations from which we could see a result.

When all was quiet in the enemy's harbours, with his battlecruisers safely in dock and showing no signs of moving, the Beaufort squadrons carried out a desultory, miniature offensive against merchant shipping. Ships were sunk, but in all probability the balance sheet will assess the worth of these operations not by the tonnage of shipping destroyed, but by the extent to which they caused the enemy to divert his resources from other, possibly more offensive employment. His Fighter squadrons were kept at readiness on coastal aerodromes, and sometimes a small standing patrol of single seaters would protect a convoy throughout the daylight hours. Merchant vessels and their attendant flak ships were mounted with many guns, and trained crews were needed to man them. A considerable effort was made by the enemy to defend his shipping against the very small scale offensive which the RAF carried out at its convenience.

In daylight Spitfire wings were starting to sweep the sky over Northern France; at night heavy bombers penetrated deep into the heart of enemy territory; and throughout night and day the submarine hunters of Coastal Command patrolled the approaches to our shores. These activities were the concern of the RAF at home in 1941, and protection of our own important convoys of far greater concern to Coastal Command than destruction of the enemy's coastal shipping.

Yet if anti-shipping was of small account in the strategical planning of the war, if a torpedo squadron's most important role was to offer a passive threat to enemy naval units, it could not seem so to us, the pilots who flew the aircraft, found the ships, penetrated their defences and launched our attack. If the worth of these operations was not to be valued in the destruction they wrought, but in the extent of their diversion of the enemy's effort, to us the sinking of merchant shipping appeared to be of immeasurable importance. Aircraft loaded with torpedoes were at hand, ships steamed along the opposite coast, and we, the pilots, strained at the leash of inactivity to reach them.

In our Beaufort squadron, the first of very few, there arose a restless, offensive spirit, nourished curiously on the extreme difficulty of our task, its admitted dangers and the opportunity it offered for individual success. Our operations were unsupported by any great drive outside the squadron, where they were not a first concern, but within the squadron the offensive spirit carried all before it. We fought an inspired little war of our own, whiling away the months in which no enemy battleship presented a target to justify our existence by operating—whenever conditions allowed—against merchant shipping. But we were too small a force to make an impression on the enemy's formidable defences; to achieve success an effort on the scale of the three major offensives was required; our small formations of three Beauforts flew out hopefully to an attack for which a force of thirty could not have been too strong. A reckless enthusiasm arose within the squadron, a thirst for achievement out of all proportion to its true worth; pilots were led into taking risks for which the inevitable penalty was exacted, but often not before spectacular feats had been performed. Cloud cover was ignored, torpedoes were dropped at suicidal range; pilots flew out into the fatal blue sky and sometimes, not content with the sufficient dangers of the shipping route, entered the enemy's strongly defended harbours in search of a target.

It was a gallant, indescribably gallant, effort inspired by the young and the brave, but inevitably it failed. Too many of our aircraft were missing, too few of our pilots survived; too few ships fell under their hand before they themselves fell. The squadron suffered heavy casualties for small achievement; it lost its little war.

But this harsh verdict on the worth of the squadron's work during my first tour is made neither from that detachment in which strategists may examine the balance sheet, nor under the spell of that unquestioning spirit which sustained the squadron through these operations; it is made under the strong influence of a significant and successful anti-shipping campaign carried out later in the Mediterranean, in comparison with which our desultory operations in the North Sea must inevitably appear an insignificant failure.

When the time came for me to leave 22 Squadron in the autumn of 1941, with the award of a DFC and the rank of S/Ldr, I was one of the very few pilots to have survived a tour of torpedo operations; yet, strangely, I did not know whether to rejoice or be sad at the circumstances which had made me a lonely survivor. The squadron had suffered its heaviest losses during the winter months in which I had been lying impatiently but safely in hospital. I knew that the crash, which so nearly took my life, had indirectly saved it. Not only had it caused me to be absent from the squadron at a time when the chances of surviving even for a few weeks were remote, but it had also given me several idle months to consider dispassionately the nature of the squadron's work. As I lay in hospital, letters had reached me from the squadron giving details of operations and incidental accounts of the latest casualties; I read and I learnt. Later, when I returned to the squadron, I was at first unable to fly and was thus presented with an opportunity of studying at first hand, but with less detachment, the operations to which I knew I would soon be returning.

This review which I was able to make, first from the remoteness of hospital, later in actual contact with operational flying, resulted in no startling discovery. It produced no infallible key to success, nor yet a cure for the disease from which our pilots died; the unsatisfactory conclusion which I reached was that luck played the leading part in deciding a pilot's fate. This finding might have inspired a fatalistic outlook, but for a lesser fact which emerged from this casual inquiry; luck could be courted; it would never deputise for skill, but it might be persuaded to walk hand in hand with it through danger. It seemed to me that careful attention to the detail of individual operations not only improved their chances of success, but also the pilot's chances of survival. It never remotely crossed my mind at this time that the work of the squadron was comparatively unimportant; I was a pilot, not a strategist, and the problem of achieving success within my limited horizon was the one I was intent on solving. My object was to sink ships and remain alive to sink more ships.

So when I returned to operations I worked on the solution of the problems they offered to a greater extent than any of our pilots had done previously, hoping by doing so to enlist luck to fly with me and fight on my side. I studied the intelligence reports, watched carefully the cloud under which I flew, and varied the tactics of our attack. While the summer months of 1941 passed, I remained, surprisingly, alive, flying along under hostile cliffs, a Beaufort on either side, searching for ships which were sometimes found and occasionally sunk. The careful attention to detail was repaid, luck played its part and I finished my tour of operations to retire to the safety of a flying instructor's appointment, which was the only one offered.

But I did not feel relief at the newly gained security which I should have done; instead a growing feeling of dissatisfaction arose within me at the little the squadron had achieved. While actually taking part in operations it had seemed that we were setting the world on fire with our hazardous daylight torpedo attacks. But in detachment I began to see the picture in its true colours; it was not good to look upon. If some ships lay at the bottom of the sea, my friends and their crews were there also. If the dead had once appeared to wave encouragement, they did so no longer; instead I could feel continually their arms reaching up from their graves beneath the seas, reaching up to draw me down. I was removed from the influence of the unthinking spirit which had supported me through a year of fighting. If the spirit of the squadron had been a restless one, I myself had personified that restlessness, initiating operations, leading attacks and often taking those risks which I censured in others. I might once have reviewed the problems with detachment, I might have brought careful calculation to bear on their solution, but I could not fight with such cold dispassion. The detailed planning of a flight, the sifting of vital intelligence information, and the actual critical flying by day within sight and hearing of the enemy, had entirely filled my life. It seemed the only work which was worthwhile; without it, life seemed empty.

With confusion in my mind, I became profoundly unhappy at the prospect of instructing, so unhappy that I could not even simulate that enthusiasm without which an instructor must fail to inspire his pupils' flying. I would climb reluctantly into the cockpit and gaze with aversion at the instruments of the aircraft I had once loved; the roar of its engines, which had always been sweet music in my ears, now sawed on the edge of my nerves. The brightest moonlight night appeared pitch black if I were to fly in it. Had I remained as an instructor, I must have reproduced a series of pupils who were dead long before they were killed for, without the drug on which I had lived, I myself was dead in all but fact. Desperately I looked around for escape.

More unhappy in safety than I had ever been in danger, remote from the whirlpool of operations through which I had swum, I forgot wishfully the risks, the over-long casualty lists and the many occasions when only luck had saved me; I remembered success to the exclusion of failure, recalled the thrills of the game, and longed to return to the fight. Yet I had no wish to return to the seemingly insignificant operations which I had just left; if I were to fight again, make the great effort to achieve success, and suffer the inevitable losses from those at my side, the cost must be balanced by the gain, the operations would have to be rewarded by success.

But how to achieve this became an increasingly urgent question. For the refusal of a posting, which my disinclination to instruct amounted to, was a court martial offence; and I was by no means well received at HQ Coastal Command to which I was summoned, nor were the arguments I sought to present. These were, simply, that the failure of anti-shipping operations on enemy coasts in Europe, such as had occupied my first tour of flying duty, was due entirely to lack of proper central organisation.

There was no staff officer at HQ Coastal Command in charge of these operations, nor one at any of the three subsidiary Groups each commanded by an Air Vice Marshal. The over-riding concern of Coastal Command was with anti-submarine operations which, in those days before the introduction of the Leigh Light, tended to be somewhat unrewarding, involving as they did much flying of patrols over vast areas of sea with few sightings and even fewer sinkings.

Small wonder that the AOC of Coastal Command during my time, the genial Air Marshal 'Ginger' Bowhill, was said to walk into his operations room of a morning and, knowing all too well that his many Hudsons and Ansons out on anti-submarine patrol were unlikely to produce any excitement, would ask his controller what he was doing with his 'strike'.

This, of course, consisted of such Beauforts as were serviceable, and the result of his inquiry would be some discussion by telephone between his controller and one of the Beaufort squadron commanders. The result, if conditions were favourable, would be the dispatch of a Beaufort or two, loaded with their torpedoes, to search for a suitable target on the Dutch or Norwegian coasts.

This, to my mind, was a gross misuse of a small but highly trained force which should have been carefully conserved, not dissipated in this manner, and which with monotonous regularity kept losing crews and aircraft without sinking any worthwhile targets.

In any case, a single torpedo dropped from a Beaufort had small chance of finding its target, one reason being that it was a very temperamental weapon, another that it was never intended to be dropped singly, three running together being considered the minimum to give a chance of a hit.

A third reason was that there was no equivalent of a gun sight by which to aim the torpedo. This was done by pointing the aircraft at the moment of drop some distance ahead of the target to allow for its speed, which had to be estimated, and for the time taken by the torpedo to reach it. In fact it was entirely a matter of visual judgement by the pilot, usually in conditions highly unfavourable to concentration.

In contrast, the navy usually fired two or more precision-aimed torpedoes from such a stable platform as a submarine in order to ensure a hit, whereas a Beaufort dropping at a speed of not more than 140 knots at 60ft above the water could hardly be described as a stable platform, especially when under heavy fire at the short range of 800 yards, which was specified.

Nor could the torpedo be expected to behave as it did for the navy for which it had been designed in the early years of the century; for the torpedo the RAF used was the same old article, somewhat crudely modified to be sent into the water at higher speeds and a greater height, with a device known as 'drum control' to ensure the entry was nose first.

In fact this torpedo was wretchedly unreliable, and instead of running straight and true was apt to describe a circle, as shown by several photographs of attacks in existence. How enviable were the Japanese, by comparison, with their specially designed aerial torpedo which showed its worth at Pearl Harbour and elsewhere.

Not just three of our erratic torpedoes, but three times that number were really required to be running together towards a target if dropped from Beauforts. In fact, these aircraft should have operated not in penny numbers but as a force, and since nine or a dozen aircraft in formation could hardly be sent off without a known objective, their target should first be located by reconnaissance.

My suggestion to HQ Coastal Command was that their Beaufort squadrons should, in fact, be employed in this way, and that there should be a staff officer at Command or Group who understood anti-shipping operations. Preferably at HQ Coastal Command, I might have added, since these headquarters were at Stanmore in North London. An appointment there would have suited all my ambitions for at Rickmansworth, nearby, lived the girl who had powerfully engaged my affections during my first tour of flying—a young actress making some mark on the London stage.

These suggestions for radical changes fell on very stony ground indeed, only to appear justified when *Scharnhorst* and *Gneisenau* swept up the channel unscathed a few months later, by which time I was out of the country, most conveniently unable to give my views to the investigation which followed this failure.

I had foreseen this move by the battlecruisers when, during my time with 22 Squadron, two destroyers had run at full speed from Brest to Hamburg. Surely this was a 'dummy run' to test our defences and fighter cover, but no one on the staff at Coastal Command would listen to this idea; so just as our six Beauforts, led by myself with a strong fighter escort, missed the destroyers, so did a full Beaufort squadron fail against the battlecruisers.

Understandably, given my 'insubordinate' views, the authorities wanted me out of the way, seeking to solve their difficulties by sending me on indefinite leave. Such inactivity hardly suited me, and it was I, in the end, who broke the deadlock by proposing a posting to the Middle East which would, as so evidently desired, put me out of sight and mind.

I speculated—a pure guess, founded on no first hand information but on a premonition—that I should find the important anti-shipping operations for which I was searching in the Mediterranean. I realised, vaguely, that since the enemy had an army in North Africa, he must be keeping it supplied by means of shipping crossing the Mediterranean from Europe. I had no knowledge of the character of this shipping, whether it sailed as single ships or in convoy, if it was escorted, what route it took or what ports it used, but I imagined that strategically it must be important, since it was the only line of communication between an army and its base. It was this importance which appealed to me; neither fighter sweeps, night bombing, nor an anti-submarine campaign could be the key to victory in the African war; it was anti-shipping which must turn the tables.

Here then was the theatre, the play and my part, the lead of a Beaufort squadron in attacks on enemy shipping in the Mediterranean. How I reached that far-off theatre, persuaded the authorities not only to present an unwritten play, but to give me the lead, and how that play came to be written line by line, is the story I tell.

CHAPTER II

DISILLUSION IN CAIRO

AS I walked home through the London streets long after midnight, the realisation that I did not, after all, want to leave this country sank into my already confused mind. I had made this discovery only an hour before when, as I sat in front of a glowing fire in the warmth of a comfortable room, at Rickmansworth, a voice had asked "Patrick, do you really want to go?" a question which I had answered by slowly shaking my head; no, apparently I did not want to go, but until that moment I had not known it. Now, walking home from Baker Street tube station in the solitude of the night I became quite certain of the answer; I did not want to go at all. Why had I not been content to remain as an instructor? Why had I not accepted that training staff appointment which had been offered instead? Why had I struggled to obtain a posting to the Middle East until the authorities, wearying of the incomprehensible attitude of a recalcitrant instructor, had gladly sent me packing. Searching my mind, walking in the night, I could find no answers to these questions which a few days, even a few hours before, would never have been asked. The next day I was to embark; that night I had been saying goodbye.

For two whole months I had been on leave at home. The pilot, who appeared incapable of instructing and was unwilling to take the postings which were offered, posed a problem to the authorities which they had temporarily shelved by sending him on leave.

When the signal sending me to the Middle East arrived I welcomed it, for this was the posting I had asked for. It offered not only an escape from an atmosphere which for me was laden with unwelcome memories, but also the novelty of fighting in the air over a strange theatre of war. Until this last evening I had been steadily looking forward to going East, not with that fanatical ambition which had led me to move heaven and earth for the posting, but with a natural enthusiasm inspired by love of adventure. Buying khaki shirts and shorts, a sleeping bag and camp kit, had been exciting experiences; asking questions of friends just returned from the desert and listening to their accounts of the life, had increased that excitement.

As the time to embark drew nearer, I felt I could not reach the land of my choice too soon. I had imagined that I might go abroad free to fight and to forget. I had thought there was nothing in England I wished to remember, but now, at this late hour of my last night, I knew that I was irretrievably wrong; there was something I did not wish to forget.

Saying goodbye to someone I did not know very well, but whom I had suddenly, at the last moment, realised I wanted to know better, much better, had not been easy. How could I explain the fact that I was going at my own request; how could I deny my enthusiasm for the new posting of a few weeks ago, or account for my sudden change of heart. It was beyond me; I could do nothing, except say goodbye. "You'll come back, won't you, Patrick, you'll be back soon?" I had been asked on leaving. "Of course I shall" I answered; then encouraged a little by this unexpected interest, I took the hands which rested on the gate between us, and holding them tightly in an effort to lend conviction to words in which I felt no confidence, added "I'll be back before Christmas". And so I had said goodbye, with a promise.

The wind blew down Baker Street; it blew round and round in Portman Square, it blew up Park Lane, as I walked home. Unbounded by railings, Hyde Park seemed to be a country wood stretching white with frost into the darkness. Voices shouted hoarsely and in vain for taxis; traffic lights winked from red to yellow to green, to no purpose. The night sky was clear and starlit, but a mist floated near the ground.

I did not want to end that walk in the night; I did not want to start the journey of the next day. I was happy in a new and confusing sensation which made me see and hear things around me to which I had been blind and deaf; the final spark of a desire to live had come to put an end to an unsettling period of aimlessness and indifference.

The voyage out around the Cape in the P & O Liner *Otranto* was the most pleasant and leisurely cruise imaginable. Most pilots going to the Middle East flew out, and the flight was considered an operational trip; however, I had not completed the six months' rest between tours of operational flying which the regulations demanded; I had finished my first spell at the end of September, and so could not start operating again until the end of March. It was therefore an obvious decision to send me by ship, and one with which I certainly had no quarrel.

January 1942 was passed in the Atlantic, with a call at Freetown on the West African coast; in February we steamed into the Indian Ocean, interrupting the cruise with four exciting days spent in harbour at Durban. March came at last to find the ship steaming up the Red Sea from Aden, the voyage reluctantly nearing an end.

The seemingly endless chain of days spent out of the sight and hearing of aircraft, the salt air and sunshine, the remoteness of the far-off war, all conspired to bring forgetfulness and strength. These four months of rest, spent at first on leave, then at sea, did for me exactly what the same months of the previous year had done; those months, which I spent in hospital, had sown the seed of success.

By the time Suez was reached, I had experienced just enough of this uneventful life to make me wish for one of greater activity. The stipulated six months' rest was nearly over, and I was ready to start operational flying immediately. Quite how many Beaufort squadrons there were in the Middle East I did not know, but I knew that aircraft and crews had been flying out steadily since the previous summer, and it seemed likely that several squadrons would be formed and operating. I had assumed that a large air force was operating in the Middle East, and that in one of the many squadrons of this large air force there would be a vacancy for an experienced pilot; if not as a Squadron Commander, than as a Flight Commander, if not in a Beaufort squadron, then in some other similar unit carrying out offensive operations.

But I was quite wrong in my conception of the size of the air force fighting the desert war; I was to discover that it was at this time microscopic. The front line itself was held by two or three fighter wings, a handful of day bomber squadrons equipped with Bostons and a few army co-operation squadrons flying Hurricanes. The night bombing was carried out by four Wellington squadrons, operating from the rear, and all the coastal activities were being attended to by a few miscellaneous squadrons so far below strength in aircraft that they were squadrons in name only. The discovery of the small size of our air force was not made until I had been in Egypt for several weeks, but the result of my misconception was soon felt. I was to find that a Beaufort pilot, no matter how experienced, was not wanted.

At the Reception Unit to which the aircrews of the convoy had been sent on disembarking, speculation was rife as to what postings we should be given. Some crews had come out from England as members of a complete squadron whose aircraft had either been flown out by other crews or sent by sea in packing cases; these lucky ones only awaited the order to move to their squadron's base. But the majority were, like myself, unattached and awaiting posting. At first the future did not cause any anxiety. I was in a strange country of which I could see the endless stretches of sand, occasional camels and, of course, the inevitable palm trees; the present was absorbing in its novelty, which I explored with a traveller's curiosity.

But the days passed gradually more slowly as the novelty wore thin, until a whole week had passed without any news of a posting. We explored the nearest town, Ismailia, showed surprise at the cold March weather, wrote first letters home and felt homesick. We also heard rumours; disturbing reports were circulated that there were few flying vacancies available and that we were likely to remain idle in the 'pool', not for weeks but for months; it was even rumoured that the crews brought out by earlier convoys had not yet been absorbed.

At the end of the week I was summoned to the Headquarters of the RAF in the Middle East for an interview with the posting staff, and set off in high spirits to cover the sixty miles to Cairo by car. In spite of the unsettling rumours which had spread through the Reception Unit, I was still confident of being offered a flying appointment. Arriving at HQ in Cairo, I showed my pass to the sentry at the gate, bounded happily up the stairs and after making my presence known, sat down to wait impatiently outside an office whose door bore the notice 'Postings of aircrews'. I thought that at one word I would be removed from the idleness of waiting into the activity of the desert war, and at first it seemed that this would happen.

The staff officer questioned me on my experience, confirmed that I had all but completed my six months' rest and made a few notes on his blotting paper with typical staff efficiency. He then selected one of a battery of telephones on his desk and spoke to No 201 Group, which was the local 'Coastal Command' situated at Alexandria, and offered to the posting staff there a Squadron Leader with Beaufort experience in England. I listened with growing uneasiness to the lengthy and rather guarded conversation which followed, for it appeared that I was being shuttled backwards and forwards on the telephone line between Cairo and Alexandria, and that neither exchange wanted me. In the end Command appropriately triumphed over Group, and although nothing was settled, I was to go to Alexandria for an interview. "I'm sure they'll find something for you" were the staff officer's parting words, spoken in the manner of a doctor reassuring an anxious patient, but by this time I myself was far from certain; I was beginning to have doubts.

That night I spent in Cairo, wondering if I really liked the tinned beer, if the city was always so crowded that a dormitory bed, not a room, was all that could be expected of its hotels, and also wondering—not very confidently—what the future might hold. But the next day I set out on the train journey to Alexandria with the same optimism as on the previous day I had set out for Cairo; it was unimaginable that 201 Group would not want me.

At Alexandria I succeeded in finding a room in an hotel, for it was less crowded than Cairo, and after exploring the town, sat around feeling rather lonely. Two months' leave, the long voyage out and the idle days spent at the Reception Unit had made me impatient for activity; the rumours I had heard and the result of the interview in Cairo made me wonder if I was to have it.

The next morning I made my way to the Group Headquarters, which occupied a building overlooking the harbour. Waves lapped beneath the windows of the office in which I waited, and outside the battleship *Queen Elizabeth* and cruiser *Valiant* could be seen, neither looking very happy as a result of some enemy mining activity. Several merchant vessels rested on the bottom at drunken angles, a reminder to me of the anti-shipping war which I had come out East to fight. But it seemed I was not allowed to fight it.

The postings staff listened, not very attentively, to a recital of my qualifications, then passed me on to the Air Staff, to whom I repeated my story, with some elaboration. Air Staff listened non-committally, promised nothing at all, and told me to return the next day for an interview with the Air Vice-Marshal commanding the Group. I left these unsatisfactory interviews very disappointed, but not really apprehensive about my future; however I soon was to be.

That evening I sat alone in the lounge of my hotel, a glass of the inevitable tinned beer in front of me, feeling a little suspicious at the result of the morning's interview and not very optimistic about the outcome of the one on the next day. Army officers, their battle dress covered in sand and eyes bloodshot from the dust of the road, passed through the lounge to start the first evening of their leave from the front. Pilots, some from the desert, others from aerodromes nearby in the Delta, passed through on their way to the bar, from which issued a steady hum of conversation punctuated by the clink of glasses and the popping of beer tins being opened. The general high spirits increased my depression. A suspicion was beginning to enter my mind that the struggle for my posting from England, the parting and the long journey out, had been made to no purpose.

Just as depression was setting in, and I was wondering whether to go to bed or join the throng at the bar, two Beaufort pilots walked in, Alastair Taylor and Tony Leaning, both of whom I had known at home. Empty tins accumulated on the table in front of us, glasses were filled and refilled, midnight came and still we were talking. The corner of the lounge became a Mess at home, with three pilots talking shop. Tony and Alastair interrupted each other with a succession of questions about home, while I plied them for information about the Middle East. How many Beaufort squadrons were there? Had they sunk many ships? Were there any vacancies? All these questions and many others were answered, but if I went to bed happy that night it was not on account of what I had learnt.

At breakfast the next morning I felt doubly depressed, in my head and my heart. A late bedtime and much beer combined to produce a splitting headache, and the information I had received the previous evening did nothing to raise my spirits. My worst suspicions concerning the future were confirmed, for the story I had been told of anti-shipping operations in the Middle East would have been laughable if I had been in a mood for comedy.

There was one solitary Beaufort squadron in Egypt, No 39, to which Alastair and Tony belonged; it was continually short of aircraft and at present over strength in crews. It already had a Commanding Officer and two Flight Commanders, Alastair being one, and so there was no vacancy for me. Instead of the steady anti-shipping offensive which I had expected, it appeared that operations were few and far between; the squadron had made no more than two torpedo attacks in the whole of its existence, one in January and the other on March 9th, only a few days before. Then Alastair had led a force of nine Beauforts against an Italian cruiser squadron escorting a northbound convoy; although a strong force of long-range fighters were protecting the ships, several hits had been scored without the loss of a single Beaufort. However, this operation was exceptional. Beauforts were in such short supply, their maintenance being so difficult on account of the sand, and made no easier by a shortage of spares, that the squadron could rarely produce more than two or three serviceable aircraft. For a special 'show' great efforts would be made, and after weeks of work on the aircraft, a small force of six or perhaps nine might be available. There was, apparently, an intention of forming a second Beaufort squadron at some vague date in the future, but this possibility was remote, since there were insufficient aircraft in Egypt to maintain one squadron, much less to form another.

It was with very little hope that I went that morning to keep my appointment with the Group Commander, and my pessimism was to prove well-founded. The Air Vice-Marshal was conciliatory but firm. He listened to my account of anti-shipping operations in England, talked himself about the difficulty of keeping his only Beaufort squadron up to strength in aircraft, and after a polite exchange of views which I could see would have only one conclusion, finally told me there was no vacancy for me in the Group.

But I was determined to go down fighting, and pressing my claim for a flying appointment as far as I dared, suggested that if I could not be posted to 39 Squadron, I should be attached to it. To this suggestion the Air Vice-Marshal remained adamant. His view was that the squadron was running efficiently under a Commanding Officer and Flight Commanders in whom he had confidence, and that my presence would achieve nothing, indeed it might easily upset a happy unit. This view was reasonable, and I left unwilling to let the matter rest, but with nothing more to say. I think the AVM must have seen my disappointment, for he volunteered the promise that when another Beaufort squadron was formed, at some unspecified date, I should be given command of a Flight. Meanwhile I was to return to Cairo, where he was sure the Posting Staff would find me a flying appointment; he was very sorry... I was dismissed.

The door closed behind me and on all my remaining illusions; I walked out of the building mechanically, unwilling to believe what in my heart I knew to be the truth; I felt like a beggar who had been refused a charity; I had come a long way to be unwanted.

My re-appearance at Headquarters in Cairo did nothing to ruffle the Posting Staff officer's smooth manner; he had, no doubt from long practice, acquired an imperturbable bedside manner to deal with patients such as I, but this time I was determined to be troublesome and no longer to be shuttled about the Middle East either up and down telephone wires, or in and out of offices, an unemployed pilot touting for a job. However my violent complaints, which had been carefully rehearsed with appropriate choice of strong language, were not immediately required. It transpired that my fate had been decided in my absence and that I was to be attached to the Air Staff at HQ, until a suitable flying vacancy occurred in 201 Group, an occurrence which I knew was remote not by weeks, but by months.

With unwilling resignation I went to the Air Staff offices to make my arrival known. There I was shown my office and taken in to see the Air Commodore under whom I was to work. At this interview, a last spark of fight reappeared in me. The sight of the desk I was to occupy, with its trays piled high with files and correspondence, the echo of typewriters tapping in nearby offices, and the formal atmosphere of Headquarters, so reminiscent of a city business and so different from the life I wanted, all conspired to give me the courage of desperation. I protested in measured terms at what I considered to be my poor treatment, but once more my request for a flying appointment was refused. The Air Commodore showed little sympathy with my aspirations and put me firmly in my place which was, he said, whether I liked it or not, to be at an office desk from nine o'clock in the morning until six at night for some months to come. I withdrew, dispirited and gloomily indignant, and sat smouldering for the rest of the morning at the hated desk, until one o'clock struck, the doors of my prison opened and I escaped.

As I walked at midday down the main street of Cairo, picturesquely called 'King of the Nile', the sun was shining from a clear blue sky, but its warmth did not bring me happiness. I passed on my way a Mosque, from whose tower an old, white-bearded man was calling the faithful to prayer in a thin, high voice. Bright red poinsettias were in bloom in Garden City, finely coloured carpets were displayed in the shops; but I was blind and deaf to the new sounds and colours of a strange city, for my thoughts were far away in England.

Although the sun beat fiercely and the sky overhead was an unclouded blue, I was still walking through that cold starlit January night on which I had said goodbye. My feet might have covered many thousand miles in the intervening weeks, but my mind had not kept pace with them. I still felt keenly the edge of the turbulent wind which blew through London's streets, saw clearly the ghostly trees of Hyde Park swallowed up in the low-lying mist and heard the hoarse voices which cried in the night. The hands which I had held on parting still clasped mine firmly, and the voice still asked me to come home.

How was I to explain in my letters why I was not fighting? How could I account for the fact that I was working in an office? How could I have said I would return before next Christmas, when I knew that the standard tour of duty overseas was three long years? I suddenly knew there were no answers to these questions, which I had thought would never be asked. I knew that I had been foolish in my speculation, and a little unlucky. That morning had been the first at my office desk: how many more were to follow, how many years to pass before I returned home?

CHAPTER III

ESCAPE TO THE DESERT

THE RAF Headquarters in the Middle East occupied a large block of converted flats in a district of Cairo known as Garden City. This name was, to my prejudiced mind, hardly justified by the little less dust and the little more green to be found there than anywhere else in Cairo. The Air Staff offices were on the third floor, and the three 'Ops' staff offices were next to each other, all facing west. From the balcony which they shared the Nile could be seen, and in the distance the desert stretched away to the horizon; beyond that horizon, three hundred miles away, was the front, but from the atmosphere of peace in these offices one would never have thought that battles were being fought there.

The Operations staff consisted of the Air Commodore, who had so firmly put me in my place, and three Wing Commanders each representing one type of operation, bombing, fighter and army co-operation, and known respectively as Ops 1, 2 and 3. Coastal operations had been on such a small scale in the Middle East that they had not previously been represented on the staff at all. When 201 Group had declined my services, Postings had offered me to the Senior Air Staff Officer who, having a spare desk in one of his offices, decided to give me the temporary appointment of representing coastal operations such as they were.

Ops 1, with whom I shared an office, had arrived on the same convoy as I had in another ship. He had served in a bomber squadron in England, but his heart was not in flying, nor yet in office work; it was in horses and the merry life associated with their pursuit. He regarded his desk telephones only as the means of conversation with other horse fanciers on local 'form', placing commissions with his bookmakers and arranging parties before the races, for the races and after the races. The trays on his desk accumulated files, some marked 'important', others 'urgent', which were transferred indiscriminately from the 'in' to the 'pending' tray, while the only document to receive serious and immediate attention was the racing page of the Cairo newspaper. Ops 1 was quite contented; he felt, no doubt, that the office gave a better headquarters for his particular 'operations' than a tent in the desert, and was only out of temper when someone would enquire for a lost file, which would invariably be found in the bottom of his 'pending' tray.

Ops 2 had come out from England on the convoy before mine with a vague promise that he would be given command of a fighter wing in the desert, a promise which had not been honoured. Since he had been working in an office in England for the last two years and, leaving a wife and family behind, had volunteered to go abroad only from the attraction of flying, he was a disillusioned man, reading files mechanically, dictating letters half-heartedly and generally giving the impression that he was serving a life sentence in this prison. I had no difficulty in sympathising with Ops 2.

Ops 3 did steady good work, and hated every minute of it. He had commanded an army co-operation squadron in three campaigns—in Eritrea, Libya and Greece—and so knew intimately the operations with which he dealt from the remoteness of his office. His squadron, flying first Lysanders and later Hurricanes, had a fine record to which his DFC bore witness. However, he had been in the Middle East for nearly three years, much of this time spent in the discomfort of front-line desert fighting, and he was a very tired man from whom it was almost impossible to raise a smile. He wanted not to fly again, nor to fight, but just to go home. He had not seen England since the outbreak of war, had sometimes been for months without letters, and his nearest approach to English fields had been the countryside of Greece through which his squadron had retreated from aerodrome to aerodrome until the sea was reached and they had escaped as best they could. He had been away a long time, he had fought, and he wanted now to go home. He worked and he waited.

Since mine was a new post very little work came my way. In the first half hour of the day a few files passed across my desk from left to right, from 'in' tray to 'out' tray, always jumping the 'pending'; an increasing number of files found their way from Ops 1's desk on to mine with which I was quite glad to deal, and very occasionally a bell would ring to summon me into the Air Commodore's office, where I would do my best to answer a question or more often volunteer to find out. But I could hardly consider my job essential, in fact my time was hardly occupied at all.

At first I was puzzled and surprised at the lack of urgency in the atmosphere at Headquarters; it might have been understandable to find inactivity in one of the other staffs more remote from flying, but in Air Staff, which I had expected to be the heart of operations, bustling day and night, it seemed inexplicable, and it worried me.

Eventually I began to realise that the responsibility for the air war in the Middle East was not resting on my shoulders, nor yet on anybody else's in the Air Staff; from my office in Headquarters I began to form a true conception of the war in the desert, which was as different from the vague notions I had harboured in England as green grass from desert sand.

The Italian army, in its initial advance in the summer of 1940, had come right forward to the Egyptian frontier at Mersa Matruh, little more than a hundred miles from Alexandria. It had been supported in the air by the modern Italian air force, with which we had nothing comparable in Egypt. Our air force was equipped largely with obsolete biplanes; Gloster Gladiators were the excellent but outmoded fighters and the ancient Vickers Victoria was the heavy bomber. This advance by the Italian army coincided with the withdrawal of our European army at Dunkerque and the subsequent Battle of Britain, so few squadrons could be spared from home for the Egyptian front. However, with all the help which our microscopic Middle East air force could give, General Wavell succeeded in driving the Italians back in disorder, and Egypt was temporarily safe. The senior Axis partner had then taken control of a situation which the Italians had grossly mishandled. General Rommel with his Afrika Korps crossed the Mediterranean to stem the retreat, since when the position had never been comfortable either for our army or for Egypt.

Rommel had at first held a line at Gazala, just west of Tobruk, but had been driven back in the previous winter to the El Agheila line, almost to Benghazi. However, this respite to Egypt's safety had been short lived, for the Afrika Korps almost immediately came forward once more with considerable weight of armour, and took up a position again on the Gazala line, this time not defensively but aggressively. In the meantime Greece had been lost, and with it much of the equipment that should have been now facing the enemy; Crete had fallen, giving the enemy air bases from which he could cover the whole Eastern Mediterranean; this was the situation in March, when I sat wonderingly and worried in my office in Cairo. Egypt had not felt so uncomfortable since the uncertainty of General Wavell's strategic retreat which had opened the desert war, and this discomfort was not without reason.

Although the Gladiators and Victorias—which had originally opposed the Italian advance—had now been replaced by more modern aircraft, the air force in the Middle East was still an unbelievably small force. England was building up her fighter strength, possibly with the intention of holding the air over a second front in Europe; Bomber Command at home was increasing the number of its squadrons and re-equipping them with the new four-engined aircraft in order to carry out intensive night attacks against German industry; Coastal Command was mustering all its resources to fight the critical war against submarines in the Atlantic. In spite of the great efforts made by the aircraft industry, there really were, at this time, no surplus forces in England to support the Middle East.

However, the immediate threat to Egypt was not underestimated by the Allied High Command; it was realised that a large, well equipped air force was needed to support the army at the front and oppose the increasing strength of the German air force in North Africa. Since England could not produce this large air force, a joint Anglo-American decision had been made that the Middle East should be supplied almost exclusively with American aircraft; the majority of these were to be sent by ship in packing cases to West Africa where they would be assembled and flown to Egypt, while others would fly directly across the Atlantic. A chain of aerodromes was built across Central Africa from the Gold Coast to the Sudan, arrangements were made to receive, assemble and ferry the American aircraft, and all appeared well for the future. However, some months were to pass before the Middle East was to feel the benefit of this arrangement; those months were the critical present.

While the RAF was waiting impatiently and nervously for the promised reinforcements, pilots were waiting no less impatiently, and rather angrily, for aircraft to fly. Either a miscalculation in the casualty rate had been made, or more likely the delay in the arrival of American aircraft was longer than expected, but whatever the reason, aircrews were pouring into Egypt, for whom there were no flying vacancies. Many of these were products of the Empire Air Training Scheme who had just completed their training at South African Flying Schools, and had come up to the Middle East full of enthusiasm to fight. Now their numbers accumulated in Reception Units without a chance of a posting to a flying appointment. I felt sorry for these crews without aircraft for I was in spirit one of them; I could sympathise with their discontent.

Conversations with the veteran Ops 3, who unsmilingly claimed he had fired the first shot in the desert war, the reading of reports, and information I received from friends, all painted a true picture of the situation before which my misconceptions faded away. I began to understand the small activity and lack of urgency which reigned in our Air Staff offices, which at first I had found so difficult to account for. The Group Headquarters, which were subsidiary to 'Command', made all the detailed decisions on the operation of their forces; they asked little from Headquarters except aircraft with which to carry out their many tasks, a request to which the only answer was a promise.

Office days passed slowly, weeks seemed interminable, yet the month came to an end, for March to become April and still find me sitting at the hated office desk. Blue uniform was discarded for khaki; more dust than ever blew in the streets and the Garden City became even less green. The sun beat down more fiercely, the pavements reflected its heat. The surrounding desert warmed for the Egyptian summer, and Cairo stifled in its breathless atmosphere. Office hours were now arranged to exclude the middle of the day, but as lunchtime drew near, the Ops staff would sit before their desks sweating in their shirt sleeves; tempers became frayed by the heat. The desert slowly became an oven, in which Cairo baked. I found I could no longer sleep at night, for I was still worried.

I could not live contentedly this Cairo life; it might offer comfort and safety, but I was continally comparing these advantages with the bare, hazardous existence which a desert squadron offered, and always finding the flying life infinitely preferable. In my hotel the grapefruit were bigger than footballs, tangerines as abundant as grapes, lumps of sugar were the size and shape of dominoes; Egyptian food was plentiful, but I had no appetite for it. Three hundred miles away there was the front, where armies were opposed; tanks clashed, guns fired and overhead aircraft flew and fought. An eggcup full of water and bully beef in a tent on some desert aerodrome would have tasted better to me than all the canned beer and fine food in a Cairo hotel. The unattainable appeared, as always, very attractive.

Having heard the grievances of the solitary Middle East Beaufort squadron at first hand from Tony and Alastair, I had been trying ever since I had been on the Air Staff to have some of them righted, but with little success. The main difficulty was a shortage of aircraft, and it was once again a question of supply. Beauforts were flown out to the Middle East from England by way of Gibraltar and Malta, or rather it was intended they should be, but in actual fact very few of them passed Malta.

Since the beginning of the year the enemy had steadily been increasing his raids on the Island, until by April great hordes of bombers and fighters were making incessant attacks throughout day and night. Many Beauforts took off from Gibraltar, but few left Malta. If one succeeded in landing safely on the dimly lit flare path, and this was a rare occurrence, it would almost certainly be damaged by bombing as it stood on the aerodrome while the crew snatched a few hours' sleep before flying on to Egypt.

Here was yet another reason for the shortage of aircraft in the Middle East; the air lifeline between England and the East was being cut by the raids on Malta, which were making this vital stepping stone difficult to use, causing squadrons in Egypt to be starved of aircraft and making it impossible to form new units. The very small numbers of aircraft which England was reluctantly sending East were being decimated before they reached their destination.

Beauforts were particularly unlucky in running the Malta gauntlet, since they were day-operating aircraft and their crews not very experienced in night flying. To have attempted to land at Malta at this time in daylight would have been suicide, for the sky over the Island, even the aerodrome circuit, was owned by the enemy, so all reinforcement aircraft were timed to arrive at night. Even then it was only possible to show a very dimly lit flare path, which had often to be switched out altogether in the face of a heavy night raid. The reinforcement Wellington crews, who were trained almost entirely at night, did not consider finding the Island in darkness or landing safely on its meagre flarepath an easy task; but the Beaufort pilots, who had little practice in night flying, were continually crashing their aircraft in a desperate attempt to land, and sometimes failing completely to find the Island. Those few who did land safely might awake from their few hours' sleep to find their aircraft riddled with bomb splinters, and their efforts worthless.

However, the Malta reinforcement route was only temporary, and it was intended eventually to send aircraft from England direct to West Africa, either by air or sea, where they could then join the promised flow of American aircraft across Central Africa; meanwhile the present extravagant method of reinforcement had to be retained while the organisation of the new route was progressing.

Beaufort crews, whose aircraft were crashed or blitzed at Malta, kept arriving in Egypt as passengers in some other aircraft, but aircraft, not crews, were wanted and they were sent to join the long list of unemployed in the 'Wastage Pool', which to my mind was no longer a pool, but rapidly becoming a lake. The situation at Malta might improve, or supply through the West African route might begin; meanwhile the solitary Beaufort squadron was chronically short of aircraft, and nothing could be done to help it. I knew I could do nothing; it worried me, but something else was beginning to worry me much more.

At first from boredom, later out of interest, I used each day to spend some time in Operations Room, reading the reports of the previous day's fighting. Ops Room was like a great confidential newspaper, with maps and blackboards kept up-to-date and notice boards bearing reports of the latest operations. News of the fighting at the front did not vary much from day to day, but it seemed that the enemy was steadily becoming stronger; a greater strength of tanks was being felt and patrols were becoming more offensive, probing our defences with armoured divisions. But the line at this time was considered stable; there was little serious fighting, and it was understood that our army was 'quietly confident'. In the air over the desert there was also no great activity; our day bombers made raids, our fighter wings covered them, and also made independent sweeps. The enemy air force was carrying out a similar programme; neither side could claim air superiority, but the enemy was offensive on the ground and so his air force operated offensively also. There was, in fact, a very evenly contested claim for the sky over the desert, but the sky over the sea went uncontested; it was undoubtedly the enemy's.

Since the fall of Crete and the subjugation of Malta by bombing, the enemy had become virtually the owner of the Mediterranean. Our naval forces were finding it impossible to operate in open sea in face of the strong opposition which the enemy could send against them. Since there was only one road and one single-track railway between Alexandria and the Western Desert, the main means of supply to the army in Libya was by coastal shipping, so great efforts were made to protect this route, efforts which took up all the resources not only of the Navy, but of 201 Group. The movements of our ships were watched by reconnaissance aircraft operating from Crete, and Alexandria itself was regularly covered by high flying aircraft which were difficult to intercept, so our naval forces could scarcely leave harbour without being challenged.

A cruiser squadron escorted a much needed convoy through to Malta in March, driving off a superior Italian naval force and surviving repeated attacks by aircraft, but such operations were exceptional and somewhat desperate. The survivors of this convoy, escorted to its destination at great risk, had been sunk in harbour almost immediately after arrival by determined bombing raids. As the end of April approached, the situation looked grim. It seemed as if Malta would fall, and that nothing could be done to help her. There was nothing light hearted about this war in the Middle East; we were losing it, and I could see one reason.

In the Operations Room were two maps, the larger showing broadly the general situation in the Mediterranean, the other giving in detail the latest information from the front. Positions of tank concentrations, the number and types of aircraft on the enemy's aerodromes, and news of his latest offensive sortie, all made interesting reading on the smaller map, but not nearly so interesting to me as some information on the other. There, almost every day, would be indicated some enemy convoy crossing the Mediterranean, whose position had been reported by our long-range reconnaissance aircraft. Typewritten slips of paper were pinned to the map in the position where the ships had last been seen, giving the number of ships, their course and speed. One merchant vessel of eight thousand tons, escorted by a single destroyer, is on its way to Benghazi; three merchant vessels, unescorted, steam southwards; a solitary ten thousand ton tanker crosses to the enemy. All went unopposed.

The enemy had a plan. He was preventing Malta from carrying out offensive operations, either with aircraft or naval forces, by a steady bombing of the aerodromes and harbour. He was making great efforts to prevent any convoys from reaching the Island, and it did seem that Malta, like Crete before it, would fall. The incessant bombing offensive was calling for a huge concentration of aircraft in Sicily, it was being costly in casualties, but it did ensure a free passage for ships to cross the Mediterranean with supplies for the North African army. Rommel was holding easily and contentedly a line which was not chosen by chance, but by design; the line which he held at Gazala was just far enough east to prevent our anti-shipping aircraft from reaching his convoys.

A Beaufort, operating from the furthest forward aerodrome, in Cyrenaica, had insufficient range to reach the shipping route and return to its base; only our long-range reconnaissance aircraft, carrying extra petrol tanks instead of a bomb load, could comfortably cover the Central Mediterranean, to bring back the tantalising reports which I read on the map. Even if a ship did appear within range, operating from a front-line aerodrome was far from easy. The enemy watched closely the coastal aerodromes near the front, and at any sign of an anti-shipping force concentrating, he might send over a bombing raid, or wait until the striking force was in the air, then send fighters to intercept it.

The enemy was undoubtedly in a very favourable position. Rommel was waiting patiently until he accumulated sufficient forces to advance, when he would come forward with full strength to take Egypt. That was the plan, as I saw it, and it appeared to be uninterrupted by anything we were doing. Our own heavy reinforcements came slowly by the long route round the Cape, our aircraft were promised but did not arrive. The army held the line precariously, helped by the small desert air force, while all the time Rommel was accumulating supplies which we could do little to prevent. Submarines operated, but with difficulty, in waters whose sky was swept by enemy reconnaissance aircraft; Wellingtons made a nightly trip to Benghazi, but I placed little faith in the night bombing of this well defended target to disrupt the enemy's communications. It seemed to me we were losing this war, and I worried about it.

As Cairo grew hotter, and the map became more depressing, I decided to escape from my office and visit 39 Squadron, which occupied an aerodrome on the Cairo-Alexandria road, called 'Landing Ground 87'. Some aircraft were available to staff officers at Communications Flight at Heliopolis aerodrome, where I arranged to borrow a Lysander. After being shown over the cockpit, for I had never flown a 'Lizzie' before, I taxied out for the first time over a sand aerodrome and took off rather carefully, since I had not flown at all for nearly six months. I was in the air over Egypt at last.

Landing Ground 87 was one of several almost identical aerodromes situated some twenty miles south of Alexandria and west of the road. They were nothing more than prepared patches of desert, levelled and cleared of scrub, with small villages of tents in one corner and aircraft dispersed in the desert nearby. After circling low over several of these landing grounds, looking for Beauforts, I eventually recognised their familiar shapes, and put my Lizzie down rather more firmly than gracefully on their aerodrome, my first landing on sand.

Tony, who was expecting my visit, came out on to the aerodrome to greet the strange aircraft which he had seen circling, and while he taxied the Lizzie away to a dispersal point in the desert, I walked over the soft sand through the colony of tents to make my presence known at the squadron Headquarters.

The CO of 39 Squadron was a Wing Commander to whom the running of a Torpedo Squadron was something of a novelty, for the whole of his long flying experience had been gained in Flying Boats. At first he seemed to regard my visit with suspicion, knowing perhaps that I would give anything for a chance to change places with him or one of his Flight Commanders, but after I had explained that I came from Headquarters only to enquire into his squadron's many difficulties, he became less guarded, and soon we were discussing agreeably the problems I knew so well.

No new facts emerged from this discussion, but when later I was talking with the squadron's crews over beers in the mess bar I received some information which puzzled me. I was already aware of the fact that the squadron had not made a sortie since March 9th, of which I had heard all the details from Tony and Alastair at our first meeting in 'Alex', but I learnt now for the first time that Group had ordered a large force to be prepared for some operation which was to take place shortly. Nobody seemed to know quite what Group had in mind, and knowing that Malta was impossible to use and the ships were otherwise out of reach, I thought it rather strange that the squadron should be preparing for an operation. However, conversation passed to another subject and I thought no more about it.

That night I lay on a spare camp bed in Tony's tent, the first night in the sleeping bag I had bought with such anticipation in London, and I slept soundly for the first time in many weeks. The next morning, I climbed into my Lizzie and flew unwillingly back to Heliopolis and the hated Cairo; I had achieved nothing at all, only seen enough of squadron life to make me more discontented than ever with my office desk. Admittedly, the squadron appeared to be in a better state than I had expected, with more aircraft available than usual, the result of several weeks of intensive maintenance effort uninterrupted by any operation, but it all seemed to be to no purpose; what could they do? I wondered.

A few days later, on a visit to Ops Room, I noticed an unusually large convoy indicated on the map: four large merchant ships escorted by destroyers were steaming southward within a hundred miles of Malta. The usual scale of air attack was being made on the Island, no less than one hundred and eighty aircraft of different kinds paying it a visit on the previous day. However I did not pay particular attention either to the size and position of the convoy or to the scale of the raids on Malta; such information was becoming usual, it was no longer worrying me.

The next day I glanced at the map again, but rather casually, for I was losing interest in this strategical war, of which I could only be a helpless spectator. The map was losing its appeal, and I had transferred my allegiance to a blackboard, which indicated the position of aircraft on the Central African reinforcement route. American aircraft were beginning to reach West Africa in steadily increasing numbers; some were being unpacked, others assembled, while a few were actually in the air and on their way; the blackboard showed a trickle, which would in time become a flow. Soon it would be possible to form new squadrons and re-equip old ones: the wastage lake would evaporate with relief into the air. Meanwhile it was a race for Egypt between the blackboard and the map, and I was beginning to prefer to look on the less depressing picture. But the casual glance which I gave the map that day immediately turned into a horrified, unbelieving stare; I stood still before it and gazed at tragedy.

Pinned to the position of the convoy, which I had noticed on the previous day, was a slip of paper bearing not the usual report sent back from a reconnaissance aircraft, but the astounding information that an attack had been made by Beauforts. Nine Beauforts had set out, three were safe. I recalled the evening spent with the squadron only a few days before, when I had wondered at the reason for preparing a force; here was the explanation clearly before me.

The map gave only the barest facts of the attack, but fuller reports of the previous day's operations were available, and these I read through very carefully. This was the first torpedo attack to be made since I had been on the Air Staff; questions would be asked about it which I would be expected to answer. As I read the detailed report on the operation from start to finish, I realised that to answer those questions was not going to be easy.

The convoy had been first sighted by a reconnaissance aircraft from Malta on the night before the attack. A Maryland, taking off from the desert early on the following morning, had found the convoy again, shadowed it and sent back reports of its position, course and speed. It was at this time about a hundred miles due east of Malta, steaming southwards, the position in which I had first seen it indicated on the Ops Room map. On receiving the Maryland's report, nine Beauforts, which had been flown up to the front at dawn, took off to attack the convoy with torpedoes, four Beaufighters accompanying them as fighter protection. The range of neither aircraft was sufficient for them to return to Egypt, and they were ordered to land at Malta after the attack.

The navigation had been inaccurate, and reaching the convoy's calculated position without any sign of his target, the leader had begun a search, flying backwards and forwards, steadily advancing and covering hundreds of square miles of sea. Eventually the Beaufighters, who had slightly less range than the Beauforts, had to leave their charge and make for Malta before their petrol ran out; meanwhile the Beauforts continued the search without their fighter escort. At last a trace of smoke had appeared on the horizon which led the striking force to their target, and it must have seemed for a moment that the leader's persistence was justified.

But the enemy was not taken unawares; the Maryland, which had shadowed the convoy for several hours during the morning, had no doubt been seen and aroused suspicion; the Beauforts had been searching so long in the vicinity of their target that their presence must also have been reported to the enemy. The result was that the little force of nine Beauforts no longer protected by even a small fighter escort, was met by a horde of single seaters which were not the convoy's normal fighter cover but had been sent out from Sicilian aerodromes especially to intercept the attackers.

Several of the Beaufort pilots fought their way towards the target and succeeded in dropping their torpedoes, but the odds against them were overwhelming. Very few of our pilots escaped from the fighters around the convoy, estimated to be a hundred strong, and of these few only three arrived safely at Malta. Having miraculously escaped from the convoy battle, the surviving Beauforts might reasonably have thought themselves safe, but on arriving at Malta they found the Island covered by a sweep of Messerschmitt 109s. Several of our aircraft were shot down into the sea within sight of their aerodrome; only three landed, and of these three only one was undamaged and able to fly back to Egypt the next day; that Beaufort was Tony's.

Nothing could conceal the fact that the operation had been a disaster; only one aircraft returned to Egypt of the nine which had set out. Several of the pilots with whom I spent the evening only a few days before had made their first and last attack. Everything possible had conspired to make the operation a failure. Indiscreet wireless messages from the reconnaissance aircraft, the over-long search by the striking force within sight of the enemy's reconnaissance, the ill-chosen position of attack within single-seater range of Sicily, and the decision of the leader to continue without fighter escort; all had been grave errors or misfortunes, for which a high price had been exacted. The attack on March 9th was considered a success, but this, on April 14th, was a failure; failure followed success, and that was not the order in which I liked to see them. I began to worry again, not over strategy this time, but over tactics.

The next day I was sitting at my desk, gazing blankly at the wall in front of me, wondering if I wanted to visit Ops Room and reaching the conclusion that I did not, when a file was brought in, marked "urgent". I glanced at the cover, moved it mechanically from the in tray to pending, and continued to brood on the disaster. I was in no mood for files; to me nothing was urgent but the demand for aircraft. I reflected bitterly that the Headquarters might be better occupied building great paper aircraft than writing so many valueless letters; I conjured up a vision of the Air Commodore busy with paper, scissors and glue; it was funny, but it did not make me smile.

At the other desk Ops 1 was working out the results of the previous day's racing, his pencil scribbling a mass of figures over the blotting pad. I thought I had better leave before I was rude to him, and decided to visit Ops 3, with whose unsmiling attitude I had something in common that morning. On my way to his office along the verandah, I looked in on Ops 2, who was reading the Cairo Times and thought the news pretty good. It appeared he never visited Ops Room, it was rather far away and he preferred the newspaper. I left hurriedly before I had time to explode and ask if he thought the loss of six Beaufort crews was good news.

Ops 3 was having some difficulty in writing a letter home; I thought I could guess why, and also for whom the letter was intended. I could understand his wanting to go home after being abroad for three years, after surviving three campaigns, while all the time somebody waited for him in England. No wonder he was finding that letter difficult to write, no wonder he could rarely raise a smile. I could sympathise with Ops 3 that morning, for I sometimes faced reality and asked myself the question: when shall I be going home? but never dared to face the true answer, always trying to satisfy myself with a vague repetition of the words "before Christmas", never daring to examine how that might be achieved. This was something else which worried me.

Not being able to help Ops 3 with a problem to which I had no solution, I decided to visit Ops Room, where I found the usual depressing picture, painted in the same drab colours. The large map showed enemy ships crossing the sea, their position reported by Marylands out on reconnaissance; the smaller map showed the enemy still holding the same line, still offensively, while the ownership of the air over the desert was still being evenly contested. The usual scale of air attack had been directed against Malta; a typewritten slip pinned to the Island read "188 JU87s, JU88s, ME109s..." I read no further, I had read the same report daily for a month. The blackboard indicating the position of reinforcement aircraft was a more encouraging document and showed a small but steady improvement; more Kittyhawks and more Bostons were reaching Egypt. I wondered grimly if Ops 1 would take any bets on this race.

My gloomy forebodings brought me to glance at another blackboard, this one indicating the number of aircraft in each squadron available for operations. If there were few squadrons in the Middle East, those few could produce a very meagre force of serviceable aircraft, and opposite the Beaufort squadron's number was a mocking "nought"; the eight aircraft which had been lost had only been raised after weeks of incessant maintenance work, and it would be many weeks before the squadron could make another attack.

I turned my back on the black picture which Ops Room presented and returned to my office, calling in to chat with Ops 3 on the way. He had just received his mail, and greeted me with one of his rare smiles; several envelopes of the same coloured paper and addressed with the same handwriting lay on his desk: his accumulated mail and the cause of his good humour. Somebody was still writing after three years; that was good news for him, it cheered me also, and I went on to my office with the intention of doing some work.

"Urgent" said the printed slip attached to the file; it was to my mind the only urgent matter I ever dealt with in that office. The file contained a brief minute from the Air Commodore, which read: "Inform me of the experience of the CO and Flight Commanders of the Beaufort squadron". I did not have to read twice to realise what this was all about; however, it did not ask for my views on the recent disaster, and I was glad, for I was uncertain what they were. I favoured a policy of attacking the reinforcement shipping whenever possible, but only if conditions were reasonable and certainly not if the odds against success were to be as heavy as in this last attack. The operation had needed strong forces, a position of attack outside enemy single-seater range, and a raid-free Malta. Group, who had organised the operation, had probably been making a desperate experiment in the use of the small forces available. No blame could be attached to the CO, or to either of his Flight Commanders, one of whom had been flying and was a casualty.

Writing my reply to the Air Commodore's minute, I suddenly connected the word "casualty" with "wastage", remembered the lake in which I was floating, and realised with a slight shudder down my spine and a contrary feeling of joy in my heart that this vacancy caused by the loss of a Beaufort Flight Commander was the one I had come out East to fill. I had come not to worry about matters of strategy which did not concern me, nor to criticise from the ease of an office chair the tactics of other leaders, but to replace this lost pilot, to use my experience where it would have most effect, and once again to be a pilot in a squadron, making much of every success, wishfully forgetting failure, fighting once more a little war.

It was my turn to be grinning as I went in to disturb Ops 3's careful letter reading and tell him what I had just done. I had sent a minute back to the Air Commodore, marked "Very urgent", answering briefly his question, pointing out that there was now a vacancy for a

Flight Commander in this particular squadron, and stating at some length my qualifications for the post. That night Ops 3 and I drank large quantities of beer; he felt he was almost in England, I felt I was already in a squadron. I slept soundly that night, and I no longer worried.

After several days of agonising waiting, in which I sneaked occasionally into the Air Commodore's office to watch the file's progress from the bottom to the top of his in tray, the answer came back to me. The file was not this time put in my pending tray, in fact it did not even reach the in tray before being snatched out of the clerk's hands. Would the 'old man' remember my protests of a few weeks ago at being tied to an office chair, would he remember the dignity with which he had told me that I could do more valuable work at Headquarters than in a squadron, or had he a sense of humour? It appeared that he had; a grim one. Written in his neat handwriting and signed with his illegible signature was a brief minute of a single line, which read: "Gibbs to go to the Beaufort squadron", and in brackets afterwards "What's left of it".

I passed the file round the Ops Staff, I cleared my trays and I said goodbye. I left with no backward glance at my office desk, at which I had done only one piece of real work, handling only one urgent file, but how carefully had that little matter been dealt with. I paid a last visit to Ops Room, where the map for the first time seemed to represent real land and sea, for I was to fly over them. The reinforcement blackboard showed a handful of Beauforts which would be ready within a week; I resolved to get them for my Flight. This was a day of days; the sun beat down and the city stifled, but it mattered not at all, for I had miraculously escaped from the purgatory of a staff appointment and was to fly in a squadron once more.

Walking home from Headquarters on air, I remembered light heartedly my last-minute reluctance to leave England, the heart-breaking interviews on my arrival in Egypt, each ending with less hope for the future than before, and the bitter disappointment at being given an office job. I forgot former worries, counted my blessings and knew I was outrageously lucky. I packed in my hotel, looking my last on comfort and fine food, and wrote a letter to England telling the exciting news; then deciding that a letter was inadequate for the occasion sent a cable. "Change of address" I wrote "Now No 39 Squadron".

CHAPTER IV

SETTLING IN SAND

39 SQUADRON, when I arrived in the last week of April, consisted of a collection of broken-down Beauforts and dispirited crews. On my visit to the squadron from Headquarters only a few weeks before, high spirits had abounded; through the preceding weeks the crews had been watching with satisfaction the number of serviceable aircraft increasing; they knew an operation was being planned, and remembering the success of March 9th when cruisers had been attacked and fighters encountered without loss, not one of them wished to be left out. But the disastrous operation of April 14th had wrought a change in the squadron; many of its best crews and leaders had been lost, the few survivors were shaken in confidence, and only one of the carefully prepared aircraft had returned. Sufficient aircraft to allow the squadron to operate would not be available for some weeks to come, and crews were looking forward to that time not with anticipation, but with doubt.

The enemy's ownership of the air over the sea was making operating against his ships with the small forces at our disposal fiendishly difficult. In England we had scarcely succeeded in outwitting enemy single seaters by flying always under a layer of low cloud, but here in the Mediterranean, the sun shone continually from a blue sky in which no cloud appeared; if fighters were met, it meant not an escape into friendly cloud, but a fight to the finish. In open sea the enemy's ships were nearly always protected by at least two or three long-range fighters, either Messerschmitt 110s or JU88s, and as they approached the North African coast, single seaters would be sent out to give additional cover. The attack on March 9th had shown that Beauforts could hold their own with long-range fighters in a running fight, but the result of the operation on April 14th confirmed a fact I already knew only too well, that small formations of unmanoeuvrable twin-engined aircraft were no match for the enemy's single seaters.

The enemy's supply ships were unlikely to come within a Beaufort's range until they were nearing the African coast, when they would always be found under an umbrella of the unwelcome single-engined fighters. Not only were the Beauforts certain to meet strong opposition over the target, but liable to be intercepted on the long flight westwards which they made to reach it, or even on their return from the attack. This flight had to be made parallel to the Cyrenaican coast, at this time held by the enemy; it was known that there were efficient radiolocation stations both on the African coast and in Crete, so the presence of aircraft flying westwards could not be hidden. A surface escort of two or three destroyers was usually found protecting a supply ship, but these were considered of small account in comparison with the air escort; it was fighters, not flak, which were the menace.

But it needs more than opposition and heavy losses to depress a squadron, and I looked around for the real reason for the lifeless spirit which had taken hold of our crews. It seemed to me that the very rarity of our operations was partly to blame; the squadron so seldom made an attack that opposition, danger and losses were not everyday occurrences and taken for granted, but rare happenings which, being almost unknown, were feared the more. In England we had operated at least once or twice a week; here, the squadron might make one attack in a month. Crews waited through these weeks of idleness, wondering exactly what the next operation might hold for them.

Inactivity under a hot sun did nothing to mend the squadron's broken spirit. As the days passed the sun beat down more strongly, and the wind did not always blow freshly from the sea, but sometimes hotly from the scorched desert. Landing Ground 87 was on the edge of the notorious Amarya dust bowl, where the sand would often be blowing when the rest of the desert was quite calm, and often we would sit around in the Mess, covered in fine sand which penetrated the canvas of the tent, looking like a collection of snowmen. Once the sand started to blow in earnest, nothing could be done to prevent it entering our tents, ruining our aircraft, getting into our food and our hair. There was no remedy but to wait until the sandstorm ceased. When sandstorms did not plague us, swarms of flies took their place; they were everywhere in great hordes, not the timid fly which we know in England, but an incorrigible pest with a painful bite which throughout the day seemed determined to make our lives a misery.

Since hardly any aircraft were serviceable there was little flying in

these, my first weeks in the squadron, and most of our crews would
spend regularly short periods of leave and several evenings each week
in Alexandria to relieve the boredom of desert life. I spent most of
my time in the Flight Office, trying to spur on my Flight Sergeant to
make greater efforts with the aircraft maintenance, or visiting the
dispersal points to encourage the airmen working in these unfavourable conditions, and trying to raise a semblance of enthusiasm in the
aircrews of my Flight.

But the sun, the sand and the flies gradually wore me down; I began
to feel ill from the heat; I was only able with difficulty to walk from
my tent to the Mess, and from there to my Flight Office; I had no
appetite for the food and existed mostly on soda water. All the time
I was in the desert this sickness never really passed; on some days I
felt more energy, on others I could raise no life. I did not want to visit
Alexandria before I had completed my first operation, and waited
impatiently as aircraft came from the Reserve Pool at long intervals
to replace the losses of the last attack. Meanwhile, a general uneasiness reigned among the squadron's crews, a feeling that they would
again be asked to do the impossible, and to me it seemed likely that
this would happen.

Only large forces could successfully overcome the defences of the
enemy convoys, and I knew only too well that an adequate number
of aircraft would not be available for some weeks at least. In particular, the long-range fighters, which were so much needed to escort our
Beauforts, were not forthcoming. There was in Egypt only one coastal
Beaufighter squadron, which was so fully employed in protecting our
own supply shipping on their passage up and down the coast between
Alexandria and Tobruk, that it could rarely spare any aircraft to come
with us. The Beaufighter situation in Egypt was identical with that of
the Beauforts; it was intended to form more squadrons, but at present
insufficient aircraft were available. I could see clearly that since there
was no cloud cover over the Mediterranean the only way to operate
reasonably against the reinforcement convoys was for the Beauforts
to carry with them their own cloud in the form of a strong Beaufighter
escort. This cloud was unlikely to materialise for some months to
come, and meanwhile we had to operate as best we could.

The shortage of our own aircraft increased the difficulty of operating; if fighter escort was not available, Beauforts operating in strength
could to some extent lend each other support, but we could hardly
even produce more than three serviceable aircraft, a force which was
not strong enough to look after itself. The number of Beauforts in the
reserve pool in Egypt was as small as the number of pilots in the

wastage lake was large, and our aircraft losses took weeks to replace. The squadron should always have had twenty aircraft on the aerodrome, but often there were half that number, and of these actually held a large proportion would be under repair. Maintaining Beauforts in flying condition in the desert sand was a heartbreaking task, and although the squadron engineer and the airmen made great efforts, very few aircraft were available each day for any operation which might be ordered.

I knew that in the course of time more aircraft would be available; Beaufighters would be spared to give us the necessary strong escort, and we would then be able to challenge any target within our range with a good chance of success for small losses. Meanwhile to most of our crews the intervening months gaped before them like an uncrossable, bottomless chasm, into which they felt they must inevitably fall. Yet I had been forewarned of these difficult conditions by my previous visit and the reports which I had read daily at Headquarters, so I had not been surprised to find at LG87 unenthusiastic crews and few serviceable aircraft, but I found something else soon after my arrival which was unexpected and came as something of a shock; the Beaufort would hardly fly in Egypt.

I had been looking forward ever since my arrival in Egypt to flying a Beaufort over the desert, and sat impatiently for the first few days in the Flight Office waiting for an aircraft to become serviceable. At last one was ready, and I taxied out on to the aerodrome to make my first flight from LG87 with anticipation of experiencing the same thrill that flying a Beaufort had always given me at home.

I took off, leaving behind me a miniature sandstorm blown up by the propellers, and immediately thought I detected a reluctance in the aircraft to climb. At first I put this feeling down to a mistaken impression on my part, due to not having flown for some time, but when I levelled out at a thousand feet, with undercarriage retracted and flaps up, I found with horror that my impression of lack of urge was confirmed beyond doubt; the aircraft, like the squadron's crews, appeared lifeless. I recalled the 200 knots which I had often read on the airspeed indicator of a Beaufort at home, and the genuine 235 knots which I had touched once on the level while being chased by fighters, yet this aircraft was struggling to reach the meagre speed of one hundred and thirty knots. As I flew around on the circuit, I saw plainly another reason for our pilots' reluctance to meet single seaters; their aircraft would not fly, for the Beaufort was not really flying, only just holding itself in the air.

This discovery of a Beaufort's poor performance in the desert really disturbed me, but it appeared that nothing could be done to improve it. It was due partly to the extra drag caused by the bulky air cleaners, fitted to keep sand out of the engines, and partly to the hot atmosphere, which prevented the Taurus engines from giving their full power. However, this was yet another problem which time would solve, for a new version of the Beaufort was in production, known as the 'Mark II', of which great things were expected. Certainly nobody awaited the arrival of this new Beaufort with more eagerness than myself, for I had counted the good performance of our aircraft as the only inspiring feature in an otherwise depressing picture, and now I found myself let down. It seemed that there would be nothing to relieve the desert depression for some weeks, perhaps months, to come, but almost immediately something did; I found John Creswell.

Having flown the only serviceable aircraft in my Flight and not really recovered from the shock, I looked around, not very optimistically, for an efficient crew. Nearly all the pilots had flown out from England complete with their own crews, and so there were very few spare observers or air gunners in the squadron. I knew well the worth of a good crew, for in England I had flown with a team which I had thought irreplaceable. It was largely to that crew's efficiency that I owed my survival and this chance of starting a second tour of operations, so I was determined again to pick a team who would keep me in the air and flying in the right direction.

After interviewing most of the squadron's spare aircrews, I found a wireless operator and air gunner who suited me; they had previously flown together as a crew, but their pilot had been posted away and the observer was sick. I found it less easy to find a suitable observer, a position in the crew which I thought most important, particularly for a leader, but eventually I did find one, and in rather curious circumstances.

In these first few weeks in the squadron I often visited Ops Room which was, of course, not a room at all but just another tent, in search of intelligence information. At home, where we had searched for our own targets, an up-to-date knowledge of the defences on the enemy coast had been one of the keys to success and survival, but here in the Mediterranean the method of operation was somewhat different. Our targets were always searched for and located by independent reconnaissance, so coastal intelligence information was unimportant. A simple order would be made for us to attack a certain target in a certain position, and the reconnaissance report would furnish all we needed to know. So I found very little in Ops Room of immediate interest, except John Creswell who, although wearing the badges of a Sergeant

Observer, appeared to be working as office boy to the Intelligence Officer. On enquiring why he was not a member of a crew, I was told that his pilot had been killed when their aircraft had been shot down over Halfaya Pass several months ago. Creswell had taken control when his pilot was hit, and succeeded in making a crash landing on a piece of desert unfortunately owned by the enemy. On extricating himself from the wreckage, he was immediately taken prisoner and spent several weeks in the enemy's hands, receiving very little food, but otherwise fairly comfortable. The enemy had then been forced to retreat hurriedly, leaving behind their prisoners; Creswell, once more safe in our hands, had been taken to hospital at Tobruk suffering from semi-starvation.

Intrigued by the story, and impressed by Creswell's air of efficiency, I asked him if he would like to navigate in my crew, an invitation which produced a grateful reply that he would. Apparently he was working as unwillingly in Ops Room as I had been at Headquarters, and with as little chance of escape, for there appeared to be a slight prejudice against Creswell as an observer on account of his very youthful appearance; he was in fact just twenty-one, but looked scarcely seventeen.

However, when talking to him I became persuaded that his navigation would be accurate, not least because he evidently had a talent for maths, having been apprenticed to a bank at home, and he was certainly impressive in operating a slide rule. I also thought I saw in him something more than mere efficiency, and wondered exactly what that quality was.

No sooner had I found myself a full crew, than a brand new aircraft appeared at LG87, the first Beaufort Mark II to arrive in the squadron. This was one of the few to run the Malta gauntlet successfully, and it was rumoured that several more were waiting in the Reserve Aircraft Pool and would soon be ready. Curiously, several of the pilots who had flown the Mark II in England did not like it, and Alastair, the other Flight Commander, was willing for me to have not only the first arrival in my Flight but also any other Mark IIs which might come to the squadron in future. My own view was that the Mark II could not possibly have a more disappointing performance than our present Beauforts, and I was willing to prefer it before I had even flown it. However a test flight confirmed my opinion; the Mark II had a better climb, was faster and handled more smoothly than its predecessor. The engines, American 'Pratt and Witneys', were more powerful than the previous Taurus, and were fitted with an endearing device by which they could be persuaded to give an extremely high 'boost' for a short time; this seemed to me to have a special application to meetings with single seaters!

Encouraged by the performance of this new aircraft and the acqui-
sition of what I believed to be a good crew, I waited impatiently for
an operation, but still no target appeared and we remained idle on our
aerodrome in the rear, waiting. The squadron always operated under
an advanced Headquarters of 201 Group, called 235 Wing, which
occupied an aerodrome at Sidi Barrani. This aerodrome, known as
'LG 05', was just south of the coastal road and some three hundred
miles west of LG87. The two or three hours which it would take for
our aircraft to reach 05 after a call might enable a target to steam out
of range, so we normally kept three Beauforts and crews at readiness
there, and also a permanent maintenance party to look after them.
The whole squadron was based in the rear partly to keep it out of
range of enemy bombers, partly to facilitate the maintenance of its
aircraft by keeping them near the main stores and workshops, which
were in Egypt.

Activity at 05 was not restricted to our own aircraft, for occasionally the enemy might pay the aerodrome a visit by day or night, and
it was not unknown to see a JU88 or ME109 flying round on the
circuit! Although Sidi Barrani was actually 150 miles behind the
current front, and so reasonably immune from enemy activity,
complete safety was unknown anywhere in this stretch of desert, and
our Beauforts had often been attacked even when flying between 05
and our base. If reasonable care had to be exercised east of Sidi
Barrani, extreme caution was required when flying westwards towards
the front. Since it was essential in these operations to obtain the full
range from our aircraft, we nearly always had to fly from 05 right up
to the most forward aerodrome available, where our aircraft would be
refuelled before finally setting out to an attack. The advanced aerodrome which the 'coastal' squadrons used had not a number, but a
name, Bu Amud, and was situated on the coastal road just south of
Tobruk.

Several of our crews had been even further forward than Bu Amud,
when in the previous winter the army had advanced, and the squadron
had used as its advanced base an aerodrome at Berka which was
almost within sight of Benghazi. For a few days it had seemed that the
squadron would be able to reach its targets easily, well out in open
sea, but this happy state was short-lived, for the army did not consoli-
date its position on the line at El Agheila and was soon back again
at Tobruk. Hearing the stories about that episode which were told in
our Mess, I longed to take part in this desert fighting and waited
impatiently for my chance to take a force of aircraft up to 05 for an
operation.

Meanwhile the heat at midday became intolerable, the flies multiplied and the sand blew for endless hours off the desert. I still felt ill, sometimes better, sometimes worse, but never feeling the energy which I needed to keep my own spirits high and to raise the enthusiasm of the crews. Scorpions crawled up the sides of our tents, the wind persistently blew from the hot south and the interminable battle to produce serviceable aircraft proceeded endlessly. Pilots were reluctant to pass the slow aircraft as serviceable, and air tests almost invariably ended in a negative report which would result in the aircraft being returned to maintenance section for several more days of work, to be followed by another air test which might produce the same result. The Mess bar did a great trade in beer, crews spent aimless evenings in Alexandria, while I waited at LG87, still existing mostly on soda water; I did not want to go into Alexandria, I wanted to go home.

In truth, though I would never have admitted it, I was not a little apprehensive of starting operations again with a new crew and in conditions of which I had no experience. I was bent on solving personal problems now, no longer worrying about matters remote from my control but fighting a little selfish war for my own life. I was not quite confident in my crew, and apprehensive of the dangers of operating under a clear sky. In weak moments, on days when the heat was suffocating and inactivity played on my nerves, I might occasionally have regretted leaving the safety and comfort of my office in Cairo. There was not the unquestioning spirit and reckless enthusiasm here which I had known in my squadron at home to make dangers seem inconsiderable and success the only objective; I longed to have my first operation behind me and my confidence restored.

CHAPTER V

STARTING AGAIN

WHEN at last an order came from Group to send three aircraft up to 05 to stand-by for an operation, I persuaded the CO to let me lead, and packing my camp bed and sleeping bag into the only Mark II in the squadron, I set out with my new crew to see for myself the western desert about which I had heard so much.

On this first flight to 05 there was little navigation necessary; a road and a railway led almost directly to our destination. Creswell told me it was wise to keep south of the railway, since the coastal guns were manned by Egyptians, whose trigger fingers were as restless as their aircraft recognition was suspect, so we flew over the desert south of the coast, the railway and the road. Occasionally we would skirt a landing ground on which some squadron or maintenance unit was based, but away from the railway and the road there were no signs of activity in the great expanse of sand stretching southwards.

Sidi Barrani's 05 was an enormous square aerodrome just south of the road, with many different kinds of aircraft dispersed around its boundary. 203 Squadron seemed to be the most strongly represented of the coastal squadrons, with half a dozen aircraft on the aerodrome. This squadron, which was the only daylight reconnaissance squadron in the Group, was unusual in having two types of aircraft; one of its Flights was equipped with Blenheims, the other with the American Marylands. The Blenheim Flight carried out daylight anti-submarine patrols over the rather dangerous stretch of sea between Cyrenaica and Crete, while the Marylands, with their greater speed and range, made the long reconnaissance flights far into the Central Mediterranean, searching for shipping. Between this Maryland Flight and our squadron there was a close link, for it was their crews who normally found our targets.

235 Wing Ops Room, one of the usual cluster of tents along the boundary, was the scene of continuous and varied activity; crews were being briefed before their flight, others came in to report on their various missions; outside on the aerodrome engines were being tested, aircraft took off, while others were landing; great plumes of sand were being whipped up off the aerodrome surface by the slipstreams from their propellers, and the noise of engines could always be heard, sometimes a roar from the aerodrome, sometimes faint in the distance, but never completely dying.

In the Mess the plain fare and shortage of water which prevailed illustrated the difference between front-line and base aerodromes; the three hundred miles from Sidi Barrani to Alexandria was a full day's journey by road, while from LG87 to 'Alex' took only an hour; our squadron could send a lorry for provisions daily, while 05 had to be content with a weekly supply for its large floating population. Yet this aerodrome could not be said to be at the front, which was still another hundred and fifty miles further west, so I could now easily believe the stories which I have heard from pilots of front-line aerodromes, where there was said to be very little fresh water, perhaps a cup full each day, no variation from bully beef for breakfast, lunch or supper, and not a mere shortage, but a complete absence of beer.

I did not have to depend for long on reports for my impression of conditions on front-line aerodromes, for on our second day at Sidi Barrani to my great surprise a target was found for our three Beauforts. In the few weeks which had elapsed since I left Headquarters, small but important changes had taken place in the general situation, with which I was now out of touch. Since very little information reached LG87, I had missed the news of the latest developments, which had always been available at Headquarters. Here at 05, I could again see the position which I had seen daily in Cairo, for Wing Ops Room was not only a centre of action but also of information.

Malta was still being attacked, but not quite so heavily as before; ships were still crossing the Mediterranean to the enemy, but by a more easterly route, sailing from Cape Matapan, the most southerly point of Greece, straight across the open sea to Benghazi. This change of route, which was thought to be due to the success of our submarines in the Central Mediterranean, brought the ships just within range of our Beauforts. However, the passage was so arranged that these targets were hardly within our range at nightfall on one day, but at dawn on the next morning they would be near enough to the coast of Cyrenaica to be given single-engined fighter protection.

There were two alternatives for attacking ships on this new route;

either a force could be sent out in the late afternoon to make an attack at dusk, afterwards returning in the dark, or single aircraft could take off in the early hours of the morning to arrive over their target at daybreak, just as the light was becoming sufficient to make a torpedo attack.

At dusk the targets were at extreme range, and aircraft returning from the attack would have no petrol to spare to search for their aerodrome in the darkness. Assistance from wireless stations at the front was very limited, and it was impossible to display much light on the flarepath at Bu Amud, or to place flashing beacons on the coast for fear of inviting attention from enemy intruders, who were active over the front on most nights. In these conditions the return flight from a dusk attack would be an unpleasant one for the pilot, with gauges indicating decreasing petrol, little wireless information to guide him, and the suspicion always lurking that he might not find his aerodrome in the darkness.

The dawn attack also had many disadvantages. Formation flying was impossible in the dark and aircraft operating singly would have little chance of hitting their target with the one torpedo which they carried, while the enemy could easily concentrate on a single attacker the fire which during a combined attack would be spread between several aircraft. Also there would be only a very limited time in which to search for the target at dawn, for, as the visibility increased towards sunrise, single seaters would be taking off from North African aerodromes to escort the ships into harbour, and they could be expected in the target area soon after daybreak.

I was particularly keen that we should operate as a force, since I knew from experience that there was strength in numbers. A combined attack by several aircraft not only afforded the best chance of scoring a hit, but Beauforts operating as a force could lend each other support if attacked by fighters. I thought that now targets were at last steaming within range, a determined effort should be made to sink them, and considered that the uncertain operation by single aircraft at dawn was hardly likely to inconvenience the enemy. It still seemed to me that to cut the enemy's supply line completely would be to turn the key, and eventually open the door for our army to advance in North Africa.

So I did my best to persuade the CO of 235 Wing to press for an improvement in night-flying facilities at the front. If there were a brighter flare path, some well placed wireless stations to send out accurate bearings, and an occasional flashing beacon on the coast, I was certain that we could return individually and safely from a dusk attack. He agreed to put forward these suggestions, but meanwhile, since neither I nor the other two pilots with me relished the idea of a return in darkness at the limit of our range and with little light to greet us, he decided on operating single aircraft at dawn.

A Maryland had found our target at midday, far out at sea, and further reconnaissances were made during the afternoon to confirm its course and speed. Our three Beauforts left 05 for Bu Amud in the evening, timing the flight to arrive at our destination just before twilight, so that the enemy would not have time to detect our aircraft on the aerodrome before nightfall. We would arrive at the front at dusk, and with luck should be over the target at dawn on the next day, our presence unknown to the enemy.

The flight from LG87 to Sidi Barrani had been made over country which I had thought a wilderness, but it was thickly populated compared with the desert over which we now flew. Only an occasional cluster of tents or moving column of transports broke the monotony of the desert tableland, until we reached the 'wire' at Fort Maddralena. This great fence of barbed wire, which marked the Libyan frontier, had been erected by the Italians to prevent the native population from escaping out of their colony! And in peacetime it had been patrolled regularly from the air. The fort itself was a stark, grim building, whch had previously been the headquarters of the Italian desert patrol. We circled to make our presence known to the 'Control' there, then flew on, very low to avoid detection and extremely vigilant, until just as the sun was going down below the horizon in front of us, a straight stretch of the coastal road came in sight, and beside it the aerodrome of Bu Amud.

Unlike those at the rear, this landing ground had no aircraft at dispersal points, nor the familiar cluster of tents on its boundary. We were the only visitors, and the few inhabitants lived underground in great cellars which had been built most considerately by the Italians. Leaving our three aircraft on the surface, ghostly shapes in the fading light, we descended underground, while a party of airmen refuelled our aircraft and made last-minute adjustments before night set in.

A small party of airmen, detached from 235 Wing for short periods, was sufficient to service the few aircraft which used the aerodrome, and less than twenty airmen between them laid the flare path, cooked the meals, drove the tractor which towed the petrol tanker, and manned a few machine guns to defend the camp. A solitary officer was in charge, whose main occupation was to try to understand and make himself understood on the field telephone which connected Bu Amud with Ops Room at 235 Wing.

In the cellar we had supper, consisting of the inevitable bully beef and some tea made with very doubtful water, then retired early into our sleeping bags with the uncomfortable knowledge that we would be called in the early hours of the morning.

The ringing of the field telephone woke me at about midnight, and I listened sleepily and not very enthusiastically to the shouting match which followed between the Ops officer and 235 Wing. A Wellington, which had no need to use a forward aerodrome on account of its long range, had been sent out from 05 during the night to re-locate the ship which the Maryland had sighted earlier in the day, and 235 Wing had now received a wireless message from it giving the target's latest position, course and speed. After every word of a long message had been spelt out over the field telephone by the phonetic alphabet our instructions were eventually made clear. Our three aircraft were to take off at short intervals and make an independent search of the sea which the target should have reached at dawn; if sunrise came without the target being found, we were to return without delay. I roused Creswell, who drew in the ship's track on a plotting chart according to the information given in the reconnaissance report, worked out the time it would take us to reach its position at dawn, and from these calculations produced a time of take-off for three-fifteen in the morning. After this we all rolled back into our sleeping bags, and the cellar was soon resounding again with the deep breathing and occasional snores of three Beaufort crews.

The night was warm and the sky clear as I walked with my crew across the sand to our aircraft at half past two in the morning. Airmen were at the dispersal point to help us start up, but we were early, and I stood for a few minutes on the wing of my aircraft looking out over a scene of darkness and silence. The silence was soon broken by the sound of a lorry which was making intermittent progress over the aerodrome surface, relieving the darkness at every stop with the dim light of a hurricane lamp, until finally a long line of these lights stretched across the sand to make our flare path. A roar from the engines of one of the other aircraft broke the peacefulness of the scene, and climbing into the cockpit through the roof, I started my engines, warmed them up and taxied out on to the aerodrome. This was to be my first operation in the Middle East, and my first flight at night for many months. Turning to face down the flare path into wind, I cast a final glance around the cockpit to check the positions of switches, levers and instrument pointers, hesitated for a moment, then opened the throttles gradually; the engines roared into life and the aircraft, gathering speed, thundered down the line of lights to rise and climb away into the night.

To avoid crossing enemy territory, and so making our presence known, we first flew northwards directly out to sea, and then, after half an hour's flying, turned on to a westerly course, parallel to the coast of Cyrenaica held by the enemy. There, in the distance, we could see an occasional coastal light, intended to guide the enemy's ships or aircraft, and once a brighter light in the sky suggested some flare dropping by our own aircraft behind the enemy lines. The faint light of flames from the exhausts flickered behind the engines, and the exhaust rings glowed dully like two great eyes peering out of the darkness. First one, and then another hour passed with this uneventful instrument flying, and the African coast disappeared behind us as we flew westwards over the sea. The engines beat monotonously together, the pointers of instruments remained steady on their dials, and I flew on comfortably in the smooth night sky.

At the beginning of the third hour my gunner broke the silence with the welcome news that the eastern sky was becoming lighter behind us. Turning in my seat I could just see the clear horizon in the East, but none was yet visible ahead, and for another twenty minutes I had to continue flying by instruments into a western sky which was still in darkness.

At last, the whole sky became coloured with grey of dawn, and I was able to fly comfortably while searching the water all around for a sign of our target. Creswell estimated that we had reached the correct position, but no ship appeared in the sea over which we flew, and we started to search northwards, flying up the target's track, expecting at any minute to see it appear on the horizon ahead. But when the sun rose, there was still no ship to be seen in a great expanse of sea, and after continuing to search against our orders for another five minutes, we turned reluctantly for home.

At the end of the second hour of the homeward flight, Creswell handed me an alteration of course, on which I turned southwards, and soon the Libyan coast appeared as a gradually thickening line on the horizon. We made a good landfall just west of Tobruk, to which we gave a wide berth, for the gun crews there, alert from frequent enemy attacks, were known occasionally to fire on their own aircraft. I was tired at the end of a long flight, but the sight of this famous little town, with its ruined buildings and cratered streets, raised a feeling of pride which would have made me fly on until I fell asleep at the controls. But the flight was nearing its end, for Bu Amud could be seen even before Tobruk passed out of sight, and as I circled to land I could see the two other Beauforts already on the aerodrome and being refuelled.

One of them had made an attack, the other, like myself, had

searched without result and returned with his torpedo still loaded. The successful pilot had found the target, not in the half light of dawn when he might have achieved surprise, but just on sunrise, and very heavy fire from the destroyer escort had prevented him from closing to short range. After the attack the target had been seen steaming on without change of course or reduction in speed, and it was assumed that his torpedo had missed.

This result seemed to me to be an example of the small chances of success which this type of operation could expect. One aircraft out of the three operating might find the target, and occasionally that single aircraft might take the escort by surprise and score a hit, but it did not seem to me that this method of operation would ever seriously inconvenience the enemy, much less cut his supply line completely. I was more than ever convinced that we must operate as a force if we were to be successful.

To delay longer than necessary at Bu Amud was to invite attention from the enemy, who in the course of the day would almost certainly spot our aircraft standing on the aerodrome, so, after snatching a quick breakfast in the cellar, we flew off east again to Fort Maddralena and 05. On our arrival there, the Wing CO decided to dispense with his torpedo force for a few days, since the Marylands had sighted no targets coming within our range, and after having the torpedo unloaded, we returned to the comforts of our own aerodrome.

Although nothing had been achieved on this operation, to me it was far from worthless. I had seen for myself the conditions of operating both at 05 and the front; I had coped successfully with the night flying in which I was so inexpert, and had at last put the first operational flight of my second tour behind me. I felt now a great confidence in my crew, and no less in the aircraft, for the Mark II had behaved perfectly throughout the whole operation and during the flights between aerodromes. With more aircraft becoming available, more targets within range, the time did not seem so far distant when I should be leading a strong force of Mark IIs out against some worthwhile target, with Creswell navigating, and perhaps with Beaufighter escort.

As I wallowed in my hot bath in Alexandria, with an evening before me to be spent not in sand but in civilisation, with a real roof over my head and a soft bed at its end, I felt for the first time that the future might hold what I was searching for.

CHAPTER VI

THE FIRST SHIP IS SUNK

IN the following weeks, the routine of life at LG87 proceeded uneventfully. Three aircraft were sent up at intervals to 05; very occasionally they operated, but more often remained there for a few days and then returned. Once a dawn attack was attempted, but not one of the three aircraft found the target; on another occasion a north-bound ship was sighted, steaming towards Crete and well within our range in the middle of the day. A force of three Beauforts took off from 05 to attack this unusual target, but for some reason they failed to score a single hit, although Ken Grant, one of the best of our younger pilots (who was leading), claimed to have surprised the defences and taken good aim from short range. This failure was a disappointing result to one of the squadron's very rare daylight attacks, for which I could find no good reason, except that perhaps three aircraft were insufficient and a force of six was needed to make certain of a hit.

However, it seemed that the squadron might soon be able to produce a stronger force, for it had sustained no losses while gradually receiving from the Reserve Aircraft Pool sufficient aircraft to bring it up to strength. In my Flight there were now no less than six Mark IIs, and the pilots, who at first had been sceptical, were beginning to appreciate their qualities. Soon all the pilots in my Flight inclined to my way of thinking, and the Mark IIs were in demand whenever aircraft went up to the front; but Alastair's Flight still remained faithful to the older Beaufort, and the squadron was divided on the subject into two friendly camps.

As the end of May 1942 approached, conditions for the squadron began to appear more favourable, indeed it seemed that almost from

the very day I had escaped from Headquarters, fortune had changed
in our favour. The enemy's ships, although never presenting easy
targets, were now at least coming within our range; operations were
still few and far between, but there were occasional flights up to 05
and much more casual flying than before to keep our crews in practice.
The squadron's spirits rose visibly in these weeks, when operating
conditions were reasonable, flying plentiful, and casualties unknown.
The 'snowmen', who sat around in the Mess when the sand blew, were
no longer looking forward with distrust to their next operation, instead
there was competition among crews for a place in the force to be sent
up to 05. The wonderful sea bathing at Sidi Barrani began to hold a
greater attraction for our crews than the night life of Alexandria. 39
Squadron was growing up in a way it was good to see. I myself still
felt ill in the heat and sand, and when I next took a few days' leave in
Alexandria, it was spent entirely in bed.

The situation at the front was changing now not weekly but daily.
The enormous German Air Force, which since January had been
based in Sicily, carrying out attacks on Malta by day and night, had
gradually been moving away ever since the end of April. Many of the
squadrons from Sicily were now in North Africa, while others were
said to have been sent to Russia in an attempt to stem the reverses on
that front. The German Air Force in the desert strengthened by these
reinforcements was becoming very active, and Rommel's army more
aggressive than ever. Aerodromes at the front were being attacked
during the day, and our rear bases were being bombed at night. There
was an increase in the enemy's reconnaissance activity, and high flying
Junkers reconnaissance aircraft would fly over Egypt at 45,000 ft to
photograph our rear aerodromes and troop concentrations. All these
activities pointed to an early attempt by Rommel to advance, and it
seemed to me that the enemy's plan was being carried out with
dangerous precision. Rommel had now accumulated sufficient forces
and equipment and was waiting only until full air support became
available on the withdrawal of the remaining squadrons from Sicily, to
advance in strength and take Egypt. I realised that the coming weeks
would be critical.

But if a shortage of aircraft in our own Air Force made it seem that
we would lose the coming battle, it was to be a lack of aircraft which
indirectly caused Rommel's eventual defeat. The enemy had held
without difficulty the present line with an air force comparable in size
to our own, but for his army to advance stronger support from the air
was necessary; to provide this air support, the German squadrons were
withdrawn from Sicily, where they were replaced by inferior Italian

squadrons. No doubt the enemy considered that with Malta reduced to ruins by four months of incessant air attack, the Italian Air Force would be able to maintain sufficient pressure to prevent the Island from rising again to take up the offensive. In this he made a fatal error, and it was the inability to supply strong air support to the army in the desert, and at the same time maintain the previous scale of raids on Malta, which eventually cost Rommel what must have appeared to him an assured victory.

During the winter months of 1942, Malta must have been the problem child of allied strategy. Ships could not reach the Island, aircraft could not remain undamaged on its aerodromes, and as the first months of that year passed without sign of the air storm abating it must have seemed that the Island must fall. Its fate depended on how long the enemy could afford to maintain the pressure which needed some hundreds of aircraft on Sicilian aerodromes and was costing a heavy daily casualty list. In fact Malta was during these months immobilising an enormous force of efficient German aircraft which might otherwise have been used to the same ruinous effect in some other theatre of war, perhaps against England. When I left Headquarters in the last week of April it had almost appeared that Malta had been tacitly given up as lost. Such survivors of the last convoy, which had amazingly reached the Island in the face of attack from the air and by the Italian navy, had been sunk in harbour after their arrival, by bombing, and Malta's ability to hold out must have been estimated not in months, but in weeks.

At this very moment, when the future of Malta looked darkest, the raids became less heavy; Italian, not German aircraft predominated, the bombing became less accurate and the fighter protection weaker. The German Air Force, which had steadily faced the Island for four long months, turned away unexpectedly, just as it seemed it would deliver the mortal blow, and Malta, rising from her knees, shook herself with surprise. The allied strategists appeared to notice suddenly that Malta was not lost, but saved, and made plans to hold it.

The main deficiency in the Island's defence was fighter protection. The flight from Gibraltar to Malta was beyond the range of our single-seater fighters, but, in the past Hurricanes had been flown off the deck of an aircraft carrier, which took them to a point off the Algerian Coast from which they could reach their destination. But a carrier could rarely be spared for this work, and Hurricanes had only reached the Island in small numbers and at long intervals, bombing reduced their strength, and throughout the winter they had taken off in their two's and three's to oppose the hordes of enemy bombers escorted by the superior Messerschmitt 109s.

The sinking in harbour of the April convoy survivors must have shown that it was useless to attempt to run another convoy through to the Island without first providing efficient fighter protection to greet it at its destination. The arrival at Malta at the beginning of May of three squadrons of Spitfires flown off the aircraft carriers *Wasp* and *Eagle* indicated that at last a decision had been made concerning the fate of the Island, and that decision was to hold and defend it.

Some of the first Spitfires were unfortunate. At the time of their arrival not all the German squadrons had been withdrawn from Sicily, and the Spitfires had hardly landed and taxied to their dispersal points, when the aerodromes were raided, and many of the fighters were destroyed without firing a single round in defence of the Island. But the survivors and their successors challenged the enemy in the following weeks, and as more German squadrons were withdrawn from Sicily the air over Malta became more evenly contested. The improvement in conditions which followed the arrival of the Spitfires must have confirmed the Allied High Command in their decision to hold the Island; more Spitfires were promised, the intention to attempt to run through another much needed convoy was known, and hopes for Malta's future improved as the sky overhead became clearer.

The improvement in conditions at Malta was felt immediately in Egypt as the blade of a two-edged sword; Rommel was reinforced by the Sicilian squadrons, but our air reinforcement route via Gibraltar and Malta was less interrupted. The flight from England to the Middle East was no longer the Grand National which it had seemed in the winter months, with Malta a Beecher's Brook where many of the starters had fallen; instead, Beauforts were now able to fly through by day, and casualties were rare. Beaufighters, in which I took as great an interest as on my previous tour I had taken in English cloud, were coming into Egypt in increasing numbers, and although there were yet insufficient Beauforts to start a second squadron, another Beaufighter squadron was actually forming. Our squadron, almost for the first time in its existence, was up to its full strength in aircraft and could at last produce a force.

Thinking that we should now start work in earnest, I visited 201 Group Headquarters and discussed our operations with the Air Staff, but with disappointing results. I could obtain only a vague promise of improved night-flying arrangements at the front, and the provision of Beaufighter escort was not thought possible, since these aircraft were still being fully employed in protecting our shipping against the enemy's increasing scale of attack. The position of front-line aerodromes was now not unlike that of Malta during the preceding months, and policy concerning them was also similar; it seemed to be tacitly understood that the army would retreat, and there was an unwillingness to establish facilities which might at any moment fall into the enemy's hands.

Since the conditions of operating from Egypt appeared unlikely to improve I raised the question of using Malta as a base for the squadron, but this subject had never been a popular one at Group since the failure of the reinforcement operation of April 14th, for which the Air Staff had been partly to blame, and I could find no support for this suggestion. The fact that conditions had greatly improved in the last few weeks due to the departure of the larger part of the German Air Force from Sicily and the arrival of Spitfires at Malta appeared to have escaped notice, and I found a general reluctance for us to use the Island even temporarily as an advanced base.

The remaining German squadrons would now leave Sicily; Rommel would have not only a great accumulation of war material at his disposal in Libya, but also the full air support for which he had been waiting. It could only be a matter not of weeks, but of days, before he would strike. I knew that although our inability in the past to interrupt the enemy's sea supply line might cost us Egypt, it was not yet too late to cut that line, nor too late for the effect to be felt. To maintain his army, Rommel required a steady supply of stores, which could only reach him by ship. He no longer required the frequent convoys which had enabled him to build up his great strength, but he was still dependent on a regular and steady passage of ships to maintain that strong force. If the supply line could now be cut, Egypt might still be saved; the enemy's plan, which had proceeded smoothly until it was almost complete, could still, at this last moment, be frustrated.

The American aircraft were beginning to flow into Egypt from the west, no longer singly but in tens, and they would soon come in their hundreds. Reinforcements, tanks and guns for our army, were known to be on their way. The future seemed assured, it was the present which gave concern. I was no longer in the centre of the picture, as I had been at Headquarters in Cairo, but I could feel the current of events surging around me. I knew little of the route which Rommel's supply ships took or how they were defended, but I did know that although they presented almost impossible targets for attack from Egypt, they were within easy reach from Malta. If reinforcement Beauforts could fly through by day, a daylight striking force could certainly operate from the Island. Malta had arisen from its knees to defend itself; I wanted to see it strike.

At the end of May, Group decided to withdraw the squadron from the line for a week in order that it could carry out some training. They had attributed the failure of Ken and his section to sink an easy target to faulty aiming, and thought that the squadron needed practice. A target ship was made available in the Gulf of Suez, and we transferred our serviceable aircraft, with some airmen to maintain them, to Shallufa, a station on the canal only a few miles from Suez itself.

This aerodrome was the base for several of the first Wellingtons to be adapted locally to carry two torpedoes which their crews were training to drop at night, like the Swordfish and Albacores, by the light of flares. Like us they were to move up to more forward aerodromes for operations, but their long range would make it unnecessary to take off as far west as 05, in fact the advanced aerodromes they would use were much nearer our own LG87. This initiative, seen here in its early stages, indicated the desperation prevailing in HQ Cairo to reach Rommel's shipping lanes; and it was quite without help from the Air Ministry at home, perhaps even without its knowledge, that the torpedo Wellington developed into a potent force in the Mediterranean war.

At Shallufa, we all practised aiming against a target ship steaming in Suez Bay. I myself had not had this opportunity for several years, and found that my judgment of range, in particular, needed some revising. A torpedo must be dropped well within a thousand yards of the target if it is to have a chance of scoring a hit, but at this distance, particularly from an aircraft attacking under fire, a ship looks uncomfortably close at the dropping height of 60ft, and over-estimation of range is a general fault. Not only must range be judged carefully, but the target's speed must also be estimated and correctly allowed for when taking aim. This practice was much needed by all our pilots, and actually it was soon to be repaid by the squadron's first confirmed success.

The change of scene was also welcome, with soft beds, concrete floors, and electric light all much appreciated, and this was an enjoyable week spent in surroundings which were luxurious compared with those of LG87. But we were not sorry when the time came for us to return, for LG87 was our home, and although it did not supply the comforts of a permanent station, it was luxurious compared with front-line aerodromes.

However, it was not to our own camp beds that we looked forward on our return, nor to our tents, nor yet to the questionable meals produced by our Arab cooks; it was the mail, accumulating in our absence, which was the attraction. News from home was food and drink to us, enabling us to forget the discomforts of flies, heat and sand, and taking us directly back to our friends at home who were delighting in the fresh green of the countryside and grumbling at the fresh winds and occasional showers of an English May. To receive a letter was the most important event which could possibly happen; a delay in the post always seemed inexplicable and puzzling.

Now, on my return from Shallufa, I was handed three blue envelopes, letters from England which had taken only a month to reach Egypt by air mail. As I read and re-read these letters, thoughts of England filled my mind, and that section of my private life which was most incalculable made a rare but penetrating intrusion into the realms of my Service existence. The ambition to fight seemed momentarily empty in the face of memories which renewed my regret at having left England and strengthened my desire to return as I had promised. I felt that critical days were being wasted and wondered how long it would take me to complete a tour at the present rate of operations. Searching desperately for a way to achieve my ambition to fight and to return, my thoughts turned once more to Malta, as they had done so often during the previous weeks; not only was the Island nearer than Egypt to the enemy's shipping route, but also much nearer home. I felt that Malta might be the stepping stone to the fulfilment of both my wishes, and saw clearly for the first time my way home to England; it stretched hazard by hazard across a sea of sinking ships.

The very day after our return from Shallufa, Group required three of our aircraft at 05, and I and two others from my Flight, all flying Mark IIs, went up in great hopes of making a combined attack. In Wing Ops Room I found even greater activity than usual, and the atmosphere generally a little more strained. Rommel's army was now pressing very hard on the front, and although that was a hundred and fifty miles away, the effect could be felt at Sidi Barrani. The aerodrome had been bombed on the previous night, and several other landing grounds even further in the rear had also received attention. The enemy was increasing the scale of his air attack on our coastal shipping, and Tobruk had been more heavily raided than usual. On the road which skirted the northern boundary of the aerodrome could be seen an endless procession of transport moving up to the front. June had come, and with it Rommel's expected push.

At Ops Room I was told that the usual Maryland was out searching for our target, which a Wellington had first sighted far out at sea during the previous night. Since we were not needed immediately, we went down to the beach to bathe, and returned in time to see the

'Mary' landing from its seven-hour flight made entirely over sea. The pilot reported that he had found the target, a large ship escorted by three destroyers, steaming on a more easterly course than usual. From calculation, we found that it would still be out of our range at dusk, and so the only possible operation was the unreliable dawn strike by individual aircraft. But any attempt, however forlorn, to sink this target was worth making; there was information that the ship was an important one, with Derna, not Benghazi, its destination, a fact which would account for its unusual easterly course. It seemed that Rommel was needing this ship's cargo urgently for his present offensive for by using Derna he was saving the three hundred miles of road transport between Benghazi and the front.

On this occasion the target was near enough for us to operate from 05, and after receiving a report of its latest position, wirelessed back from a Wellington out on night reconnaissance, two of us took off independently in the early hours of the morning to try and make an interception at dawn. Our third aircraft, as often happened, had contracted some mechanical trouble on the flight up which could not be put right in time for the operation. The chances of one out of two aircraft finding the target appeared to me remote, but I reckoned without Creswell.

After an uneventful take-off, I steered the courses which he gave me through the night, first northwards, as before, then westwards, until the eastern horizon grew lighter and I was able to give up flying by instruments as the colour of the western sky changed from black to grey. Just as I was thinking that conditions were ideal for a dawn attack, with the light just good enough to drop a torpedo, I saw a dark shape in the distance and on the starboard side, not very clearly, for it was against the darker western sky, but clearly enough for me to recognise it as a ship. Throttling back the engines in order to make as little noise as possible, I began a shallow dive towards the target. As we approached, the dark shape became more sharply defined as the grey hull of a small liner, and I saw for the first time its escort, a destroyer on either side and one directly ahead.

It was just light enough for me to be able to fly comfortably near the surface of the water, and flattening out from the shallow dive, I passed undetected low in front of the port destroyer to aim my torpedo within the escort screen at point-blank range from the target. But as I opened up my engines to level out from the dive, the look-out sighted me; one moment I saw signal lamps flashing morse from ship to ship, and the next moment first one gun, and then others, started firing. Just after I had dropped my torpedo and was turning away, an accurate stream of tracer poured out from the target only a few hundred yards away, and before I could take avoiding action, my aircraft was hit in the port wing. By this time the destroyers were all firing, but the grey Beaufort must have been a difficult target in the half light, and I was able to twist and turn my way out of the barrage towards the dark western sky without receiving further damage, although I was followed to extreme range by streams of red and green tracer, which kept passing unpleasantly close to where I had just been.

By the time I had recovered from the excitement of these few eventful moments, the ship was several miles away, and finding that my aircraft was not seriously damaged, I flew back to see the result of the attack. At first I was bitterly disappointed with what I saw. The ship had turned in a semi-circle, no doubt in an attempt to avoid the torpedo's track, and was now stationary, pointing in the direction from which it had been steaming when I first saw it. The destroyers, apparently, had not turned together, for they were now in disorder around the liner pointing in different directions and also stationary.

I flew on a figure of eight carefully watching at a safe distance from the convoy's guns the cluster of ships, and wondering quite what had happened. I knew, from the recent practice, that I had taken good aim from short range and could not believe that I had missed, yet the ship, although stationary, showed no real sign that she was hit. Just as I was turning to fly away northwards, knowing that a wireless message would have been sent to the shore for fighter protection and that to delay longer was unwise, a thin column of white smoke appeared from the middle of the ship. My crew were now quite certain that we had scored a hit, but I was not quite satisfied. However, the increasing light showed the result of one certain hit, not scored by us but by the enemy, a jagged hole in the port wing and aileron of my aircraft, and I saw that I was lucky that the controls were not affected. Although taken by surprise in the semi-darkness, the escort's shooting had been good.

The return flight to 05 was uneventful, and remarkable only for some accurate navigation by Creswell. After landing, we went to Ops Room to report the attack, but I was unwilling to claim a hit on account of the lack of evidence of any explosion. However, the CO having a Maryland to spare, decided to send it out to report on the ship's latest position; in a few hours' time it would bring back a photograph which would settle the question. Meanwhile I went over to the Mess for a late breakfast, in which I was joined later by Paul, the other pilot who had been out that morning; his appearance gave the impression that he had just had a fight, which, in fact, he had.

Not succeeding in finding the target at dawn, he had continued to search for it long after sunrise, and had ended by finding not a ship, but some trouble, in the form of a Macchi 202. Either the shooting of the Macchi's pilot had been extremely poor, or else Paul's flying of his Beaufort had been spectacular, for at the end of a running fight lasting for a full quarter of an hour the Macchi had exhausted its ammunition and the Beaufort had not a single hole in it.

I knew well the difficulty of fighting alone with a single seater in open sky, and Paul's tousled hair, sweat-soaked shirt and harassed expression, told me the whole story of those fifteen minutes of fighting out of sight of land, when his life had depended on the energy and skill with which he could manoeuvre his aircraft to prevent the enemy keeping a steady sight on him. I reflected, with some satisfaction, that this particular fighter had probably been sent out in answer to a call from the ship especially to deal with me!

When the Maryland came in, we could hardly wait while transport went out across the aerodrome to bring the crew in from the dispersal point, and as the lorry drew up outside Ops Room, a small crowd, which included the Wing CO himself, pressed round to hear the news. The reconnaissance crew reported that the ship was still in the position in which I had left it at dawn, still stationary, and with its stern almost under water. The destroyers were circling, possibly waiting to pick up survivors, and there were several fighters patrolling overhead.

This good news was later illustrated by a photograph, taken from the Maryland, which confirmed that the ship was a liner of about ten thousand tons with tanks visible on deck and showed that she was settling down in the water beyond any doubt. Everyone was pleased with this result, and I was equally pleased with Creswell, whose accurate navigation, after two hours' flying in darkness and out of sight of land, had brought us right over the target at a time when conditions were ideal for attack. It was his success.

That afternoon we flew back to LG87, where we found everyone in the squadron, both airmen and crews, very excited at this result, the first confirmed sinking in the squadron's history. Both our success and Paul's escape from a single combat with a fighter raised the squadron's enthusiasm to unknown heights and competition was keen for what was now considered the privilege of going up to 0.5 on the next detachment. At the end of a slight celebration that evening, in which beer featured heavily, I felt, as I walked across the sand to my tent in the coolness of the night, that if I never sank another ship, that one had been worthwhile, not only for the delay it must have caused to the enemy's plan, but for the spirit which it had raised within the squadron. At last the squadron had a success, and its crews longed to repeat it.

The next day, Group informed the CO that no more aircraft were required to be sent to 05, but that he was to 'ground' the squadron and make strenuous efforts to produce the largest possible force by June 12th. I recalled the last occasion when the squadron had prepared a special force, for the attack on April 14th, the squadron's blackest day, which we had now almost succeeded in forgetting. Again I was puzzled at the order and wondered with rather less detachment than before just what Group had in mind.

CHAPTER VII

BATTLESHIPS

SEATED around a conference table at the Headquarters of 201 Group in Alexandria, an assembly of the squadron commanders and flight commanders of the coastal squadrons listened to the opening address by the AOC. Such a conference was unusual, and since it could not be unconnected with the recent order to prepare large forces by June 12th, which was the next day, there was an air of expectancy as the AOC began to speak. His speech which was short, impressive and to the point, revealed briefly the well guarded secret that an attempt was to be made on the next day to run a convoy through from Alexandria to Malta; our presence at the conference and the need for large numbers of aircraft were immediately explained.

"I need hardly tell you, gentlemen, that the fate of Malta may depend on the success of this operation". With these parting words, the AOC concluded his address, which had emphasised the gravity of the situation in the Mediterranean and the need for great efforts from all squadrons, and left to one of his staff the task of outlining the general plan of the operation. A long and elaborate combined operation order was then read out and illustrated with the help of a previously prepared map which was placed on the table before us, indicating the route which the convoy was to take, with its expected position marked at intervals through each day and night of the operation.

The plan was somewhat involved, since several feints were to be made in an attempt to confuse the enemy and distract his attention from the real purpose of the operation. A small, and lightly escorted 'dummy' convoy was to leave Alexandria, reach a point off the coast at Sidi Barrani, and then return, while the real convoy with a similar small escort was to leave Haifa and steam coastwise to a position off

Tobruk, where it was also to turn back. On the return passage, timed to take place during the night, it was to pick up its full escort, which would meanwhile have steamed out from Alexandria to meet it, turn round again and steer a westerly course through the middle of the dangerous stretch of sea between Crete and that part of the North African coast held by the enemy.

It was assumed that the enemy, sighting the first and dummy convoy soon after it had left, would make the usual scale of attack from the air and eventually be satisfied when he saw it turn for home, afterwards losing interest in any further convoy activity. However, in case this plan miscarried and the real convoy were seen, that also was to turn back, in an attempt to give the impression that it had given up an unequal struggle. After this convoy had retraced its steps for some hours, it was hoped that the enemy would cease to pay it further attention, and that the arrival under cover of darkness of the full escort and another complete change of course would pass unnoticed.

While steaming coastwise, the convoys, both dummy and real, were to be given air escort by single-seater squadrons of the Fighter Group, operating from aerodromes spaced at intervals along the coast, and protection from submarines and by Fleet Air Arm Swordfish. Such steps were those normally taken to protect coastal shipping. But, when the real convoy met its full surface escort, consisting of a cruiser squadron and a destroyer flotilla, and made for open sea, it was to have the strongest possible fighter protection, first from single seaters and then from the longer-range Beaufighters, until it finally steamed out of their range altogether. In the most dangerous part of the passage, on the third day of the operation, when the convoy was open to enemy air attack both from Crete and North African bases, it would be out of reach of our longest-range fighters and have to rely on AA fire for its main defence.

As the convoy steamed westwards, the distance from the North African aerodromes would gradually increase until it was eventually beyond the range of aircraft operating from the nearest enemy base. However, although drawing away from one danger, the unfortunate convoy was going towards another, for an attack by Italian naval units could be expected in the open stretch of sea, and it was here that our Beauforts were to play their part by attempting to turn back an enemy fleet before it could reach its target. If this section of the passage could be negotiated, there still remained several hours of steaming within range of the Sicilian aerodromes, in which Malta would endeavour to give the ships fighter protection.

Altogether, the whole operation, from start to finish, bore the stamp of desperation not to say wishful thinking. The convoy was to spend several days in enclosed waters facing air attack on a scale its small fighter escort could do little to reduce, and later might be opposed by a strong Italian battle fleet, against which its light escort of cruisers and destroyers would be out-gunned; through every day and night of the operation, it could expect incessant attacks by enemy submarines. The operation was being made no easier by the fact that Rommel had all but broken through on the front, where his Air Force, strengthened by recent reinforcements, was being very active indeed. All possible air support was being given to the protection of the ships, but in face of other demands, the forces which could be spared were very small; it was once again a shortage of aircraft which was spelling defeat.

The role of our squadron was to wait at readiness at 05 for the Italian Fleet to put to sea, and immediately it came within our range, to fly out in full strength to attack it, landing afterwards at Malta. It was thought that the enemy fleet might sail prematurely, either on a report of the dummy convoy steaming westwards, or on the first passage west of the real convoy, and that a torpedo attack by our Beauforts would turn it back to port and so leave the central passage free. But to me it seemed that the efficiency of the enemy's aerial reconnaissance and his powers of deduction were being underestimated, for I doubted that he would either lack frequent and accurate reports on the movements of our shipping, or misinterpret their significance. Although the Italian Fleet was notoriously lacking in aggression, it seemed unlikely that it would be deterred from its purpose by the small weight of our attack. It was again apparent that the operation was not only desperate but speculative; straws were being clutched wishfully in an attempt to prevent Malta sinking.

The only bright feature in what I considered to be an otherwise black picture was the information, which transpired in the course of the conference, that another Beaufort squadron, No 217, was now at Malta, having been flown out from England especially for this operation. Not only did the presence of this force mean that the strength of aircraft which could be sent against the Italian Fleet was doubled, but it appeared to be a first step in a direction to which I had long been pointing; if a squadron could be based there for attacks on battleships, it could remain to attack merchantmen. However, on inquiring further into the intended use of 217 Squadron, I found that it was really on its way to Ceylon, and only staying at Malta until this one operation was complete; there still appeared to be no intention of using the Island as a base for an offensive against the enemy's supply line.

Although general attention was focussed on the immediate operation I looked on it only as a means to an end, and considered that the enormous cost of reinforcing Malta was not justifiable unless it were afterwards used as an offensive base.

The squadron, after intensive efforts on the part of the maintenance crews, was able to produce no less than twelve serviceable Beauforts, but this number, greater than we had ever produced before, was really inadequate for the task. As usual, not a single Beaufighter could be spared to escort us, for both the Coastal long-range fighter squadrons would be putting all their resources into providing cover for the convoy. The Beauforts would have to fly out alone, risk the chance of meeting fighters and attack the target as best they could; we were to be one of the slender straws at which drowning Malta was clutching.

On the first day of the operation our twelve Beauforts were flown up to 05 by the pick of the squadron's crews, a plan of attack was made, and we settled down to wait. It was not until the third day of the operation, June 15th, that we expected a call, for on that day the convoy would begin its passage into the Central Mediterranean and the Italian fleet might be expected to steam down from its base at Taranto to intercept it. So while the other coastal squadrons were active during the first two days of the operation we waited as interested, very interested spectators, with our aircraft dispersed in one corner of the vast aerodrome, loaded with torpedoes and ready to strike.

At 05 the steady flow of routine operations of normal times was replaced by a whirlpool of continuous and intense activity, for the detachments of a few visiting aircraft which were usually dispersed around the aerodrome boundary had now become the full strength of every coastal squadron. Wing Ops Room was as crowded as a railway station on bank holiday, with fighter pilots coming in with news from the convoy, Maryland crews bringing back their reconnaissance reports from the open sea, and we, the crews of the Beaufort squadron, waiting anxiously for the news that the Italian Fleet had left harbour.

On the first day the dummy convoy was duly sighted by the enemy's reconnaissance aircraft and attracted considerable attention from the air during its passage up the coast. It reached its turning point just off Sidi Barrani as night fell, and, standing outside our tents at 05 before turning in, we could see the light of flares in the sky over the sea and hear the gunfire of the escort replying to the enemy's air attack. On the second day the dummy convoy had retired according to plan, and the real convoy was coming up the coast level with Tobruk. As I had feared, the enemy were not slow in noticing its presence, and as the day passed, the fighter crews brought in reports of increasingly severe air attack; however the convoy was still under single-seater protection and was reported to be holding its own. On both days Marylands had been out covering the Central Mediterranean and sea reconnaissances had also been made from Malta, but there was no news of the Italian Fleet leaving its harbour at Taranto.

When on the afternoon of the second day there was still no sign of the enemy fleet putting to sea, the Wing CO released the squadron, which normally stood by throughout the day at an hour's readiness to operate, and we all went down to the beach to bathe. To me, this bathing in the clear blue sea was almost the only attraction which Egypt had to offer, and the beach at Sidi Barrani one of the most beautiful, enchanting places I have ever seen. Along the coast stretched a green belt of desert vegetation, an English lawn in comparison with the unrelieved sand of the interior, then came a narrow border of white salt hills, and finally the beach itself of fine soft sand. The sea, which was deep blue on the horizon, became within the curve of the bay turquoise, varying shades of blue and sometimes pale green, with the surf from its breaking waves matching the white salt hills and pale sand. Always there was a fresh breeze from the sea, and when sand was blowing up in the interior, making eyes sore and grinding between teeth, the beach would be a calm refuge; it was the only place where I ever welcomed the hot sun which beat down day after day from the cloudless sky. We bathed, lay in the sun, then went back into the sea again, forgetting completely in the peace of an afternoon on the beach the grim bustle of activity on the aerodrome a few miles away. It did not occur to us that just at this time the Italian Fleet was setting out from harbour.

On returning to the aerodrome we found even greater activity in progress than when we had left a few hours before. The convoy had now turned back to meet its cruiser escort, which it would join at nightfall, when the whole force would turn again to steam westwards under cover of darkness and start the critical third day's passage through the channel to open sea. The enemy had been making attacks on the ships at intervals throughout the day, but the convoy had always been within range of our single seaters, and it was not until the next day that the Beaufighters would furnish its only protection from the air, with Blenheims keeping watch over submarine activity.

However, it was not in our own convoy that 39 Squadron was most interested, but in the movements of the enemy warships, and in our absence on the beach the expected report had been received from

Malta that one of her reconnaissance aircraft had sighted an Italian fleet steaming south from Taranto. Since this force was not yet within a Maryland's range from 0.5, a reconnaissance aircraft from Malta would shadow it until one of the Wellingtons from the aerodrome could pick it up during the night. It was now certain that we would make an attack on the next day, and only our time of take-off remained to be decided on the result of the night reconnaissance.

After darkness had fallen, the sound of gunfire could be heard both from the distant front and far out to sea; the convoy had turned and was fighting its way westwards, and a battle was raging in the desert. Rommel, now supported by a strong air force, was pressing harder than ever; our army was known to have evacuated some forward positions near Tobruk during the day, and Bu Amud had been abandoned. A feeling of uneasiness was present in the previously cheerful atmosphere of the Mess, and uneasiness gave way to something approaching depression as during the evening reports were received of a definite retreat on the front and rumours were circulated that the convoy had sustained loss.

I myself went to bed early, knowing that a call in the early hours of the morning for a dawn take-off was probable, but sleep was continually interrupted. At intervals through the night bombs burst near the aerodrome, our guns opened fire on the raiders, and whenever the sky was clear of the enemy, the roar of our own aircraft filled the air. The steady note of aircraft on the circuit and the sound of distant gunfire never ceased, while the rumble of transport and clatter of tanks on the road continued endlessly; the land, sea and air battle had started in earnest, and 05 was in the middle of it.

The squadron took off at seven o'clock on the next morning with orders to attack an Italian battle fleet in the Central Mediterranean and afterwards land at Malta. The Wellington, which had shadowed the enemy fleet during the night, reported that it had split into two separate forces, both steaming southwards about twenty miles apart, and it was apparent that the intention was for one force to draw off the convoy's cruiser escort, while the other engaged the defenceless merchant ships. Our target was the larger of these two forces, consisting of the battleships *Littorio* and *Cavour*, accompanied by a small screen of cruisers and a full destroyer escort; if we could turn this force back or delay it, it would be possible for the cruiser squadron to engage the smaller enemy force while the merchant vessels steamed on unmolested.

A Maryland, which had taken off before us, was to relocate our target, shadow it and send back wireless reports of its latest position, course and speed. In spite of this assistance the task of finding the target in open sea after several hours' of flying out of sight of land was the most difficult part of the whole operation, and although I would have liked to have been leading the actual attack, I was glad that this heavy responsibility rested not on me, but on the CO, who was himself leading the squadron. However, I was a little worried for his experience was entirely with flying boats, he had never previously led an important torpedo attack, and I had never before followed, but always led myself; I knew from experience exactly what action I would take in certain circumstances, and the fact that he might at any time lead me into a situation which I would have avoided, made the flight from the start an uncomfortable one for me. Soon discomfort gave way to real apprehension, not only for myself but for the whole force.

The twelve Beauforts took off as the sun was rising, formed up on the circuit in four sections of three aircraft, and set out to sea, flying low over the water northwards, altering to a westerly course with the enemy coastline rather too close for safety. The CO was leading two sections of the older Beauforts, the second section led by Alastair, on his right, while I was on his left at the head of six Mark IIs, with Tony's section following mine. It was our intention to divide at the target and attack in two waves of six aircraft, but I was soon wishing that we could divide at once, for the duplication of aircraft types gave rise to trouble.

I found that in order to keep station, I had not only to throttle the engines right back, but also to put down a certain degree of flap, which was normally never used except for landing. Looking down at the airspeed indicator, I found to my horror that we were flying at the unbelievably low speed of one hundred and twenty knots. Not only was this slow speed making it difficult to keep formation, but to my mind extremely dangerous, for we were flying parallel to the enemy coast, not quite within sight of land but well within range of single seater fighters, and I thought that this particular section of the flight could not be completed too quickly; if these waters were dangerous to the convoy, they were no less so to us. Messages were being flashed from my following aircraft, all Mark IIs, suggesting that we should fly faster, for our cruising speed was uncomfortably near stall for a fully loaded aircraft flying low and in formation, and the pilots were finding it difficult to keep station. I asked Creswell to flash a similar signal to the CO's aircraft which, however, resulted in an acknowledgment but no increase in speed, and I was forced to accept the implication that his aircraft would go no faster.

After an hour of this uncomfortable flying, the squadron's formation, which had started by being faultless, had become somewhat ragged and there were already several stragglers. At intervals I made further signals to the CO's aircraft, but although they were received, no improvement resulted, and we continued to fly at the same dangerously low speed. Finally I grew angry, for I could see we were heading for disaster, and told Creswell to amend the previous polite request for an increase in speed to the peremptory warning: "For God's sake go faster", but still the leader flew on with his speed unchanged. I grew anxious, for it seemed to me that he was leading us into danger, and in fact danger did appear almost immediately in the form of single-seater fighters.

Just after Creswell had told me that the last urgent message had been acknowledged, my air gunner reported several Macchi 202s and Messerschmitt 109s approaching the formation from the north. I searched the sky, but could not see the enemy aircraft, for they were behind us, but in the distance on the seaward side I was surprised to see the ships of our convoy steaming slowly westwards, while on the other side the North African coast could just be discerned as a faint blur on the horizon. We were flying exactly half way between our convoy and the coast and the fighters which now appeared on the scene had probably been taking part in an attack on the convoy's air escort, the unfortunate Beaufighters, and were returning home when they sighted us. I could not catch a glimpse of the enemy aircraft myself, but my gunner told me that several of them were standing off at some distance away, as if uncertain whether to attack. Although it was bad luck that our formation had been spotted, it was not too late to take measures to defend ourselves, and, despairing of the CO increasing his speed, I signalled to my followers to close up in tight formation and led them on ahead.

Then the fighters started to attack, and I began to weave, making small but frequent alterations in direction and height, flying always on a westerly course and never far from the surface of the water. Our aircraft, with petrol tanks almost full and carrying heavy torpedoes, were not very manoeuvrable, and since we could not fight a running engagement but had to continue towards our target, we were even more at a disadvantage with the single seaters than usual. This sort of fight is nerve racking to a pilot, who can rarely see his adversaries, and must depend entirely on his rear gunner for information, and it is particularly unpleasant to a leader, who is responsible for the safety of his followers. Now my gunner kept up a steady running commentary on the fighters' movements, enabling me to time a turn correctly and so unsight our opponents when they came in to attack; occasionally tracer trajectories would pour past my wing and I would hear the chatter of the twin guns replying from the turret. There was nothing thrilling about this fight, it was unrelievedly grim.

The other aircraft of the formation were covering each other well by cross fire from their turrets, and at first it appeared that we might be able to hold our own. I could, in fact, easily have led the Mark IIs over the horizon to safety, we had so much speed in hand, but I was unwilling to leave the older Beauforts to be out-numbered and throttled back to remain in support. Soon the number of enemy fighters increased and they became bolder, until with half a dozen single seaters threatening our tail, my gunner began to have difficulty in keeping track of each of them and giving me sufficient warning of an impending attack. They began to adopt more aggressive tactics, closing in to short range, confusing our return fire and avoiding action by attacking simultaneously in pairs from opposite sides. The situation which a few minutes before had appeared to be under control took a turn for the worse.

The aircraft on my right was the first to go down in flames. This success seemed to encourage the enemy fighters to become more aggressive, and I found it increasingly difficult to avoid their repeated attacks from short range. One of the CO's formation went down into the sea, sending up a great column of water before vanishing from sight beneath the surface, and several other aircraft were beginning to straggle. My left hand man disappeared suddenly without my seeing him go, for I was more than fully occupied in looking after my own aircraft which had already been hit several times in the wing. The squadron, which had set out that morning as a well drilled formation of twelve Beauforts, was, after an hour's flying, sadly changed in appearance; it was neither looking, nor feeling, very happy.

The temptation to open the throttles fully, perhaps use the emergency lever, and run away from danger at three hundred miles an hour, was very great, but I knew the attack could not last for ever and if we could keep together a few minutes longer safety might be reached. We were drawing the fighters away from their aerodromes and soon they must either exhaust their ammunition or run low in petrol and be forced to break off the engagement.

After a fight which lasted no more than ten minutes by the clock, but seemed an hour in the time of the world of anxiety, my gunner reported first one, and then another of the single seaters breaking away and making for the coast, until, with the sky once more clear of the enemy, I was able to return to my position on the left of the CO. By this time the squadron was one in name only, for there were gaps everywhere; some aircraft were straggling, others were turning back, presumably hit in some vital spot, until at the end of two hours' flying only five Beauforts remained of the twelve which had set out. If the original formation of twelve had been inadequate for an attack on battleships, this little force of five Beauforts was ludicrously small, but our orders were to attack, and our target was an important one. We had flown through one danger, we could face another, so we continued: five Beauforts which had been twelve, flying steadily westwards.

After three hours had passed since setting course from 05, Creswell told me that by his calculations we were nearing the expected position of our target. My wireless operator had already intercepted the expected wireless report from the Maryland giving the Italian fleet's latest position, course and speed, and a small change in our own course shortly afterwards indicated that the CO's operator had also received the message. When the squadron had re-formed after the fighter attack, a Beaufort had joined up on either side of mine, their section leader—like my two followers—having fallen out, and I was again leading a complete section of three, while the CO had a single follower. We were flying thus as two sections, one behind the other, five lonely aircraft in the middle of a great expanse of sea, when the target came into sight on the horizon.

It was hazy in the open stretch of sea, and the enemy warships, which were painted a very light grey, merged in with both sea and sky and might have passed unnoticed but for the lines of white foam churned up in their wake. Creswell sighted the fleet first, when it was about twelve miles away, and the enemy must have spotted our aircraft almost immediately afterwards, for fire was opened on us from extreme range, and well before individual ships were distinguishable. These long-range anti-aircraft guns fired no tracer ammunition, and only the tongues of flame which flashed from the distant haze, the black smoke puffs appearing as if from nowhere in the air nearby and columns of water thrown up by shells exploding on the surface, gave evidence that the fleet was putting up a long-range barrage. Under fire we adopted a looser formation, enabling each aircraft to weave independently and present a difficult target to the guns, never steady for a moment, yet always flying so low over the sea that it could not be silhouetted against the lighter sky.

As we drew near, the fleet emerging from the haze gradually took shape and the two great battleships could be seen steaming in 'line ahead', with a cruiser screen in front of them and lines of destroyers on each side. The leading battleship was our target, for to reduce its speed by hits beneath the waterline would be to reduce the effective-

ness of the whole fleet, but in order to reach torpedo dropping range
we would have to pass through the lines of escorting destroyers, both
before and after the attack. The fleet, consisting of about twenty-five
ships in all, was steaming at high speed in such a precise formation
that it appeared like an impregnable fortress from which all guns were
pointing at our five Beauforts, attempting to assault it.

Approaching still closer, we came within range of the light multiple
anti-aircraft guns; the sky was filled not with individual smoke puffs,
but with great areas of exploding shells, vast expanses of water were
churned up around our aircraft, and innumerable lines were drawn
across the sky by tracer ammunition. Time once again seemed to be
standing still.

A disturbed night, an early call and three hours in the air, had made
me tired, and I found that I had been flying rather mechanically until
this barrage rocked me from my stupor and made me realise that I
would have to make a greater effort to pierce the defences, make my
attack and fly safely out of range. Not mechanical but inspired flying
was needed to avoid this enormous volume of fire, and sweat poured
down my face as I aroused myself to throw my faithful Mark II around
the sky, turning first one way, then the other, climbing and diving yet
always heading towards the target and never straying far from the
surface of the water.

How I passed through the destroyer screen unscathed is still a
mystery; one moment I saw in front of me a gap about a quarter of a
mile wide between two destroyers in the line flanking the battleships,
and the next moment I had passed through it and found myself flying
over a stretch of water in which no obstruction lay between my aircraft
and the target. Making about twenty knots, pitching gently in the
slight swell which prevailed, sending up a great wave over her bows
and leaving a long white wake lashed up behind her, the battleship
Littorio steamed majestically across my line of sight. I could see
individual sailors on deck, watched fascinated the anti-aircraft guns
swinging round towards me and could even distinguish the lines of
rivets on the ship's side. Hardly able to believe that I was actually
within range of such a prized target, I ceased weaving for a split
second, steadied my aircraft to take aim, and dropped my torpedo at
the battleship.

Just as I was starting to turn away, the ship's fire control must have
got my range; the whole side of the battleship seemed to go off like a
firework and become a line of jets spurting flame; the water beneath
me became a cauldron of foam seething under the explosions of shells
bursting near the surface, and the sky around my aircraft was filled

with the flashes and smoke of others exploding in the air. Opening the engines up to full throttle I attempted to escape from this furnace, but my aircraft, rocking drunkenly from nearby explosions, seemed to be standing still, and when finally there was a deafening explosion underneath the fuselage and a sickening sound of rending metal, I thought for a bitter moment that the flight had come to an end. Oil from a broken hydraulic pipeline sprayed over the cockpit, drenching my shirt already saturated with sweat; the control column became slippery in my oily hands and the cockpit was filled with the blue smoke of an explosion. Yet we were still flying; I was automatically climbing and diving, twisting and turning, with the engines roaring at full throttle, and we were passing in front of the line of battleships on our way towards the opposite line of destroyers. Streams of tracer were following us; the air was still black with explosions and the sea still a carpet of foam. My gunner, who could now see the inferno which I had just been facing, was unable to produce his usual lucid commentary but could only shout at intervals "Look out" as a stream of shells passed dangerously near his turret. Miraculously a gap appeared in the destroyer screen ahead, through which I raced with as much relief as if it were the gate of heaven itself, for beyond was the open sea, and although gunfire pursued us until we passed out of range and I continued to fly at full throttle until the target disappeared over the horizon behind us, I knew that in open sea we were in safety.

When I had settled down to fly straight and level, I called up each member of the crew in turn, and finding that although somewhat shaken they were uninjured, I turned my attention to the aircraft. The engines, after a long period spent continuously at full throttle, were once more turning comfortably at cruising speed, and their instruments, oil pressure gauges, boost gauges and rev-counters, all showed steady normal readings. Petrol gauges indicated that the engines had been drinking petrol like a thirsty giant during the time the throttles had been wide open, but there were no signs of the tanks being punctured by shrapnel, and Creswell calculated that we still had sufficient petrol in hand to reach Malta. The flying controls were in working order, and the shell which had exploded directly underneath the aircraft appeared, in spite of the considerable impact, not really to have caused any serious damage, although some of the hydraulic pipelines were evidently severed by shrapnel and my gunner reported that his turret was out of action. However, since we were now unlikely to meet enemy fighters, absence of defence did not worry me unduly, nor did the possibility that the hydraulic system working the flaps and undercarriage might also be damaged cause me any misgiving; we were still flying, it looked as if we would reach our destination, and then would be quite soon enough to deal with the problem of landing.

Having satisfied myself that the aircraft would continue to remain in the air, I looked around for signs of the other Beauforts and saw one flying on a parallel course several miles away. After pursuing it for nearly half an hour I drew near enough to read the letter painted on the side, and recognising it as the CO's aircraft took up formation on his right. Soon afterwards another Beaufort appeared from the horizon to join us, and we made the two-hour flight to Malta as a formation of three, with the CO leading. There was time for reflection now, and my thoughts turned back automatically to the target we had left behind us. Had any hits been scored, had we succeeded in our task of turning the fleet back? I wondered idly, speculating on the result with a strange indifference. The attack already seemed to have taken place long ago; it seemed no more real than some far-off battle recounted in a history book. With less detachment I reflected on what might have happened to the two aircraft which had made the attack and not afterwards rejoined formation, and whether those forced to turn back after the fighter engagement had safely regained their aerodrome. Had the Beaufighters fared better than us? Or had they too lost three quarters of their number in desperate fighting over the ships they were protecting?

These reflections, into which I was lulled by the sudden transition from the feverish activity at the target to the contrasting monotony of a flight towards safety, gave way to anticipation as the end of our journey drew near. My wireless operator was intercepting messages passing between the leading aircraft and the wireless station at Malta, by which Creswell could check our position, and for my benefit he converted this information into the time which would elapse before we should see land.

Another half hour of flying seemed an intolerable length of time; fifteen minutes before we should reach our destination was to me an eternity; time which in moments of danger had passed at an agonisingly slow speed now seemed to have been stopped completely by monotony; the view of sea and sky was unchanging, the sun appeared fixed at its zenith. I was so weary and desired the flight to end so much that relief was mingled with disbelief when I heard Creswell's assurance that we should see the Island within five minutes.

Gradually a tiny blur became distinguishable on the horizon ahead, which, as we approached, became more distinct, and out of the distant haze appeared the welcome shape of an island, Malta. From our position low over the water, only a steep cliff-face could at first be seen, but as we climbed up, the whole island came into view beneath us, appearing like a solitary stepping stone misplaced from some pond into this great expanse of blue sea. My first impression was that the island was luxuriant, for it looked so green in comparison with the bare desert, and so full of life; roads, buildings and fields were everywhere, and the coast was crenelated with little coves and bays in which the sea was an exquisite transparent green. I was thrilled at my first sight of this little rock, for I saw that this was no longer Africa, but Europe; although England was a thousand miles away, I felt immediately that on this island I would be very near home, and that was where, at the end of this long flight, I longed to be.

The ground appeared to be so hilly that I could not see where an aerodrome could possibly be made, but I knew that there were actually three in existence, of which our destination was the largest, Luqa. But the CO, who knew Malta well since he had been stationed there in peacetime, led us straight on to the aerodrome circuit, and I was able to distinguish one long runway on which aircraft were landing and taking off. While the CO made his approach, I tested the hydraulic system and found, as I had feared, that it was completely out of action. This meant that I would have to make a 'belly' landing with undercarriage retracted and flaps up, but the prospect hardly disturbed me at all, for I had often seen other pilots putting down their damaged aircraft in this manner and knew exactly how it should be done.

Making a faster approach than usual, since I had not the use of flaps to improve control near stalling speed, I held the aircraft off at a few feet above the runway, and switching off the engines and their petrol supply, braced myself for the inevitable crash. At first it seemed that the aircraft would float on interminably, but eventually it began to sink, down and down, until with a grating sound it settled down at last on its belly and tobogganed down the runway to the accompaniment of a shower of sparks and a sound of rending metal, coming to rest an inglorious wreck in the middle of the aerodrome. We all scrambled hurriedly through the roof, almost before the aircraft had reached a standstill, Creswell clutching the Panda mascot which always flew with me, and grateful to feel our feet firmly on dry land once more, we stood gazing silently and disconsolately at what remained of my own personal Mark II: words could not express what we felt. But to me it mattered not at all how I had come, through fighter attack and through flak, or ingloriously by landing my faithful Beaufort on its belly; what mattered to me was the fact that I was there. I had arrived at Malta.

As I stood gazing at the wreckage and feeling rather guilty that my aircraft should be completely blocking the runway, a Wing Commander drew up with a scowl on his face and remarked: "Dammit, man, we usually do this sort of thing on the grass"; apparently this method of arrival was not uncommon and arrangements were made to deal with the emergency. An army tank was kept close at hand, which now clanked up to my Beaufort, waited for a few minutes while the crew lashed a wire hawser around it, then nonchalantly dragged it off the runway towards the boundary, allowing some Spitfires which had been circling impatiently to come in to land.

If the aerodrome of 05 had seemed a whirlpool during the convoy operation, it was a quiet, peaceful backwater compared with the runway at Luqa. 'Dead' aircraft, damaged by enemy action or a crash, were parked on the grass, of which the majority I noticed were Beauforts. Wellingtons were dispersed around the boundary; an endless chain was made by Spitfires taking off and landing, and a section of Beaufighters were testing their engines before taxying out to take off.

I was standing just off the runway, regarding with amazement this scene of activity, when a car drew up and a familiar voice shouted for me to get in. The owner of the voice was the CO of 217 Squadron, Willie Davies whom I knew well from our days in the Fleet Air Arm together and as we drove to Ops Room, I plied him not only with the usual questions about England, which he had left only a week before, but also about his squadron. I learnt that 217 Squadron really was on its way to Ceylon, but Willie himself was returning to England after the convoy operation and handing over to his second-in-command. The squadron had only made one sortie, when twelve Beauforts had taken off in darkness early that morning and made individual attacks at dawn on the same Italian battle fleet which had been our target later in the day. Not a single aircraft was lost, but several had been hit, a fact which accounted for the number of Beauforts I had seen in the dead aircraft park. All the same, 217 Squadron had fared much better than us, and it seemed to me that this result demonstrated the superiority of Malta over Egypt as a base for these operations.

There was no proper Ops Room at Luqa, only an Intelligence Office, where utter chaos now reigned, for about twenty crews who had just returned from various missions were trying to make their reports to three Intelligence Officers in a room not more than ten feet square. While I was waiting my turn outside the office, my CO appeared and I took the opportunity of expressing my views very strongly on the dangerously slow speed at which he had led the formation. He told me that he had been unlucky in his choice of aircraft and his Beaufort would just not go any faster, but I could not help feeling that he had overestimated the danger of running short of petrol and for that reason had cruised at a speed which, although economical, was suicidal.

While we stood outside the Intelligence Office, discussing the flight and trying to piece together the full story of both the fighter attack on our formation and our torpedo attack on the battleships, our two other crews, who were so long overdue that we had given them up as lost, appeared. It seemed a miracle to me that the five aircraft which had survived the fighter attack should also have come through the intense barrage from the target unscathed and safely reached their destination. The crews of these last two aircraft had experienced difficulty in finding the Island, and one pilot, whose wireless had been put out of action by a near miss, had seen the pointers of his petrol gauges flickering around the dreaded nought when at last he had sighted land after a desperate search of a wide expanse of sea with no wireless to guide him.

By the time we had recounted our stories to each other, the room had become less congested and the Intelligence Officers were free to take our reports. Sinking with relief into an armchair, I accepted gratefully a cigarette which was offered me, in spite of the fact I never smoked. As this indicates, I was extremely tired, and had been answering with the help of my crew the Intelligence Officers' questions for nearly five minutes before I awoke to the fact that he was being politely incredulous of what we were telling him. He had been working through every day and night of the convoy operation, and was no less exhausted than we were, and when for the third time he asked me if I was sure that I had left Sidi Barrani that morning, we both simultaneously burst out laughing. It seemed that the intention to operate our squadron had the reputation at Malta of being mythical, and when news had been received that our aircraft had taken off from Egypt that morning and were to land at Malta, few had believed that we were really in the air or would actually arrive. But five of us had arrived, spectacularly and incredibly, and as our story was gradually unfolded, the operation appeared to the Intelligence Officer no longer mythical, but legendary.

Reports on the torpedo attack were conflicting, for all our pilots had been so preoccupied in taking avoiding action in the barrage of flak that they had hardly paid any attention to what was going on around them. I myself remembered little more than the momentary glimpse of a giant battleship in front of me, but details of that image had become obscured in the subsequent struggle to escape. After some discussion it was established that the whole fleet had turned during the attack, and the leading battleship had afterwards been shrouded in smoke, whether from a torpedo explosion or its own gunfire was uncertain. But I was losing interest in this post-mortem, in fact almost falling asleep in the comfortable armchair, and the reports that there were several Junkers 88s over the fleet, that the strength of the enemy fighters was estimated variously from a dozen to twenty, and that a second and smaller Italian naval force had at one time been visible on the horizon, read to me like the column of an out-of-date newspaper.

Most of us were not only exhausted, but also very hungry and, suddenly realising that our last meal had been at half past five in the morning, we went to the Mess to try and get something to eat. I had completely lost track of time, which seemed to have been playing tricks ever since the flight had started at seven o'clock that morning, but it was with a shock that I found neither lunch, nor tea, but supper being served in the Mess; it was nearly seven o'clock in the evening. After a welcome hot meal, I spent the early part of the evening in the bar, hardly able to keep awake while drinking the local bottled beer and listening to pilots of other squadrons telling their stories, from which I gained an impression of all that had been happening at Malta during the day.

For the first time I heard that two convoys were being run to the Island simultaneously, one as I already knew from Alexandria, the other from Gibraltar, the intention being to divide the enemy's attention and so increase the chances of the ships coming through unscathed. Little was known about the Alexandria convoy, except the bare fact that it had turned back in the middle of the day, inexplicably to many observers, for it appeared to have gone through the most dangerous section of its passage and no longer to be threatened by the Italian fleet. Disappointment at Malta had been intense when it was learnt that this convoy had not continued, and the news caused no little indignation among the crews of the Beaufort squadrons, who appeared to have achieved their objectives, for a reconnaissance made during the afternoon confirmed the Italian fleet as steaming northwards for Taranto with one of the battleships showing signs of damage.

The convoy from the west had come within range of the Malta fighter squadrons at dawn that morning, and the Spitfires and Beaufighters which I had seen operating from the aerodrome had been part of the force protecting it from aerial attack throughout the day. This last stretch was the most dangerous part of the western passage, for although protected by our fighters the convoy had to pass within easy reach of the Sicilian aerodromes and very close to the Island of Pantelleria, on which the enemy could base aircraft. Not only had an intense battle been fought in the air over the convoy, but an attack had been made by a force of Italian cruisers, which at midday had started shelling the lightly escorted merchant ships. Two solitary Beauforts of 217 Squadron, the only aircraft to be immediately available after the squadron's dawn attack on the eastern convoy, had gone out to attack these cruisers and actually made them retire, unfortunately not before great damage had been done. In spite of all possible measures to protect them, many ships of this convoy were lost, and the end of the day which should have seen Malta relieved showed only a few ships of the western convoy and their escorting destroyers safely in harbour at Valletta. This was a bitterly disappointing result to our desperate efforts, and when depressing reports came of fierce fighting on the front in Libya and a retreat by our army, it seemed to me that the day's operations had brought not us, but the enemy, nearer to his objective.

Although it was still light outside, I could keep awake no longer, and leaving the bar, which looked as if it would resound with the hum of reminiscences until the early hours of the morning, I made my way to my billet for the night, a building in Luqa village which had formerly been a Nunnery. Looking from the window of my room, I watched the sun, which I had seen rising over the desert that morning, going down behind the hills of Malta, silhouetting the spires and domes of its villages against the red horizon. As the light from the last rays of the sun died away, the sky changed slowly from pale to darker blue, and the stars became distinguishable in the darkened sky, in which appeared a crescent moon hanging low over the horizon. Beholding this new moon, I made a wish.

Throughout the night the sound of aircraft circling the aerodrome could be heard; night fighters on patrol or Wellingtons going out on reconnaissance. Sirens wailed at intervals, and I was awakened by the intermittent note of enemy aircraft overhead. The engines of their dive bombers roared, a staccato crackle of gunfire greeted them, and the sky outside was illuminated by searchlight beams. Bombs burst nearby, the Nunnery shook under their explosion; plaster fell from the ceiling and the flickering light of a blazing fire was reflected in a mirror. The enemy were raiding the harbour and attempting to destroy the few ships which had arrived safely. Yet I only turned over, wearily, in my bed; I was tired, and all this activity had nothing to do with me. I no longer wanted activity or excitement, only rest, and slept through the night well into the next morning.

At lunch time on the next day I heard that, now the convoy operation was completed, the Beauforts were no longer required on the Island. Now all the torpedo aircraft were being prepared to move, 217 Squadron to Ceylon and our few remaining aircraft back to Egypt.

The removal of the anti-shipping forces from the Island at a time when they could be operated most usefully against the enemy's supply line to relieve the pressure on land in Egypt, appeared to me a short-sighted policy. Although the enemy made raids regularly by day and night, of which the objectives were the harbour and aerodromes, these were no longer on such a scale that they would prevent our aircraft from operating efficiently. I still had no detailed information as to what route the enemy's supply ships were now taking, but Malta was in such a central position that I felt certain they must come within our range during the greater part of their passage, not for a period of hours as from Egypt, but possibly for two or three days of their voyage.

I was unwilling to leave without at least attempting to make the staff accept the suggestion, which 201 Group had rejected, that a strong anti-shipping force should be based permanently at Malta, so I sounded out several of the officers stationed at Luqa on the probable reception of such a suggestion, and finding their opinions encouraging, went during the afternoon to the RAF Headquarters at Valletta to approach the Air Staff. The Senior Air Staff Officer was busy, but his deputy, who saw me, listened carefully to my recital of our difficulties of operating from Egypt and the advantages of carrying out Beaufort strikes from Malta. When I had finished, he whistled slowly, tapped his teeth thoughtfully with a pencil and said that he thought there was something in the idea and that I should repeat my story to the AOC.

Before I knew quite what had happened I found myself sitting in a chair in the great man's office telling him what I thought was wrong with our Mediterranean strategy! The AOC at this time was Air Vice-Marshal Hugh Lloyd, who had become famous during his term of command for the tenacity with which he had defended Malta through the heavy raids of the winter months. I found him not only the personi-fication of aggression, but also the possessor of sufficient sense of humour not to resent my ideas; on the contrary, he welcomed them. Any offensive operation appealed strongly to him, and my suggestion that 217 Squadron should be retained on the Island and 39 Squadron moved from Egypt was well received. Neither the failure of the long awaited convoy from the East to reach its destination nor the advance of Rommel's army in Libya influenced the decision of this great leader who never thought in terms of retreat; the idea of using Malta as a means of stabbing Rommel in the back and frustrating his plan at this last moment must have been irresistible to him.

Instead of being told to mind my own business, as I had feared might happen, the AOC thanked me for the visit and promised that he would make the suggestion to the Commander-in-Chief in Cairo by signal immediately. Just as I was leaving, he enquired how I was returning to Egypt, and on being told that I would probably be flying as a passenger in the CO's Beaufort, he called one of his staff and told him to make arrangements for me to fly back by air liner that night.

This interview had been so unexpected and its result so gratifying that I was in a half-dazed condition of supreme happiness when I left Headquarters, and for some time afterwards wandered through the streets of Valletta as if in a trance, trying to imagine just what the success of this plan would mean. At Malta, removed from the excessive heat of the desert, the irrepressible swarms of flies and blowing sand, I would feel well again; I would no longer sleep on a camp bed in a tent, but on a soft bed in a comfortable stone building. I would enjoy the benefit of hot water and gaze with pleasure at rain clouds in the sky and green vegetation growing from the earth. But personal attractions faded before the operational advantages which the Island offered, and considering these, I came suddenly to my senses and realised that Malta appealed to me not because living would be more pleasant or flights less hazardous, but because it was where I should be. I saw clearly that here was the scene of the important operations for which I had left England, travelled around the Cape, passed through Egypt and made a flight through fire and over water to reach this destination; Malta was a step in my circular journey back to England, a journey which could not be completed until I had blazed a path of sinking ships on which to travel. Seeing my way home distinctly for the first time, I immediately ceased my wanderings in the narrow streets between the hollow bombed buildings, and made my way back to the Mess to write a letter, which I sent to England. "39 Squadron, now at Malta", was the address with which I headed the paper; I wrote these words proudly.

CHAPTER VIII

MALTA AT LAST!

I LEFT Malta on the night of June 16th as a passenger in a Lockheed 'Lodestar' air liner, and returned at dawn on June 22nd, flying my own Beaufort; between these two dates the future of my plan, on which my own future so much depended, wavered uncertainly. A series of incidents led up to my second arrival on the Island which would not have been remarkable individually, but together formed the links of a chain which was so strong that it seemed the hand of fate was moving me relentlessly to my destination against all earthly opposition. Throughout this week there was continual uncertainty as to whether I should be sent to Malta, and during the subsequent months which I spent on the Island it was never certain that I should eventually go home. Yet once I had actually reached Malta, I never again returned to Egypt; after flying out many times from the Island as pilot of my own Beaufort, at the head of a force making for the enemy coast to attack shipping, I made my last flight as a passenger in an airliner, flying westwards to England. My dream did come true.

The Lodestar, one of several similar aircraft which made a nightly trip to Malta to bring stores and evacuate some of the inhabitants, flew me back to Egypt in comfort. Arriving at Heliopolis at sunrise, I telephoned to LG87 for the CO's car to fetch me, and went to the Mess for breakfast. The news, which I read in the Cairo paper that morning, was bad. Our army was now definitely stated to have been driven from its defended position on the Gazala line and to be retreating under pressure from Rommel's armoured divisions; several forward aerodromes had fallen into the enemy's hands and Tobruk was again besieged. My fear that Rommel would accumulate forces too strong for our army to resist was being justified; I was tired of watching helplessly my amateur forecast coming true. As I read this depressing news, I wondered idly if the overdue reinforcement aircraft were yet coming from America in sufficient numbers to stem the tide of retreat, and remembered the race which I had witnessed in Headquarters Ops Room between the enemy's supply ships and our aircraft, their progress indicated on the blackboard and the map. These thoughts reminded me of my friends on the Ops staff, and I decided to take advantage of my presence in Cairo to visit them.

When the car arrived, I drove to Headquarters, where I found the Ops staff officers unchanged since I had left. Ops 1 asked with interest about the racecourse at Malta, which he remembered from a successful day at some peacetime meeting, and seemed disappointed when I told him it was no longer used. Ops 2 appeared to be unaware that a convoy operation had been in progress, but Ops 3, who had read a report of our attack, produced for my benefit one of his rare smiles, and asked if I had written any bright minutes while I was at Malta. I replied that I had, as a matter of fact, done some staff work on my visit, and told him the story of my interview with the AOC. Conversation then passed to the situation on the front, and I found the opinion held in Headquarters even more depressing than the news in the morning paper; not only was the army in full retreat but unlikely to make a stand until the Egyptian frontier was reached. More welcome was the information that American aircraft were reaching Egypt in large numbers; the promised flow had started in earnest. Old squadrons were being re-equipped, new squadrons were forming, and the outlook for the future was good. In two, perhaps three months' time, Ops 3 thought, sufficient air strength would be available to drive the enemy out of the sky. Meanwhile the army would attempt to hold the line while waiting for reinforcements; the future seemed assured; it was the present which was still so uncertain.

While I was sitting on Ops 3's desk, talking, the first of a series of lucky incidents occurred; the Air Commodore passed along the balcony, saw me and asked me to come into his office. He wished to hear the story of our attack on the battleships, but to me that was now an event of the past and I was more interested in winning further support for my idea of basing Beauforts at Malta. I saw in this chance interview an opportunity to tie the knot of intrigue at both ends, for I knew that AVM Lloyd's signal would be under consideration in these Headquarters at this very moment, and if I could win support from the Air Commodore he might sway the C-in-C's decision in favour of the proposal. So I led the conversation around to the problem of attacking the enemy's supply ships, and after enumerating the advantages of Malta as a base for these operations, I found my views again received with enthusiasm. The Air Commodore said he would discuss the whole matter with the C-in-C, and although he made no promise that my suggestion would be accepted, I left with confidence that the foundation of the plan was now firmly laid. After this encouraging interview I left Headquarters to drive back to LG87 in even higher spirits than on the last occasion, when only a few weeks before I had escaped from my office to join the squadron; I felt that I was already on my way to Malta.

As the tents of the aerodrome came within sight, I wondered quite what effect the casualties of the attack would have on the remainder of the squadron, and whether the spirit which had risen so steadily in the preceding weeks would once again have fallen to the level at which I had first found it. But I was reassured by the greeting which I received on arriving in the Mess, and saw with relief Alastair, Tony and Ken, the pilots of three of the aircraft which had been seen to turn back after the fighter attack. Two of them had succeeded in limping home and landing safely at 05, their aircraft hit either in petrol tanks or engines, but Ken, whose Beaufort was riddled with holes, had run out of petrol when actually within sight of the aerodrome, and was forced to crash-land in the desert with his undercarriage retracted. The operation had, after all, not been so costly in casualties as had at first seemed likely; of the four aircraft missing, three had definitely been shot down by fighters, but the fourth had been still flying when last seen, and might possibly have reached the African coast. However, the majority of the squadron's aircraft were either missing, riddled with bullet holes, or crashed, and I saw immediately a defect in the plan to move 39 Squadron to Malta; it no longer existed as a striking force and several weeks would pass before it could raise a reasonable number of aircraft.

Within the next few days the CO and our other crews returned from Malta, some in their own Beauforts, others, whose aircraft had been crashed at Luqa, flying as passengers in a Wellington which was in transit from England to Egypt. Once more the squadron settled down to its routine, not despondent at the losses, but rather proud at having acquitted itself well in a difficult task. Crews went into Alexandria for a few days' leave, new aircraft were fetched from the Reserve Pool, and the events of the past were forgotten in expectation of the future. As the longest day of the year approached, the sun beat down with increased intensity and the heat became insufferable. Occasionally the sand blew off the desert and always the irritation from flies persisted, while work proceeded endlessly on the squadron's unserviceable aircraft.

These days passed in an agony of suspense for me, for I was waiting for some indication that my suggestion had either been accepted or turned down. After my encouraging interviews with the AOC in Malta on the Monday and with the Air Commodore at Headquarters in Cairo on the next day, I had expected that the squadron would receive an immediate order to send its available aircraft to Malta. As the week passed slowly without news of the expected order, I began to fear that the very small number of aircraft which the squadron could at present produce and the failure of all but a few ships to reach Malta might decide against the plan; the resources, both of the Island and 39 Squadron, might now be considered insufficient for the task. When Saturday came at last and still there was no sign of an order to move, I reluctantly accepted the implication that my proposal had been rejected and tried to reconcile myself to two or perhaps three years spent not in the sands of Egypt but in some desert further east into which I thought the enemy would inevitably drive us. But that evening it looked as if I was to be reprieved from that unattractive future; a telephone message was received from Group instructing the squadron to prepare six aircraft to 'stand by' for some unspecified operation on the next day. This was the largest force which the squadron could raise at this time, and while the CO, who was ignorant of my activities, wondered what operation Group had in mind, I realised immediately that these aircraft were destined for Malta.

Just at that moment when it appeared that my goal would be achieved, my hopes were dashed by a glance at the operation order which the CO produced; it detailed not me, but the other flight commander, Alastair Taylor to lead the force. This was a completely unexpected obstacle, and seemingly insuperable. I had originally thought the whole squadron might be moved, then, when it had become obvious that such a move was impossible on account of the shortage of aircraft, I had imagined that a few aircraft would be sent, and I would be detailed to lead them. The enthusiasm with which I had welcomed the news turned to despondency at this unforeseen turn of events. I went to bed early that night, feeling bitterly disappointed at the omission of my name from the operation order; it seemed that I had lost the opportunity which I had struggled to create. I felt so near and yet so far from Malta.

The next morning the CO went into Alexandria to visit Group, and left me responsible for despatching the six available aircraft to 05 in the event of an order being received to do so. I was sitting in the tent, which was my Flight Office, trying to become resigned to remaining in Egypt and consoling myself with the hope that the squadron might be ordered to send more aircraft to the Island in a few weeks' time, when Alastair came in and asked me if I would like to take his place! He had been promoted to Squadron Leader on the previous day, and suffering now from the results of the usual celebration which had lasted well into the night, thought it would be wiser not to fly. Restraining with difficulty a note of enthusiasm from my voice, I replied that I would be only too delighted to do him a good turn and would certainly fly in his place. While Alastair retired happily to bed, I went happily to work. I amended the operation order, selected a good Mark II from my flight, and told my crew to pack. Luck was on my side.

At midday the expected order for the six aircraft to fly up to 05 was received, but the object was still stated to be an operation not a move, presumably for reasons of secrecy. We had packed our kit in the aircraft, tested our engines and were taxiing out on to the aerodrome when the order was countermanded.

The sun was at its height and there was not a breath of wind in the air; the interior of the cockpit was like a greenhouse, the perspex panels magnifying the sun's rays. My shirt was soaked in sweat, flies were settling on my face and I had burnt my hands on the scorching metal parts of the aircraft, when a messenger ran out from Ops Room to tell me that the order was cancelled. Taxiing wearily back to the dispersal point, I switched off the engines and sat for several minutes in the cockpit, unable to raise the energy to move. Neither I nor my crew felt capable of unloading our kit, and we decided to leave it in the aircraft until the evening. I could register no emotion at this last-minute disappointment. My spirits had risen and fallen so often during the preceding days that I was no longer capable of enthusiasm or despondency, and retired like the other crews, to spend the Sunday afternoon sleeping on a camp bed. I accepted defeat.

At five o'clock I was awakened by a runner with a message that I was wanted on the telephone. I rose and walked, not very enthusiastically, across the stretch of sand between my tent and the Mess, and picked up the receiver to find myself speaking to a staff officer of 201 Group. I listened, still without enthusiasm, but with increasing attention to his detailed instructions, for I realised that this time the order for our aircraft to move was being made in earnest. It appeared that 235 Wing had been evacuated from Sidi Barrani on account of the enemy's advance, and only a small party had been left behind to receive visiting aircraft. Throughout the day it had been doubtful whether the aerodrome could be used, it was so near the new front line, but according to the latest information it would be held until the next morning. Our orders were to fly immediately to 05, have our aircraft refuelled and loaded with torpedoes, and leave for Malta not later than midnight. How long we were to remain on the Island was not known. The staff officer wished me luck, and I thanked him for no reason, for I knew I already had it.

A hectic scramble to round up the party and get the aircraft started followed this last-minute order, for there was no time to spare if we were to land in daylight. In the end we reached 05 just as the sun was going down, but without Creswell's assurance that we were at our destination I would never have recognised the aerodrome I knew so well. The great canvas town, which was situated between the northern boundary and the road, had completely vanished; there was not a single tent within sight. Instead of the usual display of many different types of aircraft on the aerodrome, only a few Wellingtons and Fleet Air Arm Albacores stood on the boundary. The remainder of the coastal aircraft had retired with the tents of Wing Headquarters to an aerodrome at Fuka, some two hundred miles further east. What had formerly been a large and active camp was now a desolation of desert, waiting to fall into the hands of the enemy.

As I approached to land in the half light of dusk, I misjudged my height above the ground and flattened out too soon, allowing the aircraft to stall. One wing dropped dangerously before I could correct it, then one wheel touched the sand, and with the aircraft tilted at a drunken angle, I thought for one horrible moment that we were going to crash, but to my relief it righted itself and, after bouncing ungracefully towards the boundary, came safely to rest. The journey to Malta already appeared to be a hazardous one of many pitfalls, and I realised with misgiving that we were not yet half way there.

I parked my Beaufort in a corner of the aerodrome, where it was soon joined by four of the five other aircraft of the party which had landed in quick succession after me. The sixth aircraft was thought to have developed some defect, for it had been seen to turn back shortly after take-off. By the time the last aircraft had been parked, it was almost dark, and five rather bewildered crews collected on the boundary, wondering quite what to do.

Just as I was feeling that our arrival, particularly my landing, should have attracted some attention, a lorry drew up and the driver called to us to jump in. He then drove off the aerodrome on to a track leading into the desert, and after a few minutes drew up outside the entrance to a dugout which, he told me, was being used as an Ops Room. Entering this improvised Ops Room, I found a very hoarse officer talking into a field telephone under the flickering light of a hurricane lamp, and recognised immediately the conditions I had experienced at Bu Amud. But although the scene was similar, circumstances were different. 05 was situated not behind a stable line, as I had known Bu Amud, but directly in the path of an advancing enemy. The officer in charge was attempting, single-handed, to attend to the needs of about twenty aircrews, to direct the refuelling, loading and flare path parties, and to interpret the almost unintelligible orders he received from Group over the field telephone. At the same time he was preparing to move his detachment back at short notice before the expected enemy advance, after providing aircraft landing on the aerodrome with facilities until the last possible moment. Not surprisingly I found the Ops officer a very harassed man and not very pleased at the arrival of five more aircraft on his aerodrome, although he had been forewarned of our coming. However, he promised to have our aircraft refuelled and loaded with some torpedoes, which had been left behind especially for our use, while we were having supper, and I left him conducting a three-way conversation with a Wellington squadron commander, an airman from the flare path and someone on the other end of the field telephone.

Sitting on a mound of sand in the open air, watching aircraft taking off and landing, we ate our supper, which had been prepared in a field kitchen. I think we were not only tired, but also a little nervous, for there was tension in the atmosphere at 05 that night. The sound of gunfire was no longer in the distance, but close at hand, and the western sky was lit up repeatedly by flashes of explosions or the occasional light of flares. The dull frightening murmur of the enemy moving up his line under cover of darkness persisted endlessly in the background of sound, a contrast to the heavy, undisguised rumble of our transport on the coastal road, travelling not towards the front, but ominously eastwards. We were not frightened, but sick at heart that the army should be retreating; we had become attached to the aerodromes from which we flew; the desert around them had seemed our own property and their messes had been our homes. It had been difficult to visualise future operations when Bu Amud fell, and now that 05 was passing into the hands of the enemy, it seemed that the squadron had no future. Whether we should reach Malta, and what awaited us there, was still uncertain.

Our apprehension was increased by an accident which occurred on the aerodrome within our sight. A Wellington failed to rise at the end of its take-off, and crashing into rising ground near the boundary, burst into flames. A burning aircraft is a spectacle which always chills the heart of those who fly, and now, as the aerodrome became illuminated by the flickering light of the flames and the crackle of

The author in September 1942.

Opposite page from top to bottom: A group from 39 Squadron in Alexandria, including Tony Leaning (on left) and Alastair Taylor (on right) both wearing winter uniforms. Beaufort Mk IIA, AW337 flown by the author after delivery in 1942, is photographed on a desert airstrip. The same aircraft being towed off the runway at Luqa by a tank after being crashlanded by the author following his attack on battleships, 15 June 1942. *(Both Beaufort photographs courtesy Roger Hayward).*

Above: John Creswell, after being commissioned, displays his recently awarded DFC and DFM.

Beauforts in pens at Luqa
Right: being serviced;
Below: being loaded with
a torpedo; **Opposite:** Ready
for take-off.
*(Photographs courtesy
Roger Hayward)*

Opposite below: The
author photographed in
the desert prior to his
move to Malta.
*(Photograph courtesy
Norman Franks)*

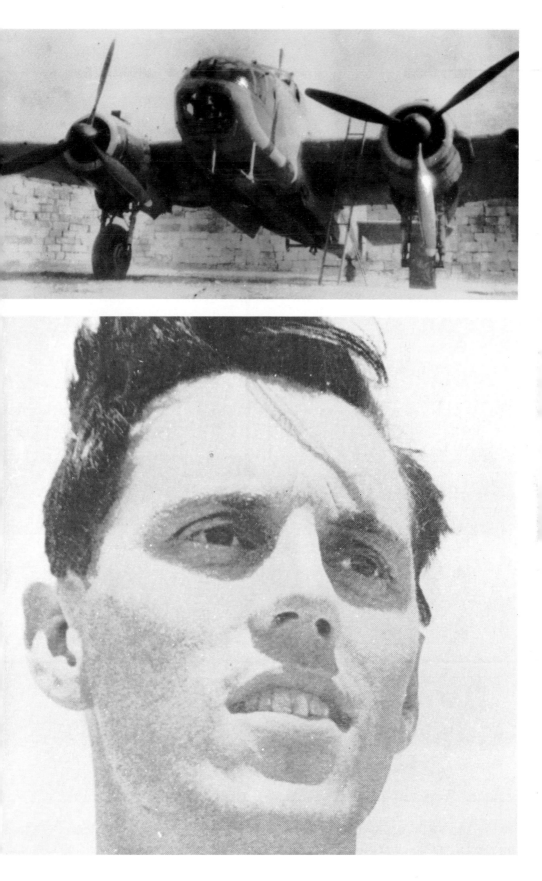

A sequence of photographs showing various stages of attack from Malta by 39
Squadron and taken at different times during the summer of 1942. The results could

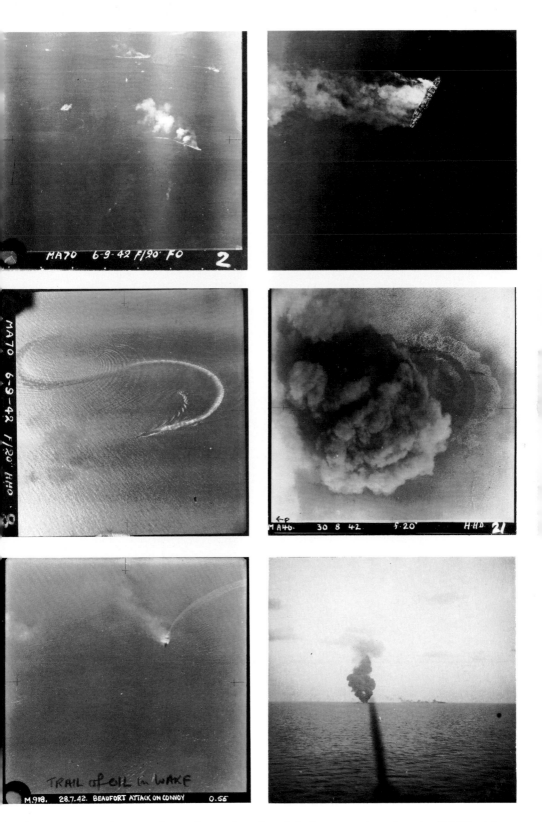

be diverse, as can be seen from the series of aerial photographs taken by PRU with some ships burning fiercely and others in obvious distress.

The author with friend outside Buckingham Palace after receiving his decoration in 1943.

ammunition exploding in the fire reached our ears, our spirits sank and conversation ceased. When a succession of deafening explosions occurred, caused by the bombs bursting, we could look upon the scene no longer, and retired in silence to the dugout.

The Ops officer was, if possible, rather more harassed than when I had last seen him, for he feared that the fire burning on his aerodrome would act as a beacon to enemy raiders. Until this unforeseen disaster he had been coping magnificently with the situation, driving out on to the aerodrome to give orders to the flare path control, hurrying back to answer the telephone, and endeavouring to despatch an anxious collection of aircrews on their missions; but now the prospect of the aerodrome being bombed was too much for him, and he abandoned the Ops Room to supervise extinguishing the flames.

While waiting for his return, I spoke to some of the other crews who were, like us, sitting on the floor of the dugout, looking dejected and bewildered, and learnt with interest that the Wellingtons on the aerodrome were not making bombing or reconnaissance sorties, as I had supposed, but ferrying torpedoes to Malta. The diversion at this critical time of Wellingtons from their normal offensive role as bombers to act as torpedo transports was significant of a change of attitude at Headquarters. At this very moment the effectiveness of bombing the enemy's port as a means of restricting his supply of armaments was being openly questioned by the strength which Rommel was demonstrating in the present battle. It appeared that the staff in Cairo had at last decided that torpedoes used from Malta against shipping might succeed in reducing the enemy's strength where the bombing of Benghazi from Egypt had failed.

I had not previously considered how torpedoes would be supplied to the Island for our operations, in fact I had considered Luqa as just another aerodrome from which Beauforts could operate. Now I was reminded that in spite of the decrease in air raids, Malta was still virtually a besieged fortress, which could be reached only by aircraft or submarines. I saw that a much more detailed organisation was required for an anti-shipping offensive from the Island than a simple order for aircraft to move, and appreciated that the delay of a few days in acceptance of the proposal, at which I had been so impatient, was really very small. The staff must have weighed many considerations before embarking on such a venture, particularly at a time when all possible resources would be needed to stem the enemy's advance on land, and the future of Malta itself must still have been considered problematical after the almost complete failure of the convoy operation. At a time when Egypt was being threatened, great efforts were being made to support the projected offensive from Malta against shipping, efforts which I hoped we could justify.

When the Ops officer returned, we obtained the information necessary for the flight; wireless call signs, recognition signals and a weather forecast, and the observers, spreading their plotting charts on the floor, set to work with rulers and pencils to draw in the track. On the chart the position of Malta was indicated by a tiny dot, and the blank space, representing the stretch of sea we had to cross to reach it, appeared enormous in comparison. To find a small island after a long flight over sea and out of sight of land was a very different task from finding an aerodrome situated on a stretch of coastline, and there was always an element of doubt about a flight to Malta. If navigation was inaccurate and the wireless failed, an aircraft might search an area of sea in vain until its petrol supply was exhausted.

I was not looking forward to the flight with any confidence, largely because my wireless operator had reported a fault in his set which he was unable to rectify. Normally I would never have considered undertaking such a flight without the help of wireless, for it would be most unlikely that even Creswell's accurate navigation would find the Island after the long flight made entirely in darkness. Now, although I realise I was risking my aircraft and crew, I considered that circumstances justified a decision to make the attempt; so much was at stake, so much had happened, that I felt that it was too late to turn back. Rommel would take the aerodrome on the next day, within a week he might reach the Egyptian frontier and later, perhaps, Alexandria would fall; then Malta would be out of a Beaufort's range and the way would be barred.

However, although prepared to take this risk, I was determined that the attempt should bear the stamp not of rashness, but of calculation; luck, I remembered, could be courted and flew with those who, before embarking on even the most hazardous flight, were confident of landing in safety at its end. Such confidence could only be obtained from careful preparation before take-off, and after discussing the details of the navigation at some length with Creswell, I decided that to attempt to find our destination at night was asking too much of providence. Even the other pilots, who could expect to receive wireless aid during the flight, were looking forward uneasily to the task of finding the Island at the limit of our range and then landing at a strange aerodrome in darkness, which would be necessary if we observed our orders to take off before midnight, for dawn was at seven o'clock and the flight would take just under six hours. I thought a preferable arrangement would be to arrive in the first hour of daylight, and persuaded the Ops officer to ask permission from Group to delay our time of take-off. There followed the usual incoherent discussion over the field telephone, which the Ops officer interpreted as meaning that Group would not cancel the order for us to take-off at midnight, and if I cared to make other arrangements it was on my own responsibility.Thinking that a delay of a few hours in our arrival would be preferable to the likely alternative of not arriving at all, I decided that we should take off individually at two o'clock in the morning, which would result in our covering the last hundred miles in daylight.

With all arrangements completed, we said goodnight to the Ops officer, and made our way across the desert to our dispersal point. Several hours remained before our time of take-off, and all the crews tried to snatch some sleep to enable them to be fresh at the start of their long journey. Taking off my shoes, I rolled into my sleeping bag and lay on the soft sand under the wing of my aircraft, but sleep eluded me. I was unable to drive recollections of past events or speculations on the future from my mind, and when these momentarily ceased, the noises of movement in the darkness and shadows cast by the bright moon attracted my attention.

The bright light of the half moon, which I had seen hanging as a crescent low over the hills of Malta, silhouetted the shapes of our aircraft against a clear sky. Guns were never silent through the night, the murmur of movement was always audible from the front, and transport rolled ceaselessly along the road. Above the clamour of war could be heard the steady sound of the sea, waves breaking on the sands of the beach where I had lain in the sun just a week before. I was sleepless from anxiety for the future. The flight without wireless, which would normally have been a considerable undertaking, had been made by the course of the past and promise of the future into a momentous link in the chain of events which were leading me to the accomplishment of my two ambitions, to fight the enemy in the way I had chosen, and to return home before Christmas. Excitement at the adventure which awaited me at the Island was mixed with apprehension at the flight before me which was to decide between failure and success. I knew that this was my last night in the desert, but was uncertain whether I would spend the next night at Malta.

I was roused by the sound of the other crews stirring in the darkness nearby, and as my crew packed our sleeping bags into the aircraft, the air became filled with the noise of engines starting up. I had arranged to take off last, and sitting in the cockpit with the engines warming up, I watched the other Beauforts running down the flare path and rising to vanish, one after another, into the darkness, on their way.

As I taxied out to the floodlight, the feeling of tension which I normally experienced before a night take-off was accentuated by the importance of the mission. Opening the throttles rather faster than usual, a result of nervousness, one engine failed to respond fully, and the aircraft, instead of accelerating straight down the line of lights, swung across the flare path before I was able to correct it. By applying full rudder I succeeded in heading the aircraft back to the proper side of the flare path, but by this time it had gathered speed, and after bounding uncontrollably, rose unsteadily into the air. Even then, I was not yet safe, for it had risen prematurely at a speed little above the stalling point, and for a horrible interval of uncertainty I concentrated desperately on the instruments before me as the aircraft headed into the darkness, the speed insufficient to climb and the ground an unknown distance beneath us. But the crash did not come; the moment of doubt passed and as speed increased I was able to climb, until safe figures were indicated on both altimeter and airspeed indicator.

When we reached a thousand feet, Creswell handed me the first course to steer, which would take us as usual northwards, and setting this course on the compass, I settled down to steady flight. Although the moon was up, it was behind us, and there was no horizon visible to relieve my eyes from gazing continuously at the instrument panel. I settled down to this monotonous flying as comfortably as possible, lowering the arms of the seat to support my elbows, trimming the aircraft to fly straight and level and so relieving me of the need to apply pressure to the controls, and adjusting the cockpit lighting to illuminate the instruments softly but distinctly. Time, indicated by the cockpit clock, passed slowly and without incident; the monotonous beat of the engines, which by its continuity had superseded silence, was unbroken, the moon and stars were reflected in the windscreen, and the instruments bore witness to level flight on a steady course, westwards.

After three hours of this uneventful instrument flying we were little more than half way to our destination, and the remaining hours were beginning to loom unpleasantly in front of me. Repeated restless changes in my position in the restricted seat and alterations in the intensity of the lighting, for a short time kept at bay the drowsiness which I felt overcoming me. But at the end of the fourth hour I found that the steady rhythmic beat of the engines and the monotonous reflection of the unchanging instruments were relentlessly lulling me to sleep. After I had several times aroused myself with a start to discover the aircraft off its course and taking up dangerous attitudes,

I realised that I could no longer be trusted to stay awake, and asked Creswell to come back from the navigator's position in the nose to sit beside me and prevent my falling asleep. When, during the fifth hour of the flight, the sky behind us became grey with the light of dawn, I still needed Creswell at my side to put his hand on my shoulder occasionally and remind me I was straying off the course. It was not until the sun rose and the western horizon became distinct enough for me to cease flying by instruments that I felt able to dispense with my 'knocker up' and Creswell returned to his position in the nose to check the navigation by the light of day.

After the sun had risen, only another hour remained before land was due to come in sight. At first flying in daylight was a welcome change from the wearisome night flying, but as the hour neared its end and the time approached when the Island should appear on the horizon, an unpleasant sensation of anticipation mingled with dread gradually took the place of relief. I hardly dared ask Creswell for our estimated time of arrival, but he showed no hesitation in answering and told me we should see land at seven forty-five precisely. Gaining confidence from his assurance, I began to search the horizon no longer questioningly, but expectantly, and when the hands of the cockpit clock pointed to a quarter to eight still without any sign of land, I felt that not our navigation but the Island was at fault in failing to play its part by making an appearance. But Creswell still showed no lack of confidence in his calculations, and asked me to continue on the same course for another five minutes. During these extra five minutes, which seemed to take longer in passing than the preceding five hours of the entire flight, I watched not the minute hand of the clock, but the second hand ticking its way round the dial, trying to persuade myself that time really was passing and not standing still. At the end of the five minutes I was just preparing to forego all confidence I had ever placed in Creswell and regretting bitterly my decision to make the flight without wireless, when land came into sight on the port side.

Creswell and I sighted the land at the same time, but there was a lack of enthusiasm inappropriate to the occasion in both our voices as we told each other of our discovery. I said that I thought I could see land on the port side, feeling more doubtful than jubilant at the sight of the indistinct shape which was appearing on the southern horizon, while Creswell was a little more specific in his statement that the Island was just coming into sight. As we drew nearer, the shape of the coast-line became more distinguishable, but neither Creswell nor I uttered a word; we did not dare express the thought which was passing through our minds: this land was not Malta.

When we were within five or six miles of the coast, I could contain my doubts no longer, and turning to avoid approaching the land any nearer, I asked Creswell if he was sure this was Malta, being quite certain in my own mind that it was not. Although the weather was hazy, I was near enough to make out a long low coastline which was completely unlike the steep mountainous Malta I remembered from my previous visit. Creswell, I discovered, shared my doubts, but he appeared not to be unduly worried by the presence of an unrecognised stretch of land, and asked me to fly along parallel to the coast while he tried to identify our position from the map.

I was not really perturbed at this turn of events, for the sight of any land, friendly or hostile, was welcome after nearly six hours in the air, for the possibility of being lost over a wilderness of sea was now removed. This land could only be part of two coastlines, either African or Sicilian, and if we could fix our position we might yet reach our destination, for I had been cruising at an economical speed with just such an emergency as this in mind, and the gauges showed sufficient petrol for another hour's flying.

I continued to fly parallel to the coast, some ten miles out, for I did not feel inclined to make any close range investigation which might draw the enemy's attention. Even at this distance our safety was doubtful, so when at last Creswell pronounced rather hesitantly that we were off Tripoli I was only too glad to make away from the coast in a northerly direction, while he calculated the course to take us to Malta. It did occur to me that the navigation was unnecessarily inaccurate, but I decided to leave recriminations until a more suitable time. But I found the course, which he handed to me a few minutes later, was a southerly, not a northerly course, and there followed several minutes of talking at cross purposes before it transpired that I had misheard Creswell's voice through the telephones: the land was not Tripoli, but Sicily! For the second time on this flight I had been flying for several minutes in completely the wrong direction.

Turning southwards, I gave the land a wide berth on the starboard side, for I knew that Sicily was the home of many fighter squadrons and an unhealthy spot for a single aircraft in daylight. To steer the course which Creswell gave me would have resulted in crossing the coast, so to avoid this I started to work round the easterly point of the land, intending to set course after the detour. I was now firmly convinced that we were off the southern corner of Sicily, and very pleased at this, for it meant that Malta was only sixty miles away. Creswell was still showing signs of doubt, which I attributed to the fact that we had not approached the coast near enough for him to identify any particular feature. Skirting the most easterly point of the land, I turned to fly parallel to its southern coastline, still expecting at any moment to meet a formation of Italian fighters, and accordingly keeping a safe distance from the shore.

But as more of the south coast came into sight, I became increasingly reluctant to leave it behind and turn onto the southerly course which should lead away from danger towards our destination, for I, too, was beginning to have doubts. I could no longer reconcile the features of the distant coastline with my memory of the south-east corner of Sicily, and Creswell, who had the map before him, was expressing the same doubts. To set off on a course from an uncertain position with our limited petrol would be suicidal; to risk fighter attack and establish definitely our true position seemed far preferable to the likely alternative of a watery grave. So after some discussion, we decided to investigate the coast more closely, and flew northwards with some trepidation, expecting fighters to appear at any moment. As the land gradually drew nearer, tempers became frayed, and I found myself losing patience with Creswell's failure to identify some feature on the coastline from his map. It seemed that we were wasting time, using up valuable petrol without getting nearer to our destination and flying dangerously within the jaws of the enemy.

At a distance of two or three miles the coastline began to appear familiar to me, and I was just about to communicate this fact to Creswell when he pronounced that this strange land was neither Tripoli nor Sicily, but Malta! At this we both burst out laughing. For fifteen minutes we had been flying around with extreme caution, hardly daring to approach the land which was our destination.

Our failure to recognise the Island was due partly to my wishful disbelief in the amazing accuracy of the navigation, and partly to the unfamiliar view which the land had originally presented. After first sighting land on the port side, we had turned to approach from the north, and the northern coast of Malta, together with the smaller island of Gozo, had appeared from a distance to be one continuous line stretching into the haze. It was only when we worked round to the south coast that it became apparent that the land was an island, and I recognised the steep cliffs over which I had flown on my previous visit. I should really have placed implicit faith in Creswell's navigation, for land had appeared at the correct time and there had been no good reason to think it was not Malta. Apprehension and tiredness had conspired to produce in the cockpit an atmosphere of doubt which was quite unjustified. Only Creswell emerged from the episode with credit. To have make a landfall within a few minutes of his estimated time of arrival after nearly six hours' of flying, partly in darkness and entirely out of sight of land, was a magnificent achievement. I apologised to him very meekly for my doubts and never again questioned his navigation.

With the coast correctly identified at last, I lost no time in reaching Luqa, and was soon taxiing over the aerodrome surface to a dispersal point indicated by some waving airmen. As we climbed stiffly out of the aircraft to stand on the welcome ground tiredness was forgotten in relief at our safe arrival. After exchanging some sarcastic remarks on the island's mistaken identity, the crew began to unload the aircraft as if it were the end of any routine flight.

Yet I did not feel the elation which I might have expected at having forged a master link in the chain of events which was leading me in the way I had chosen; the hazards of the flight had sobered my ambition, making the future no longer appear assured. I saw future operations not as easy stepping stones across the sea, a path leading me home, but as a net in which I had become hopelessly enmeshed by my own dangerous intrigue; I had talked my way into the net to reach Malta, now I was to fight my way out again, to England. Perhaps I was tired, or perhaps the early morning did not hold the same candle to the future as late night, for the fair ambition which I had struggled to achieve appeared momentarily before my eyes in the black cloak of death.

CHAPTER IX

QUICKLY OFF THE MARK

DURING the twenty four hours preceding our arrival at Malta so many momentous incidents had piled up one on top of another that we felt ready for almost any eventuality, but the news which greeted us from Intelligence Office was something for which we were not quite prepared. Intending merely to report our arrival, enquire after the other crews and then retire to bed for the day, I walked into the Intelligence Office to be welcomed by the CO of 217 Squadron with the news that we would be required for an operation within the next few hours. Sinking into an armchair, I asked weakly for more details, and received from Willie in reply an account of all that had occurred at Malta during my week of absence.

With characteristic decision the AOC had not waited for final approval from Cairo before starting an offensive against the enemy's supply line, and 217 Squadron had already been out twice to attack merchant shipping. On the first operation Willie Davies, who had been leading, failed to find the target and returned empty handed, but on the second occasion, when the squadron had been led by his second-in-command, a ship had been sunk. Neither of these operations had been without loss. On the first, unsuccessful, sortie one aircraft had been shot down by fighters and on the actual attack three Beauforts had gone down before flak, one of these missing aircraft being the leader's. 217 Squadron, which had sustained some losses during the convoy operation, was after these two sorties reduced to a handful of serviceable aircraft, and our six Beauforts had been moved from Egypt to strengthen the force for further operations. There had been not only a shortage on the Island of aircraft, but also of torpedoes, and the Wellingtons which I had seen leaving Sidi Barrani on the previous evening had arrived just before dawn bringing sufficient 'fish' for our immediate needs. With the arrival of our Beauforts the stage was set for the first act of the offensive.

These events, about which I learnt with approval, were viewed by Willie with considerable distaste. Only a few days before, long-range tanks had been fitted to his aircraft and all preparations made for their onward flight to Ceylon in charge of the senior Flight Commander. Willie's passage to England by air liner had actually been booked when an order was received that his squadron was to remain indefinitely at Malta. This news had not at first disturbed him, for he still hoped to be able to hand over his command and return home, but when his relief became missing the situation changed and his chances of seeing England again for some months vanished. Willie had no desire to come to closer grips with the enemy; he had accomplished the work for which he had been sent out from England and now felt trapped at Malta by a turn of events which he could not have foreseen. His depression at being retained on the Island was equal to my high spirits at having arrived there, but when I learnt the reason for his desire to return home, I was able to sympathise. He had become engaged to be married just before leaving England, and thinking to be away not more than a few weeks, had arranged a date for his wedding, which would now have to be postponed indefinitely. Hearing this story, I felt not a little guilty, for the retention of 217 Squadron at Malta was the result of my suggestion and the indirect cause of Willie's plight.

However, the war was not making allowances for Willie's private life, and although his heart might be far away he was now sitting in the Intelligence Office at Luqa, waiting to make not a peaceful flight to England, but an offensive sortie to the Italian coast. Some merchant ships were known to have left Palermo on the previous evening, and 217 Squadron had been at readiness since dawn, waiting for news of their latest position. The first reconnaissance aircraft had brought back a blank report, and a second reconnaissance was now being made in an attempt to locate the target. As I listened to this account of the situation I realised that we had been ordered to leave 05 before midnight in order to be available at Luqa at dawn. Luck had been on my side again, for if the target had been located at the first attempt, 217 Squadron would have operated without us and I would have found it difficult to account for our late arrival.

Now we had some time in hand, since the 'recce' aircraft was not due back for another hour, so leaving Willie to organise the refuelling of our aircraft, I went to the Mess for breakfast. There I found the other crews, who had landed before me after uneventful flights, and before long they were in fits of laughter at the story of my arrival. They did not seem unduly perturbed at the all-round-the-clock flying which was expected of them, in fact it was accepted as an everyday occurrence. The atmosphere that morning at Malta was very different from the previous evening at Sidi Barrani; there was an assurance of victory in the air, not the depression of defeat. The Island had survived its siege, it was ready to hit back.

On my return to Intelligence Office I found a further surprise awaiting me. I was handed a signal which had just arrived congratulating me on the award of a bar to my DFC. Too much seemed to have happened to me within the last week. The attack on the Italian fleet, my aircraft hit, and a crash landing; then the two successful interviews with senior officers resulting in the acceptance of my proposal; Alastair's timely indisposition and the substitution of my name for his on the operation order; finally, the narrowly avoided accident while taking off from 05, and the uncanny accuracy of Creswell's navigation which had brought me to the Island. All had been eventful happenings following one after another in rapid succession. Now, within an hour of my arrival at Malta, I had received a second decoration. This auspicious start to the new project dispelled the doubts I had experienced earlier in the day; the chain of luck would hold, the venture would not fail.

I hardly had time to appreciate fully this latest piece of good luck before the pilot of the 'recce' aircraft came in with his report; two merchant vessels escorted by four destroyers were steaming along the coast northwards from the toe of Italy. Expectancy gave way to feverish activity as Willie briefed the crews with the plan of attack while his navigator worked out the problem of intercepting the target.

217 Squadron had originally intended operating six Beauforts, but Willie was able to produce a spare, to make with our five aircraft a useful force, twelve strong. But Group were not only sending a strong force of Beauforts, but also providing fighter cover. I was amazed and delighted to find that a Beaufighter squadron, No 227, was to accompany us. The AOC, considering it essential that Beauforts should have fighter protection, had retained this squadron especially for the forthcoming operations against shipping. Like 217 Squadron, it had originally been sent out from England for the convoy operation only, and was really destined for Egypt. Not only were the Beauforts going to operate from an ideal base, but in ideal circumstances, in large forces heavily escorted. Success of the venture seemed assured.

After arriving at Malta at eight o'clock in the morning, I was in the air again before eleven, not this time flying alone, but as one of a

formation of twelve Beauforts escorted by a similar number of Beaufighters. Willie was at the head of the force, with the Beauforts divided
as usual into sections of three, while the Beaufighters, working in
pairs, weaved on either side of the formation. One of the pilots of my
Flight was on my right, one of 217's aircraft on my left, and a section
made up by the three other aircraft of 39 and led by Tony followed
behind me.

At the end of nearly two hours, we were flying parallel to the Italian
coast, which could just be distinguished in the distance on the port
side. There was still the same haze hanging over the water which had
made recognition of the Island so difficult earlier in the day, and when
I first saw the merchant ships on the horizon, I mistook them for small
islands rising out of the sea. This momentary illusion was dispelled by
a signal from the leading aircraft to spread for the attack, and recognising the shapes in the distance as our targets, I manoeuvred my
section into position.

Approaching the target from astern, four sections of three Beauforts
deployed into attacking formation, one section behind another forming a long line of aircraft stretching low over the water. The two
merchant vessels were steaming abreast of each other, separated by
only two or three hundred yards. On either side of this little convoy
was a destroyer, perhaps three quarters of a mile away, and two more
destroyers were steaming a similar distance ahead. We were approaching from the south, the convoy was steaming northwards. The two
flanking destroyers were occupying the exact position in which we
wished to make our turn in to attack, so a decision had to be made
either to pass this obstacle on the seaward or the convoy side. As the
target rapidly drew nearer it was possible to sense the tension in the
section leaders' cockpits as they reviewed the situation: should they
attack the port or starboard ship? On which side should they pass the
inconveniently placed destroyer?

Seeing the leading section make a wide sweep to pass the destroyer
on the seaward side and attack from the port, I decided to approach
from the same direction, but to pass the destroyer on the convoy side.
Tony decided to follow me, while the remaining section of 217 made
for the other side of the convoy to attack from the starboard. In this
way we approached in three parallel columns, expecting at any
moment to be greeted by hail of fire, but the enemy appeared to be
asleep. The leading section had taken such a wide detour that I found
my section coming in to position for attack long before it, still without
any sign that the enemy was aware of our presence. Passing in between
the destroyer and the convoy, I began to turn towards the target,

knowing that at any moment peace would be shattered by gunfire. Just as I was taking undisturbed aim at the nearer of the two merchant vessels, the convoy awoke to the fact that it was being attacked, but I had dropped my torpedo and was making away before all the ship's guns were in action. Compared with an attack on battleships this seemed an easy task.

I was dwelling on my good luck to have been first in to the attack and so escaping the full volume of gunfire, and not taking very violent avoiding action, when an unexpected stream of tracer shot past my cockpit, the aircraft reeled under the force of two explosions, one engine stopped momentarily and the control column jumped out of my hands. The unutterable thought that we had been shot down flashed across my mind, to be followed immediately by strenuous efforts to keep flying. The aircraft responded to the controls, though rather sluggishly, the engines kept turning, and after a few moments of doubt, I knew all was well.

Several minutes elapsed after this incident in which my whole attention was devoted to nursing the damaged aircraft, and when at last I was able to look around me, the convoy was far away in the distance. No Beauforts were in sight; only a solitary Beaufighter, which must have seen that I was in difficulties, was weaving around my tail. I had been unable to pay attention to my gunner's comments in the heat of the getaway, but now he invited an inspection of the tailplane and Creswell went back to investigate. His expression after a visit to the turret was eloquent of the damage which I suspected from the poor response of the elevator control. One shell had demolished a large part of the rudder and tailplane, another had burst under the fuselage, but the engines appeared to be undamaged and control remained adequate. Not one of the crew had seen any result of the attack, but I thought it unwise to return to investigate in my damaged aircraft, so followed by my single Beaufighter escort, I set course for Malta, not looking forward with any enthusiasm to a landing possibly without the use of flaps or undercarriage, and certainly with very restricted elevator control.

I arrived at Luqa without further incident, and finding with relief that the undercarriage would go down, began to make a careful approach to the runway. At the usual height of about eight hundred feet I started to lower the flaps, an action which nearly resulted in disaster, for the limited elevator control was insufficient to keep the aircraft level, and I was forced to raise the flaps promptly to avoid diving towards the ground. However, without using flaps I found the control sufficient to flatten out correctly for landing, and when we

touched down firmly on the end of the runway I thought the danger
was passed. But the aircraft immediately started a violent swing to
port, and I was only able to prevent it describing a semi-circle by
applying full rudder and opening up the port engine. After an anxious
moment, in which I thought the undercarriage was going to collapse,
we eventually came safely to rest on the grass, with the aircraft tilted
at rather an odd angle: the port tyre had been flat when we landed.

As I climbed out of the cockpit on to the wing, a sight met my eyes
which caused me to stop dead: the tailplane had almost ceased to
exist. On examining the damage more closely from the ground I discovered that the elevators had not only been torn to shreds by the
explosion, but were hanging almost unsupported from their control
wires; part of the rudder was missing and one side of the tailplane
was all but completely demolished. One shell had scored a direct hit
on the tail, another had burst under the port wing, dangerously near
the engine nacelle, and had caused much more extensive damage than
the mere bursting of a tyre.

Seeing the mangled wreckage that had been my tailplane and the
jagged gaping hole in the underside of the wing, I saw enough to tell
me that I had been amazingly lucky not to have been shot down and
felt grateful for my escape to the Panda mascot which I was carrying
under my arm. It had flown with me on my very first operation from
England many months before, when my aircraft in spite of receiving
three direct hits had brought me safely back from the enemy coast
over two hundred miles of sea. After that incident the Panda had
always accompanied me on operations, sitting on a ledge in the cockpit
looking over my shoulder. Although my aircraft was continually being
hit, this mascot seemed to bring me the phenomenal luck which kept
me from meeting disaster. When not flying, it reposed in a bag
containing Creswell's navigation material, charts and rulers; perhaps
the amazing accuracy of his navigation can be attributed to the Panda's
influence. To me, it personified good luck, and I was never ashamed
to be seen walking across the aerodrome carrying my mascot.

As I left the aircraft to be towed away by tractor, I realised with
regret that another Mark II to which I had become attached would
have to join the one which I had landed on its belly in spending many
weeks in the repair section. I noticed that other Beauforts were also
parked on the grass instead of being taxied to their dispersal points;
one was lying just off the runway with a broken undercarriage,
another, which I recognised from the letter on its side as Tony's, had
a damaged tailplane.

At Intelligence Office there was the usual chaotic scene. Inside the tiny room some crews were making their reports, while others standing outside were discussing the operation. Our arrival caused something of a stir, for several crews had reported that they had definitely seen our Beaufort crashing into the sea, and we were not exactly expected to return. When all the reports were made, it was revealed that two Beauforts were missing, both unfortunately from 39 Squadron: one of my followers and one of Tony's had been seen to go down in the sea near the target. It was thought that both ships had been hit, for they had been stationary when last seen. Although this result appeared satisfactory, it did seem that these attacks were going to be costly in casualties, for beside the two Beauforts actually missing, no less than five others were damaged. We could hardly expect to achieve greater surprise and I dreaded to think of the casualties on some future occasion when the enemy was prepared for attack. The operation had, on the other hand, been an easy one for the Beaufighters, who had climbed to circle while we made our attack, for not a single fighter had been seen and all their aircraft had returned safely.

As usual, discussion of the operation did not end with the completion of our reports, but was continued in the Mess during the evening. Willie described the sight of my section followed by Tony's passing between the flanking destroyer and the convoy as resembling a train running into a station, for our aircraft had formed one long line, so evenly spaced that they might have been joined together. His section, after turning in around the bow of the destroyer, had attacked just after Tony's while the other section of 217 had been attacking the other merchant ship from the opposite side at the same time. Everyone had dropped their torpedoes at short range, and the attack appeared to have been well executed, so when the 'recce' pilot returned with the news that one of the merchant vessels had proceeded on its way and the other was stationary, but showed no signs of sinking our disappointment was equalled by astonishment. It emerged some days later that the depth of our torpedoes had been incorrectly set before the operation.

As I sat in the bar that evening, I found it difficult to realise that I had arrived only a few hours before; the whole day had been so fully occupied and the preceding week so eventful, that it seemed that I had never left the Island since my spectacular arrival just a week ago. I was, if possible, even more tired than on that first evening at Malta, and again could hardly keep awake to listen to the eternal pilot telling his unchanging story. Although tired, I was in a state of supreme happiness, in which life seemed very sweet, for I felt that whatever the result of the day's operation, at least a start had been made on the offensive against the enemy's supply ships; I had begun the journey of uncertain length and unknown hazards which was to take me home.

These thoughts recalled the signal which had brought news of my decoration, and leaving the bar I sat down in the ante-room to write a letter. It said that my new address was Luqa, Malta, and that I hoped it would be unchanged for some time to come. Slipping the signal and the letter into an envelope, I put it in the outgoing mail and realised with pleasure that it would take only three days to reach England: Malta seemed very near home.

CHAPTER X

THE SCENE IS SET

AND Rommel swept onwards. Sidi Barrani was taken on the night our five Beauforts left for Malta, only a few hours after our departure. 235 Wing, which had retired some two hundred miles to an aerodrome near Fuka, was forced to move again within a few days, when Fuka was threatened. Within a week of Tobruk's capture Mersa Matruh had fallen, and Rommel's army poured over the frontier of Egypt up to the village of El Alamein, a name never previously mentioned in the whole desert campaign.

From Malta it looked to the least pessimistic of us that Egypt must fall; it seemed that the fluctuations in the last two years of grim desert fighting had been no more than the mere whims of capricious Fortune, who was now, finally, to declare her hand for the enemy.

Rommel had held his position on the Gazala line comfortably and patiently, while receiving supplies through Benghazi, until he was strong enough to break our line and advance unchecked to El Alamein. It was reasonable to suppose he would now attempt to repeat that strategy, and hold the present line until additional supplies, received through Tobruk, would enable him to take Egypt. This plan, which had threatened through the preceding months, appeared all the more menacing now its success was proved; and this time the enemy was not separated from his objectives by five hundred miles of desert, it was within his sight.

Meanwhile, the enemy were halted rather than held within sixty miles of Alexandria. The aerodromes on the Cairo-Alexandria road, which had once been used by squadrons based five hundred miles in the rear, were now in the front line. News reached us that the remainder of 39 Squadron had given up Landing Ground 87 to some Kittyhawk squadrons, and retired to an aerodrome on the canal; the crews were idle once more, with few aircraft serviceable and no targets steaming within range. This news made me glad to be in Malta.

Our aerodrome was situated high up in the middle of the Island, the Island itself stood minute in the heart of a great expanse of sea bordered by three hostile coastlines: Italian, Greek and North African. Pounded day and night by enemy bombers, alone and almost completely cut off from material help, Malta fought on into this third year of war, towards the conclusion of what was to prove a David and Goliath struggle.

Successive months of the previous winter had been the worst for Malta since the threat of war had become a reality when Italy threw in her lot with the Nazis in June 1940. England in that year was attempting to counter a series of rapid blows which began disastrously with the invasion of Norway in the spring, and culminated in a triumphant survival of the enemy's day and night bombing offensive in the autumn and winter. Amidst the disasters of that summer, the Italian declaration of war and subsequent military action in the Mediterranean might almost have seemed remote to one so mortally engaged at home.

Italian aircraft raided Malta in the first few hours of war, while Italian troops crossed the Libyan frontier into Egypt; ever since that day there had been continuous raids on Malta and incessant fighting in North Africa; the Island and the desert, inseparable from the start of the Mediterranean war, became more closely linked as the struggle progressed. As General Wavell drew on the Italian army into Egypt in his initial strategic retreat, a tiny force of Gladiators used to go up from Malta's single aerodrome to engage the Italian raiders. In spite of the inferiority in numbers and the obsolescence of our aircraft, this first offensive in the Mediterranean, carried out solely by Italian forces, was withstood. Before many months had passed the enemy were in full retreat in Libya, and Malta was continuing to challenge the raiders. Our Navy were active in the Mediterranean, striking terrific blows at Cape Matapan and Taranto, intercepting enemy convoys and successfully escorting our own shipping; Malta was not yet isolated.

In the eventful summer I was in England, at an aerodrome which became momentarily linked with Malta by an incident which made me realise that, in spite of the ominous surge of events at home, the Mediterranean war was not quite forgotten. One evening in June a handful of Hurricanes landed at our aerodrome; the next morning they embarked in an aircraft carrier which left soon afterwards—for Malta. Operating these fast monoplanes from a carrier, first attempted during the Norwegian campaign only a few weeks before, was still in its infancy, and the pilots of the 'Hurries' were all former members of the Fleet Air Arm, chosen for their experience. I myself had once served in aircraft carriers, and found among these pilots some of my contemporaries who had been drawn at short notice from instructing especially for this work. How I envied them! Since my first flying days I had longed to belong to a fighter squadron, and at this time I was contriving to escape from instructing to actual fighting. For many long weeks after those Hurricanes left, I hoped desperately that when another carrier load was sent I should be chosen, so achieving my ambition to fly and fight in single seaters. But as time passed that hope receded, and Malta became obscured from my thoughts by the activity of a year of operating from coastal aerodromes at home, for before that summer was out my desire to fight was granted by a posting to a torpedo squadron. It was not until now, when I was actually on the Island, that I heard the end of the story of those Hurricanes which I had seen beginning two years before.

Flown off the deck of their carrier within range of Malta, they arrived safely and afterwards the Island's fighter defence was reinforced in this way whenever a carrier could be spared for the task. As 1940 came to an end with the Italians in retreat in North Africa and Malta's defences stiffened with modern aircraft and a new airfield, Luqa, hastily completed to receive them, the outlook from the Island must have appeared almost bright.

But immediately the blue sky of optimism became obscured by a cloud of German arms, particularly of aircraft, which threw a dark shadow over the whole Mediterranean. Germany, no doubt dissatisfied with the performance of her Italian ally, decided to direct operations herself; Rommel and the Afrika Korps crossed the sea to North Africa, Kesselring brought his formidable air force into Southern Europe, and as Malta reeled and gasped beneath its blows through 1941, first Greece and then Crete fell in quick succession to the strong enemy. The New Year came to find a thousand hostile aircraft on Sicilian aerodromes, the enemy established in Greece, in Crete and holding the North African coast from Tripoli to just short of Tobruk; Malta was surrounded, our Navy had suddenly ceased to dominate the Mediterranean. The same disposition which enabled enemy transports to cross the sea unscathed, prevented our ships from reaching the Island.

In January and February, while I was on my way to the Middle East, the scale of air raids on Malta was increasing. In March and April, while I worked in Cairo, the onslaught was increased. The Island's ports and aerodromes were battered day and night; aircraft burnt at dispersal points around their aerodromes, ships burnt in harbour alongside the quays. The Hurricanes out-numbered, out-gunned and out-run by the newer ME109s, could hardly survive in the air or on the ground. On April 14th, when our Beauforts had gone into Malta after their attack, only two Hurricanes had been serviceable to keep the aerodrome clear. Malta, the moated fortress, was beleagured and in April, when the enemy owned the air over the Island and the sea around it, it did look as if she, in her turn, must fall.

Yet just when the outlook was desperate, two complementary events occurred which conspired to give Malta another lease of her catlike life: Italian squadrons began to replace German in Sicily, and at the same time the first Spitfires arrived at Malta. Like the first Hurricanes, they were brought out from England in aircraft carriers and flown off at a point near the Algerian coast. The aircraft reached their destination and the carriers returned intact to repeat the operation on several future occasions.

The Spitfires' first task was to clear the daylight air over the Island, in order to make the aerodromes safe for a further supply of aircraft, and then to protect the June convoys, both East and West, on their arrival. It had not been forgotten that survivors from the March convoy, after a desperate and successful effort by the escort to bring them intact to Valletta, had been sunk in harbour by dive-bombing raids, which a heavy barrage but few fighters had been powerless to prevent. So this time a Beaufighter squadron, No 235, was sent out from England a week before the operation for the sole purpose of giving long-range cover to the ships as they approached the Island, and a second carrier load of Spitfires arrived soon after them to reinforce the single-seater cover. Fighter protection for the June convoys was assured, if they could only reach that comparative safety without encountering an Italian fleet. It was to assist the convoy's weak escort in dealing with that menace that the torpedo squadron of Beauforts had been sent out from England.

The importance attached to the reinforcement of Malta, both by the Allies and the enemy, can be estimated by the efforts made to achieve it, and the measures taken to prevent it. In the end, strength prevailed. The enemy, moving squadrons up to forward bases in Sardinia and Sicily and cleverly employing his naval forces, won the day, and only two ships of the western convoy made harbour at Valletta. From the bare result of the operation it did appear that the enemy had succeeded, that we had sustained a costly failure. But within that apparent failure remained a small but far-reaching success: the safe discharge of the cargoes of those two ships in harbour. Their petrol, ammunition and food was water to a dying man, and gave Malta yet another short but remarkably effective lease of life.

Nevertheless the failure of the expected abundance of supplies to materialise was keenly felt throughout the Island, and I found significant changes had taken place during my week of absence in Egypt. Petrol for motor transport was so restricted as to be almost unobtainable on even the most urgent Service errand; food, formerly fairly plentiful, was now strictly rationed; ammunition for the anti-aircraft guns was limited to a frighteningly low daily figure. The local brewery was forced to close down and beer vanished from the shelves of the Mess bar. Malta was tightening its belt against a very uncertain future.

Yet the Island, with the stubborn confidence which had so often in the past been its only defence, looked unflinchingly forward into that unassured future, and still, with our army in Egypt facing a defeat that must immediately drag Malta with it, seized upon some straws of optimism. A two months' blockade had been broken; it was not the scant success but the circumstances attending it which gave heart to the Island. The efforts made in England and Egypt to get ships through were a reminder that Malta was still unforgotten in Allied strategy, and that she was not to be allowed to fall starving into the hands of a waiting enemy without a struggle. Hope of another and more successful attempt at reinforcement still burned high. Meanwhile, there remained on the Island a greater force of aircraft than it had ever known before, and the three aerodromes were in full use: Luqa, by far the largest; Takali, little more than a landing strip for fighters; and Hal Far, an established base for Fleet Air Arm Swordfish and Albacores.

To construct a modern aerodrome anywhere on the tiny, hilly island must originally have appeared an impossible task; terraced fields bounded by stone walls cut narrow steps into the steep gradients; villages clung precariously to the slopes, hid in hollows or perched on the brows of hills. The contours rose and fell from coast to coast, the only level ground a beach of sand. It was into this miniature country that at least one full-sized aerodrome had to be fitted in the first year of war if the Island was to be held. The problem had been solved, and our aerodrome at Luqa was its creditable solution. Placed boldly on very high ground in the middle of the Island, it consisted of one long wide concrete runway, some twelve hundred yards long, intersected by another so much shorter that it was suitable for use only by the single seaters. The main runway, adequate in length, was unfortunate in its gradient, which gave a fall of several hundred feet from end to end. The south end was on the brow of the hill, the north further down the slope, terminating in a precipice with an abrupt drop into a disused quarry. Not a few flights had ended with this fatal dive, especially in the winter months, when it had been impossible, on account of enemy actions, to offer more than a faint line of landing lights to the pilots of transit aircraft who, being strangers to the aerodrome and tired after a difficult flight, were prone to make a small, costly error. Since then the runway had been lengthened at its southern end, and a further extension was now in progress, but landing down the hill still demanded caution, good brakes and occasionally blind hope!

Leading off the ends of the runways were taxying tracks initially concrete, ultimately gravel, which meandered up hill and down dale into the surrounding fields. At intervals along these tracks were 'pens', square spaces enclosed by three high walls, in which aircraft were kept to protect them from the blast and splinters of bombs. From the air Luqa looked like a great octopus, the main runway its body, the taxying tracks, winding through fields between quarries and farm buildings, its tentacles. In spite of its strange appearance this great monster was to squirt out far and wide a very potent ink.

Like the desert aerodromes the pens were numbered, and a list of the positions of dispersed aircraft read like a telephone directory, with two exchanges, Siggiewi, the village at the north end of the aerodrome, Safi at the south. To find a strange number without reference to the directory, a key map, might take an hour's exploration among vineyards and tomato fields, and on several occasions a search party had to be sent out to establish the whereabouts of an aircraft wrongly dispersed.

Taxying between pens and the aerodrome was, I found, the most hazardous part of an operation. The tracks were narrow, the slopes difficult to negotiate. Taxying uphill often needed full throttle to prevent stalling, downhill called for full brake to avoid running off the track over a cliff into one of the many quarries. Also there was no room for aircraft to pass on these tracks, and a pilot, after negotiating half a mile of this maze, might be confronted with a dense cloud approaching in the distance, the dust thrown up by the slipstream of an aircraft taxiing in the opposite direction.

At first utter confusion resulted whenever we tried to assemble our force of Beauforts and Beaufighters on the aerodrome, but eventually the difficulties of arranging for at least twenty twin-engined aircraft to take off in a certain order in quick succession were solved. Although inconvenient, the pens and their dispersal over a wide area were really effective in keeping down the 'mortality' in aircraft from enemy bombing, and were almost as great a contribution to the defence of

Malta as the deep shelters hewn out of the rock.

For the air raids, although lacking their former fury, still persisted both in daylight and at night. Whenever the enemy suspected the Island of an attempt to renew the offensive, a strongly escorted reconnaissance aircraft would be sent to photograph the aerodromes. Fighter reinforcement revealed the intention to run the blockade, a concentration of our medium twin-engined aircraft pointed to attacks on shipping; neither activity was allowed to proceed uninterrupted. During the winter months, before the completion of the pens or the arrival of the Spitfires, many more aircraft had been destroyed on the ground than in the air. Throughout the summer the enemy continued to concentrate his attacks on the aerodromes, but gradually the effects of this bombing became less disturbing; where the Germans had so nearly succeeded the Italians conspicuously failed.

When the sirens wailed civilians took cover, but work continued on the aerodromes until the sound of klaxons signified that enemy raiders were actually overhead. Spitfires, taking off at the first warning of an impending raid, climbed up to meet their adversaries; their engagements often took place directly overhead and within sight from the ground. The rising note of engines accelerating as aircraft dived would be heard faintly from a great distance, to be followed inevitably by a remote chatter of machine-gun fire. Usually the aircraft flew so high that they could only be seen clearly when reflected by the sun; from the ground they would appear like silvery minnows darting to and fro in the sunlight reaching to the bottom of a deep, clear pond. Suddenly out of this remote combat, seeming to be taking place just outside the boundaries of reality, a great curving plume of black smoke might be smeared thickly against the cloudless sky, writing that spelled an aircraft's destruction. While aircraft weaved and pilots fought, bombs would burst on the earth beneath. Occasionally the white canopy of an open parachute might be seen floating gracefully and unconcernedly as it descended slowly from destroyers to destruction. Twenty thousand feet separated spectators from the battle overhead, but that distance might at any moment be made to appear very small.

The Spitfires, initially fighting an uphill battle, often fell victims to the enemy's superior numbers, but gradually the day raids became less effective, their bombing less accurate; they wore the enemy down. A few carrier loads of Spitfires operating from Luqa, Takali and Hal Far challenged, and eventually routed, the strong Italian Air Force spread over a score of aerodromes in Sicily. A significant battle was won by the Spitfires at Malta that summer, yet at the time their work was taken for granted; the raids and their interception were part of the day's work.

While the fighters were never able to rest, with some pilots always waiting at readiness by their aircraft and often called on to make several sorties a day, our force might be idle for several weeks, waiting for a target. After our first attack, there was a decrease in the movement of enemy shipping. This lull gave me time to find my way about; I explored the aerodrome, bathed from some enchanting beaches, and began to learn something about the behaviour of our targets. The picture, which I had originally seen in faint outline at Headquarters in Cairo, became filled in with the detail it had then lacked, and I came to see the situation in the true colours of reality.

Many hours of every day and night I spent in Malta I used to sit in the Intelligence Office listening, questioning, discussing. There was no Ops Room at Luqa, and this little office performing that function and a dozen others as well, was the clearing house of information on all enemy activities, usually distilled from reconnaissance reports. For as well as the Beaufort and Beaufighter squadrons, two Spitfire squadrons and a Flight of night fighters, the aerodrome held a 'recce' squadron, No 69. We saw little of the single-seater pilots, for in daylight they were either standing by their aircraft or in the air, and at night lived in their own separate Mess at Sliema some miles away. But 69 Squadron shared the Luqa Mess with us, and the large aerodrome staff and we got to know its crews well.

This squadron was unique in having three separate flights each equipped with a different type of aircraft, Spitfires, Baltimores and Wellingtons. The Spitfire flight was really a miniature Photographic Reconnaissance Unit, manned by a single officer, the indefatigable Adrian Warburton, and two sergeants. These pilots, alone in their unarmed single-engined aircraft, flew the long distances at a great height over open sea or enemy territory to secure reconnaissance photographs. Almost every day, sometimes twice in a day, they covered the Sicilian aerodromes and Italian ports, bringing back a roll of film on which were vital exposures. Naples, Taranto or Brindisi might each be covered on successive days; confirmation might be required of activity at Cagliari in Sardinia, or Tripoli on the North African coast; new fortifications suspected at some insignificant Italian village; a hundred tasks kept these pilots busy.

The Spitfire flight covered the ports of departure and located our targets in daylight, helped in certain instances by Baltimores, while the Wellington flight searched for and attacked ships on night passages, using bombs. The watch on enemy shipping was continuous throughout the day and night, and 69 Squadron's aircraft became our telescopic eyes, vigilant everywhere within our range, searching while we waited to strike.

I used often to be sitting in the Intelligence Office when one of these flights was being briefed, and always contrived to be there when the pilot returned with his report, especially if he had been engaged in covering the ports. Both the 'recce' pilots and the Intelligence officers fed my curiosity from their fount of knowledge, and although there was no movement of shipping in these first two weeks, I was soon able to visualise the behaviour of the targets we were to attack.

The ships sailing from Italy to North Africa took a roundabout route. Leaving Genoa or Naples they came south, usually calling at Palermo or Messina in Sicily, then rounding Cape Spartavento, the toe of Italy, made a northerly passage hugging the coast to Taranto. There ships from Adriatic ports, such as Brindisi or Fiume, joined the route, convoys might be formed or the surface escort augmented. Then, sailing out of the Gulf of Taranto, the convoys crossed the Ionian Sea, and started the long passage southwards down three hundred miles of Greek coastline, across three hundred miles of open sea, to their destination. Previously Benghazi had been the only adequate easterly port available to the enemy in North Africa, but now that Tobruk was in his hands most transports could be expected to berth there in order to discharge their cargoes as near as possible to the front line.

Such was the route used by the enemy that summer, but it had not always been so. In the previous winter the majority of enemy transports had passed on the other side of Malta, sailing from the most westerly point of Sicily to the Tunisian coast, which they followed on their way to Tripoli or Benghazi. The small duration of the passage in open sea was the attraction of this route, but ultimately that did not compensate for the length of time it forced ships to spend within easy reach of Malta.

Blenheims, sent out from the UK and operating from Luqa, opened the offensive against the eastern route, employing the somewhat suicidal tactics of bombing at daylight at low level. The object was, in effect, to throw a stick of bombs through the side of a ship, but this involved a low, straight approach from the beam which made the attacker an easy target. Small wonder that the Blenheims were withdrawn early in 1942 on account of heavy losses. But Fleet Air Arm torpedo aircraft, Swordfish and Albacores operating from Hal Far against ships on this route, continued to have rewarding results. Their pilots, making attacks only at night, developed a formidable technique for locating their targets and illuminating them with flares which gave sufficient light for a torpedo attack. The range of these biplanes was limited, their speed by present standards negligible, but they did possess qualities suitable for this special night attack, and no praise is too high for the results their crews achieved.

Throughout the winter of 1942, when daylight operations were impossible for these slow speed biplanes, they worked at night, sometimes forced by the raids to take off or land with bombs bursting around their runways and the sky overhead lit up by flares. At the target they would be met by a steady barrage of fire, the tongues of flame from the guns and flashes of exploding shells appearing doubly intimidating against the curtain of night. Some aircraft were destroyed on the ground by bombing, others lost in action, until the force was so reduced in strength that a crew had occasionally to make two sorties in a single night. But in the end this gallant effort won its little war. Before the spring came the enemy, in the face of heavy losses, virtually abandoned this route, and the few remaining Fleet Air Arm crews left for Egypt with their work completed, only to return when conditions improved.

After this setback the enemy sent his transports through the Central Mediterranean, straight from Taranto to Benghazi, seldom allowing them to pass Malta at night within range of Swordfish or Albacores. It was on this route that I had seen so many convoys crossing the map at Headquarters in March and April, among them the convoy which our Beauforts had attacked with such a heavy loss on April 14th. This direct route had in its turn been abandoned in favour of the Greek coast and a rather shorter passage in open sea. Perhaps the enemy was alarmed by some sinkings by our submarines, so secret that we heard nothing of them, or perhaps he feared the use of Malta by torpedo aircraft of longer range than Swordfish; whatever the precise reason for this change, the fact remains that during the greater part of the time I was at Malta ships followed this route as inflexibly as if it were a canal, passing points on the Greek coast with such regularity that they might have been locks open at no other hour.

The whole passage was timed so that the ships should complete the final stretch in darkness and reach port at dawn. Convoys, sighted off the most southerly point of Greece an hour or two before dusk, would be photographed in Tobruk or Benghazi next morning. I knew from observation in Cairo how effective these tactics had already proved in enabling the transports to pass to their destination unchallenged. But this route, adopted primarily to avoid daylight attack by squadrons based in Egypt, left a flank wide open to attack from Malta. The ships, as they steamed down the three hundred miles of Greek coast, were within a Beaufort's range during every daylight hour, and if they started from ports on the west coast of Italy, might spend yet another day within easy striking distance as they sailed up the Italian coast from the toe to the heel.

As the situation became clear to me I saw immediately that the prey which had eluded attack from Egypt was within our grasp from Malta. Not only were these targets within our range in daylight, but for the first time in my experience, adequate forces were available to send against them. For if Malta was well placed as a striking base, it was no less favoured in its position on the aircraft reinforcement route. Although by this time the majority of aircraft sent east from England used the newly opened Central African route, the lighter aircraft, a category which providentially included Beauforts and Beaufighters, continued to fly from Gibraltar to Malta, where they refuelled before flying on to Egypt. While in the past winter few transit Beauforts had succeeded in negotiating this route, equally few reached their destination this summer, for Malta claimed them. Beauforts destined for Egypt or India were arrested in their passage and absorbed in our squadron to make good its losses and maintain its strength. This action was of course out of court by all the canons of Air Force organisation and became the cause of some friction between Malta and Cairo. Heated signals were exchanged between the two Headquarters, one referring our AOC to "the aircraft which he had impounded". Another mentioning "piracy". Eventually HQ Cairo was persuaded, perhaps by our results, that strength was more desirable at Malta than anywhere else, and we were allowed tacitly to maintain our squadron continually at its full strength of twenty aircraft by absorbing transit Beauforts and crews.

In this way a flow of replacement aircraft was assured, but the supply of torpedoes was not so easily settled. The twelve torpedoes expended on our first strike, some of them brought in by the Wellingtons only a few hours before, had reduced the stock on the Island to single figures. In the following weeks more Wellingtons, later joined by Sunderland flying boats and Liberator transports, continued to bring torpedoes in at night both from Egypt and Gibraltar, but we used up the 'fish' as fast as they came in, and in spite of these efforts, the stock remained low. On one occasion, when all our aircraft had been loaded for a strike, only a single torpedo remained in reserve. But sufficient was enough, and this particular well never quite ran dry.

A shortage of torpedoes was no surprise to me, for their supply had been limited at home as well as in Egypt; few spares for our aircraft I had expected: Beaufort parts were notoriously scarce. But the possibility of a petrol rationing, as natural a consequence on a besieged

Island as a shortage of food, I had completely overlooked.

Now that the attempt at reinforcement had failed, the petrol available for air operations was rigorously controlled; so many gallons could be consumed each week and no more. Fortunately the weekly figure never actually dropped low enough to limit operations. Spitfires went up to oppose every daylight raid, night fighters patrolled above the Island in darkness, and the 'recce' aircraft kept an unbroken watch on enemy activities; whenever a ship steamed within range in daylight, Beauforts and Beaufighters went out to strike.

But the need for economy had a great influence on the conduct of operations from Malta at this time. "Is it worthwhile?" was no remote academic question, but a very real one, requiring a reasoned answer and the balance sheet of operations, which had meant so little to my squadron in England, was constantly being examined. A force of Beauforts and Beaufighters would consume a vast quantity of petrol on a sortie, and a dozen valuable torpedoes might be expended; to balance the account, a clear-cut success was needed. So considerations of economy, although never actually restricting our activities, did demand very careful planning of each operation, an insurance against waste. "Which is the most favourable position for attack?" "What strength of aircraft will ensure success against this target and escort?" "Who will be leading?" were questions carefully deliberated. Waste might jeopardise the future, one false move and the game might be lost.

In these first two weeks on the Island, which passed strangely without a target steaming within our range, I never came near to appreciating this situation; my mind was focussed on immediate problems which obscured the wider view. As the months of the summer passed, experience gradually broadened my outlook, but it was not until long afterwards that I saw the scene in true perspective; it was then in retrospect, from England.

Immediate problems included arranging for the efficient maintenance of our aircraft and organising the aircrews. What remained of my original Flight became absorbed in 217 Squadron, of which I now became second in command to Willie. This was a curious, unique Squadron, in name 217, originally destined for Ceylon, with a part of 39 divorced from its Headquarters in Egypt, and an ever-increasing number of aircrews arrested in transit to replace losses. Superficially we were little more than a scratch collection of aircraft and crews, with neither Headquarters nor airmen, without Flights or Flight Commanders, yet 217 was in everyway a fighting squadron, and despite three changes of name in as many months, a high casualty list calling for a steady flow of new crews, and as uncertain a future as any squadron has ever had, it retained its identity to the end. When I left in September there was not a single pilot remaining who had started with me in June, but I still left behind in Malta a fighting squadron.

A squadron is often said to be as good as its aircraft, and we attached great importance to the maintenance of our Beauforts, which was carried out by the aerodrome's permanent ground staff. Most of these men, less favoured than the aircrews who stayed only for short periods, had been on the Island since the outbreak of war with Italy, spending no small part of this time in the underground shelters, tunnelled from rock. With food rationed, beer and cigarettes unobtainable, quarters cramped and roofless, their lot was unenviable, yet from their uncomplaining behaviour bombed Luqa might have been any peaceful English station. I think the arrival of the Spitfires gave them new heart; certainly they worked magnificently on our Beauforts under the hot sun, often throughout the night, and once they got to know the strange aircraft and engines, their work was the very best. From many long flights made entirely over sea, we never lost a single aircraft from engine failure. What more can I say?

For several reasons Willie and I made Headquarters the Intelligence Office. Not only was it in one of the few buildings on the aerodrome still standing with its four walls intact, but one of the very few favoured with an effective roof, not it is true the original, but one improvised from corrugated iron sheets, already pierced here and there by splinters. This office was also blessed, or perhaps cursed, with two field telephones, one to the camp exchange, the other a tie line to Group HQ in Valletta, both indispensable to us. There was a large room adjoining where our crews could congregate for briefing, and the 'recce' squadron, with whom we had to keep in close touch, had its Headquarters in the same building.

Presiding over the office which we invaded was the Intelligence staff, consisting of a Flight Lieutenant and two army officers, the latter lent from their Regiment to help in the convoy operation and never afterwards returned. Before our arrival the intelligence work had been largely restricted to reporting on enemy bomb damage, and our intrusion, far from being resented, was welcomed as making a change to a less defensive occupation. But the new war, which now began in this office, was no grim silent struggle, but a battle of wits, innuendo and practical joking; reality was tackled only when necessity absolutely demanded.

The two army officers were Lieutenant Gammidge, who quickly became associated with the well-known Holborn department store of a name differently spelt but pronounced similarly; and Lieutenant Tucker who became addressed as Ponting, merely because this was the name of the rival store to Gamage's in Kensington. No store could be found for the Flight Lieutenant, Kerridge, but he immediately became Porridge, such was the schoolboy humour which enlivened our days and nights, making the office of this trio an oasis of light-heartedness.

The walls were plastered with drawings illustrating the more curious side of life at Malta, and with caricatures of the staff made by Gamage, the latter discreetly taken down before an AOC's visit. Willie, too, was a good mimic, with a very special sense of humour only slightly affected by the set-back in his love life. Although it was more than tactless to bang a door in Malta, on account of the effect of noise on the much bombed, he delighted in throwing stones on to the iron roof of the office, then coming in to observe the occupants recovering from shock.

Luckily the partners in the firm of Porridge, Ponting and Gamage were long suffering and more than tolerated us, the intruders in their office, who sat in their chairs, used their clerks and drank their cocoa. In fact they extended help to us far beyond the bounds of their official capacity, and in these first days when all was strange, we leant heavily on their experience. They became soon an inseparable part of the team which operated against ships, seeing every operation through from start to finish, supplying the link between the reconnaissance and strike. In their office the game might at any moment begin with the return of a pilot from a 'recce' with the report of a ship at sea, a game played at break-neck speed until it ended with the return of our crews from the attack.

Even when all was quiet on the enemy coastline, it was rarely so in the Intelligence Office, where activity of some sort was continuous; the war, particularly the telephone war, never ceased. By telephone I remonstrated with the Flight Sergeant in charge of our aircraft, received orders from Group, gave instructions to the Torpedo Officer, and without moving made a hundred necessary journeys for which there was no transport. In the office I sat working every day at the table on which Creswell would lay his chart to draw in the tracks along which we flew; here the operations were planned, the ships attacked. The office was the centre of the aerodrome, the Island and the sea to the enemy coasts; the only world which existed for me was enclosed by the circumferences of a circle, the limit of a Beaufort's range. But at night, after an attack, while the night fighters patrolled overhead, I would sit at the same table writing letters to another world attempting desperately to describe my own.

I worked here on the aerodrome high in the middle of the Island, poring over signals, maps and reports, flying out over the great expanse of sea to the three hostile coastlines. In the summer of that year the Mediterranean was a wonderful field of opportunity for a squadron operating in daylight against ships, and Malta was indeed the centre of the theatre I had visualised. My desire had been granted, the opportunity was mine and it now only remained to play the part. As the days passed and the scene became set, the actors waited nervously for their call, until at last the lights went down and the curtain rose on the play which had no ending.

CHAPTER XI

CURTAIN UP

AT midnight on July 2nd three merchant vessels escorted by destroyers left Brindisi for North Africa. Their sailing caused no surprise at Malta; it was, in fact, anticipated.

A PRU Spitfire, making a routine cover of the port, had brought back news of these ships' arrival a week before, since when the progress of their loading had been observed by a daily reconnaissance. When, a few days later, the arrival of destroyers in the outer harbour was reported, the day 'recces' were made more frequent and the cover extended to a night patrol outside the port, carried out by Wellingtons.

While the ships loaded, plans were made at Malta to intercept them, and by the time their departure was imminent twelve Beauforts loaded with torpedoes and half that number of Beaufighters were waiting ready at dispersal with their crews at hand to answer an immediate call to strike. But the enemy unaccountably delayed. Loading was complete, the merchant ships had joined their destroyers in the outer harbour, yet the convoy did not sail. The AOC himself came up to Luqa on three successive days to impress upon us the importance of the operation which appeared certain to take place on the next day; reconnaissance reports were awaited with nervous expectation and even the elastic atmosphere of Intelligence Office became strained. Finally Willie and I, who now shared a room, were awakened in the early hours of the morning and summoned to the Intelligence Office, where the expected report brought in by a Wellington crew greeted us.

The plan so carefully laid beforehand was now put into operation. Crews were called, fed and assembled for briefing an hour before dawn, while airmen, similarly roused, prepared the aircraft. After briefing, buses took the crews round the maze to their dispersed aircraft, and soon the roar of aero engines warming up in the pens filled the night air. As the hills of Malta became silhouetted in the grey half-light of dawn, our aircraft taxied slowly up on to the aerodrome like angry hornets creeping protestingly from their nest, and taking off in one continuous stream, Beauforts followed by Beaufighters, joined formation on a circuit of the Island. Then the force, diving to sea level, set course for its objective and vanished over the eastern horizon towards the first rays of the rising sun.

The disposition of the force was the same as on the last attack: the Beauforts in arrowhead formation in sections of three, with Beaufighters weaving in pairs on the flanks. Willie was leading, my section flew on his right and Tony's was behind me. Group had decided to intercept the target between the Greek islands of Cephalonia and Zante, and Willie's orders were to make a landfall at Cape Geroghambo, the north westerly point of Cephalonia, and then to turn and search southwards along the coast. To forestall any unexpected change in the convoy's route or speed which might upset this interception, a Baltimore had been sent out ahead of us to locate the target and wireless back its latest position. With visibility at a maximum, there seemed no reason to doubt that we should find our objective.

But the last half hour of the long outward flight passed strangely without the expected wireless message being received. In due course land appeared ahead, the mountains of Greece towered above our low-flying aircraft, and Willie, making an accurate landfall at Cape Geroghambo, turned to fly southwards within ten miles of the coast. As we passed down the full length of Cephalonia and then started to cover the coast of Zante, it seemed that every second would show our target to have been hiding below the horizon in front of us. The tension of the preceding days spent in waiting reached breaking point; pilots' eyes scanned the horizon and gunners swung their turrets in anticipation of fighter attack; and still no target appeared. Reaching the limit of his search, the most southern point of Zante, Willie turned for home empty handed, and I followed rather reluctantly, for I had a strong desire to explore the channel behind these islands, which I knew was occasionally used by shipping. Throughout the long uneventful homeward flight over sea, out of sight of land, passing monotonously beneath the customary blue sky, I wondered just what had happened to those ships.

We landed at midday, after five and a half hours in the air, parked our aircraft in their pens and went to the Intelligence Office to make a negative report. There something nearer pandemonium than the chaos which usually prevailed during an operation reigned. The ships so carefully watched during the preceding days and nights had been completely lost at this critical moment. The Baltimore, after taking off at first light, had just reached the Greek coast when it experienced engine trouble which forced it to turn back with the mission uncompleted. This failure, which had not only resulted in the convoy proceeding on its way unchecked but also made Malta the poorer by several thousand gallons of fuel consumed by our aircraft, was causing apoplexy at Group HQ. 69 Squadron were ordered to send out 'recces' at half-hourly intervals, the telephones rang with recriminations, everyone wrote reports. Willie, judging this a suitable moment, threw some stones on to the roof of the office, afterwards opening the door to find at least twenty harassed people climbing out from under a single small table.

We, although disappointed, were glad to feel guiltless of this failure, for we had made our landfall on time and searched the prescribed area thoroughly. We reported, found there were no further instructions for us, then left the office as quickly as possible to get some lunch; afterwards most of us retired to bed, for we had been up since three o'clock in the morning and were tired.

At four o'clock Willie and I were lying on our beds, sound asleep, wearing nothing but towels around our waists, looking, as Willie remarked later, like a pair of pious Hindoos, when a runner woke us with a message that we were wanted immediately in Intelligence Office; the convoy had been found. A PRU pilot had just come in to report the three merchant vessels escorted by no less than eight destroyers steaming through the very stretch of water we had searched so diligently a few hours earlier. The convoy's appearance so far behind schedule was attributed to a reduction in speed, or perhaps even a halt made in the early morning to pick up additional escort. However, Group were not at the moment showing concern in the convoy's past but in its future. "Should Beauforts stand idle on the aerodrome at Malta while enemy ships steamed within their range?" was a question to which the only possible answer arrived in the form of a signal ordering all available Beauforts to attack before dusk. That we had received no warning to stand-by for an operation gave Group no concern; it was the Intelligence firm which took the strain.

The office became frantic once more as crews were rounded up and aircraft made ready. Of the twelve Beauforts used that morning, only nine were now serviceable, and as the squadron could only raise six crews who had not made the earlier flight, three were called upon to fly again. In any case either Willie or I would have to lead, and he asked me rather diffidently if I would do so, a request I could have countered by demanding the toss of a coin between us. However, I knew well that there was really only one flight which held any attraction for Willie, the flight home, and feeling in my heart that every flight east might eventually lead me in the direction I desired, I agreed to go, making it a condition that I should borrow his personal aircraft since mine was not serviceable after the morning flight.

This time Group had not given us an area to search; the signal briefly ordered "all available Beauforts of 217 Squadron to attack before dark" and left the detailed arrangements to the squadron commander. Since Beaufighters were not included in the force it was evident that the attack was intended to be carried out in the half light of dusk, when the convoy's fighter escort would have left for the night. Knowing that such an attack demanded very exact timing, I consulted with Creswell and together we hunted through pages of the almanack and poured over a chart on which he had already drawn the route which the convoy would take and marked off its expected progress at hourly intervals, calculated from the position and speed given by the latest 'recce' report. At three o'clock it had been seen making ten knots off Zante, five hours later it would pass the island of Sapienza, off the south-west corner of Greece and start the passage in open sea; sunset was at eight-twenty in that latitude. As Creswell and I bent over the chart working out the problem it was nearly five o'clock; just an hour later we were in the air and setting course from the Island.

To settle down to steady flight was a relief from the wild scramble which preceded our take-off. From the very moment the operation was ordered we had been racing against time, for the convoy, according to Creswell's calculations, would be enveloped in darkness at a quarter to nine, and the outward flight at cruising speed woud take not less than two hours and forty minutes; it was essential to set course not later than six o'clock. Creswell calculated with the speed of an automaton, crews were briefed with the barest essentials, then packed into the waiting buses and rushed out to their aircraft. I was just leaving the office when Willie came up to wish me good luck, at the same time thrusting into my hand a packet of caffeine tablets which he said might help in keeping me awake.

Our first course was set for the most southern point of Sapienza, the convoy's position at eight o'clock, where we intended to turn south and approach our target from astern. Two hours passed in steady cruising, then the sun went down behind us and the eastern sky began to darken with alarming rapidity. There was no margin for error in this flight, and I was beginning to glance anxiously from the cockpit clock to the darkening sky when Sapienza appeared dead ahead, and we turned to follow the convoy route.

Land vanished in the dusk behind us and the most critical part of the flight began. With the last of daylight dying in the western sky and darkness creeping up from the east, the time remaining to make a torpedo attack could be estimated not in minutes but in seconds.

I was flying on a course a few degrees East of South in order to keep the shipping route between our force and the light western horizon, when grey shapes suddenly emerged from the leaden sea and became silhouetted against the dying sky, a line of ships that were our targets. Although conditions were ideal for a surprise torpedo attack, we had come upon our objective at the last possible moment, and there was no time to be lost in claiming our precarious advantage.

Running down the east side of the convoy, cloaked in darkness, I signalled to my section to spread, and turned in to the attack. The three merchant vessels in front of me were steaming in a staggered line ahead, protected on either flank by four destroyers. Choosing the first ship of the line as my target, I passed in front of the leading destroyer and was actually taking aim before a rocket shot up from the ship in front of me, a signal that it was being attacked. Guns immediately opened up from every side, for by this time the other Beauforts must also have passed through the destroyer screen and been facing their targets.

I was just turning away when an accurate stream of tracer poured out from the ship towards which my torpedo was running, and a shell burst with a shuddering explosion under the tail of my Beaufort which promptly stood on its nose at less than a hundred feet above the scarcely discernible surface of the water. My heart may have stopped dead, but my hands jumped to actions which momentarily saved us from joining the submarine war. Somehow disaster was averted, the aircraft recovered from the dive and climbed away over the further line of destroyers into safety.

Behind us continued the prettiest pyrotechnical display I have ever seen given by enemy ships. Colours were favoured by the convoy for its tracer ammunition, and since it was almost dark they showed up frighteningly well; streams of green and red played up from every ship, not to mention an occasional multi-coloured Verey light, shot up for some unknown reason.

By the time I had climbed to a thousand feet, several miles separated my aircraft from the convoy's guns and I was a little happier, but even then none too happy. As usual when my aircraft was hit, it was the tailplane which had suffered, and this time the elevator appeared almost completely jammed, luckily in the position of level flight. The control column moved sufficiently to allow a gentle dive or climb, but further movement in either direction was prevented by some obstruction, past which I dared not attempt to force it for fear of increasing the unknown damage and making bad worse. I knew I was lucky to be still flying and decided not to consider the difficulties of landing until the more immediate problem of finding the Island in darkness had been settled.

Night, creeping up unnoticed in the heat of the attack, fell before the convoy vanished from sight in a blaze of colour, and I found myself flying automatically by instruments on a course given me by Creswell which led into the dark western sky. Whether any hits had been scored I neither knew nor cared, for tiredness was setting in at the end of a long flying day. I was looking forward with distaste to the monotony of the return flight, not quite confident of finding the Island or landing safely at its end, when suddenly I remembered the packet of caffeine Willie had given me, and took a few tablets. Their effect was immediate; energy returned, fears dissolved and reactions quickened; above all, time, which usually seemed to stand still in the air at night, began to pass at the speed of thought. A series of wireless bearings were received by which Creswell could check the navigation, and soon the cone of searchlights always put up over Malta, when enemy activity allowed, to guide friendly aircraft appeared briefly some fifty miles ahead. With our destination in sight the business of finding the Island after three hours' flying out of sight of land and in darkness seemed to offer no problems at all, but the landing was again beginning to walk as a ghost before me, a ghost which I proceeded to lay immediately with another large dose of caffeine which exhausted the packet.

I had never before taken caffeine, which was usually provided only in special circumstances for the crews of long-range aircraft, and could hardly be expected to know that the packet given me by Willie contained a dose designed to keep awake not a single person, but a complete crew of four! However, ignorance on this occasion resulted in some perfectly blissful flying, without which I would probably never have landed safely at all.

On our arrival we found not only unusual patches of cloud drifting over the hills, but the inevitable air raid in progress, and were forced to circle the Island waiting for light on the runway. Meanwhile, illumination was not lacking elsewhere: bombs burst with blinding flashes, fires were started and at intervals chandelier flares lit up the sky as they floated slowly to earth. For the first half an hour our view of this show from the gallery was probably preferable to a position in the pit, but then the entertainment began to pall, not on account of monotony, but because our gallery seats were becoming uncomfortable; petrol was running short and the raid showed no signs of ending.

Asking Creswell to flash an urgent request to the flare path for light, I approached the aerodrome with determination, our Beaufort picked up and dropped several times by searchlights, and probably fired at occasionally by our guns. Reducing the circle of the Island to a circuit of the aerodrome proved unexpectedly difficult, for the limited elevator control made the aircraft impossible to turn sharply and clouds were perpetually drifting between my line of sight and the flare path, which seemed to be playing a game of hide and seek. Creswell flashed a further message asking for more light, a request politely granted by the enemy, who immediately dropped a whole series of flares right over Luqa, their light making the 'octopus', not to mention our Beaufort, both look and feel very naked and vulnerable.

The flare path, despite the raid, was now lit at full strength, and the floodlight for landings was flashed on at intervals, but I could only catch sight of the aerodrome for a tantalising second before it dodged behind cloud. To add to the discomfort, I had occasionally a strong suspicion I was being followed, not by one of the other Beauforts now on the circuit, but by an enemy intruder.

Finally the game which had started so lightly ceased to amuse; with the pointers of my petrol gauges indicating single figures, the situation became critical. Had there been a further supply of caffeine at hand, my ghost, no doubt, would to this very day still be circling Luqa oblivious of a slight deficiency in petrol. But now I began to despair of reaching the runway, and considered making a forced landing on the sea. I did actually make an approach to a field illuminated by enemy flares, but from two hundred feet I saw enough to make me change my mind, and abandoning this method of suicide, climbed up to try the aerodrome once more. The degree of desperation prevailing in the cockpit can be judged from the fact that Maltese fields are no bigger than postage stamps and always surrounded by heavy stone walls.

Just at the moment when my petrol gauges were reading nought, and I had become indifferent to my fate, the enemy raiders left the Island, a green light flashed up from the flare path and the floodlight's beam shone steadily over the runway. Expecting an engine to fail at any second, I lowered the flaps to make a short approach, and for the second time that day nearly dived to destruction: the elevator control was insufficient to keep the aircraft level with flaps down. I had the flaps up again in a flash, and recovered somehow from the dive, but not before an unpleasant lack of height was indicated on the altimeter.

Exhausted, I started another approach, this time without using flaps. Keeping the flare path straight in front of me I gradually lost height, at the same time trying to bring the speed down to a reasonable figure for landing, but control grew so ineffective as speed was reduced that I dared not lower the undercarriage. Finally, after a frantic struggle in the last hundred feet, more by prayer than by skill I contrived to bring the aircraft low past the floodlight. As we rushed into the beam, I switched off the engines, an agonising interval followed as we floated up the runway, then came the crash, and with it safety. Yet another crash landing marked the end of another flight, and we were down at last.

The crowd which surrounded the crashed aircraft almost before it had come to rest was not a reception committee interested in the four weary figures which scrambled out; other Beauforts were still circling overhead, their petrol dangerously low, and the runway had to be cleared without delay. So it came about that I found myself, in company with John Creswell and the others, assisting in removing the obstruction I had made. The tank pulled, we pushed, and within half a minute of its arrival, the crashed Beaufort was on the grass well clear of the runway. As the floodlight beam shone out again over the aerodrome for another aircraft to land, we inspected the damaged tail plane by its light and found the elevator almost completely jammed; most of the very small movement at the control column must have been used in taking up slack in the wires. For a few moments we stood gazing stupidly at the aircraft which had brought us home, Creswell holding my Panda mascot as if it were a baby; then a runner came up with a message for us to report at the control tower and we set out across the aerodrome, talking in monosyllables.

There the AOC and some of his staff were waiting to hear an account of the attack. I introduced my crew then left most of the talking to Creswell, who proceeded to paint a lurid picture, worthy of a film scenario, including an account of an explosion on one of the ships which I strongly suspected of being a product of his imagination. Observers, and also gunners, are always prone to exaggeration, no doubt from a warped sense of loyalty to their pilot. Whenever the force scored a hit, my crew claimed it for me, whenever we failed, they found excuses. Now I intervened to keep Creswell's account within the bounds of possibility, and when at last the story ended sent him and the gunners to Intelligence Office to repeat the information for the official report always made at the end of every sortie. Alone with the AOC I was able to give Creswell the credit which he deserved for the faultless navigation to the target, without which the attack, whatever its result, could never have been made.

Incidents such as this, the AOC coming up to the aerodrome after a long day spent at his desk in Headquarters in order to receive personally the returning crews, were typical of the spirit prevailing on the Island, which was personified by Air Vice-Marshal Hugh Lloyd himself. That night he had been on the aerodrome when the raid started, and ordering onlookers into the shelters had himself remained on the flare path to direct operations. His orders had kept the beacon of searchlights alight at intervals during the raid to guide our aircraft in, and caused the flarepath to be lit when our petrol was running dangerously low. While raiders circled above interspersed with friendly aircraft he had made the aerodrome a lighted target to help us, and stood on the runway in the open while flares hung overhead and the bombs fell, making every effort to bring his aircraft safely down. Now, at the end of this interview, the AOC returned to the flare path to see the remaining Beauforts come in and I made my way to bed feeling that for him I would that very minute take off again and make another six-hour flight. He was inspiring.

As I sat on my bed, so tired that I could hardly raise the energy to undress, Willie gave me an impression of how the scene had appeared from the ground. He had spent much of the time in a shelter, to which he was repeatedly being banished by the AOC, but occasionally he had escaped notice and stood by the floodlight, watching my progress with anguish and amazement. If my flying had seemed blissful in the air, it had been excruciating to Willie on the ground. Apparently my aircraft had spent long periods either enveloped in cloud or out of sight behind the hills, and several times had actually passed down the surrounding valleys well below the level of the aerodrome, threatening the architecture of nearby villages. When at last I had appeared to be coming in safely my aircraft had been seen to vanish suddenly behind Luqa village in a steep dive, no doubt the occasion I had tried to use the flaps, and the onlookers had waiting stoically for the crash which did not materialise.

Willie, of course, had been showing rather more concern for my safety than the normal solicitude of a CO for his crews, and this was not wholly accounted for by the fact that I was flying his own personal Beaufort. He was hoping to hand over the command of the squadron to me and return home, an arrangement he had already suggested to the AOC, who had promised to consider allowing his release on compassionate grounds. So of the many welcomes I received on my return, Willie's was undoubtedly the warmest. I often wondered later whether that packet of caffeine was given me with an ulterior motive;

at any rate, the fact that his marriage took place before the month ended owed something to every one of those tablets!

Whether we sank one of those three ships I never knew, for Benghazi and Tobruk were covered by reconnaissances from Egypt, but rumour had it that the next day's cover failed to account for one. Of the nine Beauforts that set out, seven returned. One of the two missing aircraft was seen to dive into the water near the target, presumably hit by flak, and the other, also hit, had begun the homeward journey, sending out a last SOS in a position midway between the scene of the attack and the Island. We sent out aircraft to search this area all the next day, but neither floating wreckage nor dinghy were seen in that wilderness of open sea.

Another lull began now, but this time it was a prelude to a rather more orderly storm of activity than the last. Nearly three whole weeks passed without a target presenting itself, then ships moved and we went out against them, making three sorties in a week.

This respite from operations was invaluable, for it enabled the screws of our organisation, which had creaked and groaned under its first test, to be tightened. It was, of course, not our squadron but the reconnaissance arrangements which had failed and so put the whole machine out of gear. The squadron's organisation had at first worked smoothly; crews had risen from their beds, taken aircraft from their pens to join formation over the Island and arrive as a force off the Greek coast at the appointed time. It was the appointment which had been wrongly made; we had waited for but failed to meet our target and later in the day were forced to send an improvised force to pursue rather than meet it with a hurriedly prepared plan of attack.

The squadron never had sufficient crews and aircraft to form two separate forces, and since one flight of five or six hours' duration was all that could be expected of a crew, and often all that could be obtained from a Beaufort without further servicing, it was never really capable of making two attacks in one day. The demands of the last occasion had been exceptional, but now I considered that every step should be taken to avoid a repetition of those exceptional circumstances in the future; appointments between important targets and large forces of aircraft should not be wrongly arranged.

The solution was to take matters more slowly and by doing so bring the enemy more surely within our grasp. The force had originally been sent out on the evidence of a night reconnaissance only, a member of the staff having assumed that the ships would maintain the speed reported; this assumption, although reasonable, had proved incorrect.

Night 'recces', particularly when there is no moon, can be very incomplete; the speed of a convoy can be assessed fairly accurately, but the composition is difficult to establish with any degree of certainty. No doubt the convoy had been making the speed reported by the Wellington crew at the time they had last seen it, but subsequently it had certainly slowed down, most probably to pick up additional escort, for only six destroyers had waited in Brindisi, whereas eight were observed escorting the convoy later in the day.

On the other hand, the evidence of the day 'recce', on which Creswell had based the navigation for the second sortie, had proved accurate, and the short time elapsing between the last sighting of the convoy and our arrival had left little opportunity for it to evade attack. So it was resolved never again to send out a force on the sole evidence of a night reconnaissance, except in very special circumstances, but always to have the target covered in daylight by PRU. This decision meant sacrificing the chance of attacking in the first hours of the day, for the Spitfires could not normally take off before first light and might not return with their report until two hours later. However, our force could come to readiness while the 'recce' aircraft was out, in order to take off with as little delay as possible when it returned.

Two hours might pass before the 'recce' aircraft returned from the target, and usually another two and a half hours would be needed by our force to reach it; since the majority of these supply ships did not make more than ten knots it was hardly possible for them to disappear in the short time available. However, they might speed up or slow down, so to insure against this happening, we continued to use a Baltimore and continued to sweep a length of the shipping route instead of making for a single position. We made our landfall at a point several hours steaming in front of the target's expected position, then turned and ran up the route towards it, an arrangement which not only made finding the target easier, but also suited our tactics which demanded an approach from either dead ahead or dead astern. As a further insurance against some quite unforeseen occurrence, such as the target stopping completely or turning back, a Baltimore was still to go out just ahead of the attacking force, but was only to break wireless silence if the target was found in a position outside the area we intended to search. In this way we hoped to conserve the chance of surprise which a wireless message might jeopardise. Altogether a very fine net was woven, ready to be cast over enemy ships, and in practice this system did work well, for we never afterwards failed to keep our appointments.

A week before the next attack, when all the reconnaissance plans were laid and we were waiting eagerly to put them to the test, the squadron received an unexpected reinforcement: a complete flight of Beauforts arrived from England. This flight, six aircraft strong, led by a Squadron Leader with a Flight Lieutenant as its second-in-command, was a most timely addition to 217 Squadron's dwindling strength, made more welcome still when it transpired that their aircraft were Mark IIs and their leaders of considerable experience. Jimmy Hyde, the Squadron Leader, had been a contemporary of mine in 22 Squadron in England, and 'Hank' Sharman, his second-in-command, had also served for a short time in the same squadron before becoming an instructor in torpedo dropping. This flight was actually part of 86 Squadron, which was being sent out complete from England, but it was arranged that their aircraft and crews should work with 217 Squadron until the arrival of the second flight.

With the promise of a complete Beaufort squadron fully staffed with Squadron Leaders and Flight Lieutenants, the AOC consented to Willie returning home, a decision duly celebrated in Crème de Menthe, almost the only obtainable alcohol. But passages in the airliner which left nightly for Gibraltar on the first stage of the flight to England were much in demand, and Willie was still forming the anxious part of a queue when we made our next sortie.

Single ships steamed down the Greek coast on July 21st, 24th and 28th; we found, attacked and hit every one of them.

The first target, a vessel of ten thousand tons, was sighted by PRU shortly after dawn steaming south from Cape Maria di Leuca, the heel of Italy. Again, this was no chance sighting; the ship had been watched in port during the preceding days and the usual indications of the intention to sail had resulted in this final reconnaissance which found her at sea with an escorting destroyer on either side, and no more efficient aerial protection overhead than a single inoffensive flying boat.

Within a few minutes of this report being received at Intelligence Office, Creswell was working out the navigation, while I briefed the crews who had been waiting ready in the adjoining room. Soon the maze was vibrating with the roar of running engines, and moving clouds of dust indicated that aircraft were taxiing out onto the aerodrome. Taking off first, I turned to circle, while a stream of aircraft poured off the runway to climb up and join formation on either side of me; then, at the head of a force of nine Beauforts and six Beaufighters, course was set for Zante.

Two and a half hours later a welcome thickening of the thin line between sea and sky was apparent, which soon became a coastline and finally an island; Creswell had, as usual, brought the force directly onto its landfall. Turning, we ran northwards low over the surface of the water, some five miles out from the coast, all the time peering anxiously over the horizon for a sight of the target. No wireless message had been received from the Baltimore, which had gone out ahead of us according to plan, so there was no reason to suppose the target would escape us. But as Zante was left behind, and mile after mile of the Cephalonian coast became rapidly eaten up in our sweep northwards, I began to lose confidence for, as on the last occasion we had covered this area, the limit of our search was drawing near without a sign of the target. I dreaded to return empty handed and find that our carefully laid plans had gone astray, for this time a second strike sent out on our return could not possibly reach the target before nightfall; it was the last chance to attack and it seemed to be slipping from our grasp; but that did not happen.

As we came abreast of Cape Geroghambo, a ship appeared on the horizon twenty miles ahead. Relief replaced anxiety in the cockpit, which in turn gave way to excitement as the distance separating us from the target decreased rapidly and the merchant vessel with its two dark grey flanking destroyers became clearly visible. As the two following sections of Beauforts, led by Hank and Tony, broke away to take up their positions, the Beaufighters started to climb from the surface of the water and I, spreading my section into line, turned in to attack from the seaward side. Hank's section followed me, Tony came in from the land, and almost before a shot was fired nine torpedoes were in the water running towards their target; we had achieved complete surprise. As I was aiming my torpedo, the merchant ship had actually started to turn in a last-minute attempt to avoid our attack, but gunfire was unaccountably absent, and although several guns were firing before the last section turned away, the volume of fire was never that expected from an armed merchantman and two destroyers.

I had almost forgotten that the seconds spent in waiting for the result of an attack could be so brimful of anxiety as the long minutes spent in searching for the target, for my aircraft had been hit so often in recent attacks that its safety had claimed my attention to the exclusion of all other thoughts until the target was left far behind. But as I turned away from this attack, with the unaccustomed freedom of an undamaged aircraft, doubts and hopes raced through my mind, I found my wish granted: the merchant vessel was shrouded in smoke.

The defences had been weak, the attack well executed and the result was all we could hope for; a glance was enough to show that at least one of our torpedoes had found its mark, and with a light heart I set course for home, knowing that to delay might give time for fighters to come out from a nearby aerodrome and turn the success into a disaster. As we reformed to start the homeward flight, with Hank and Tony leading their sections into position on either side of me and the Beaus coming up behind us, I saw that not a single aircraft was missing; the force was returning exactly as it had set out.

The Beaufighters, who were slightly faster than our Beauforts, left us after the first half hour of the return flight and went on ahead, since their protection was unnecessary over open sea. So by the time our nine Beauforts in close formation dived in triumph low over the island before breaking up in spectacular fashion, our success was already known at Luqa.

The Beaufighter crews had brought back enthusiastic reports of the attack which they had watched unchallenged from an elevated position above the convoy, for after dealing summarily with the single unfortunate flying boat patrolling near the target, they had circled over the ships dropping beer bottles! It was hoped that these missiles, which fell with a frightening scream, might be mistaken by the enemy for bombs and cause him to divert his attention from the torpedo aircraft approaching low down.

This scheme had been suggested after the first attack by a Beaufighter observer, who had watched the whole volume of the convoy's fire being concentrated on us so effectively that it had claimed two aircraft and damaged five others, while the Beaufighters, circling over head, had been engaged by neither fighters nor flak. The role of the Beaufighters was primarily to protect us from enemy fighters, but that menace, always expected, had not yet materialised and their leader, anxious to give us more active help, had agreed to try the effect of beer bottles. Although this 'bombing' eventually proved ineffective, its inception was a most valuable first step towards effecting a gradual but far-reaching change in the Beaufighters' role, from passive protection to taking an active part in the actual attack.

The 'recce' Baltimore, landing before the Beaus, had also brought back news of our success, for having located the target within our line of search, it had kept wireless silence and remained nearby, not only witnessing the whole attack but taking a photograph of the burning target. Even the most conservative reports from crews actually taking part in an attack are liable to be optimistic, so although the Beaufighters and the independent Baltimore crew were emphatic in claiming a hit for us, I remembered the unfounded optimism after the first

attack and waited for the film to be developed. However, the photograph which was sent up from Headquarters a few hours after our
return showed distinctly the burning ship just as I had last seen it, and
confirmed fully the reports.

In the celebration which inevitably followed this good news, a large
hole was made in the remaining supply of Crème de Menthe, for our
first success coincided with the eve of Willie's departure; he left that
night for England.

The next operation was at once more successful and disastrous; the
target was hit and afterwards burnt out, but half the torpedo force was
lost.

Jimmy Hyde led this attack. It had not yet been decided whether
86 Squadron should retain a separate identity or become merged in
with 217 Squadron; Group were waiting for the arrival of the second
flight before making a decision. Meanwhile we agreed to pool our
resources and work together, a commonsense arrangement since one
flight was useless by itself and 217 Squadron was already needing
reinforcement.

Jimmy held the same rank as I, and superficially was of the same
experience. After a tour of operations in 22 Squadron at home, we
had both completed periods of rest and were now back in the line once
more. But his experience had been gained mostly at night, for he had
been active in the squadron's versatile days of all round the clock
operations, which included some torpedo attacks by moonlight, night
bombing and minelaying. I had spent most of that period in hospital
and Jimmy, completing his tour shortly after my return to the squadron, had missed a new era, just beginning, in which we had been
employed exclusively in torpedo attacks carried out in daylight. Not
only had he very little experience in leading daylight attacks, but no
experience at all of operating in the Mediterranean, so when I learnt
that he wished to lead I tried as tactfully as possible to dissuade him.
I was unwilling to risk breaking the run of success or losing the confidence which the squadron's crews were beginning to show in my
leadership. Although more experienced than Willie, I had followed
him without question, and it seemed reasonable to suppose that Jimmy
would be willing to lead a section on his first operation from Malta
before leading the complete force.

However, the quality which more than any other had won Jimmy his
DFC was stubborn resolution; he was determined to lead, and I was
forced, very much against my judgment, to agree that he shoud lead
alternate attacks. The inevitable occurred; Jimmy went out on his first

sortie from the island at the head of six Beauforts and six Beaufighters, and although the target was hit, Jimmy himself and his whole section were lost.

The target, intercepted off Cape Geroghambo in the identical position of the last attack, was a single merchant ship whose escort of two destroyers was this time supplemented by two E-boats. I had been very much opposed to the choice of this point for the interception, for I thought it hardly likely that enemy ships would fail to be on their guard as they passed the scene of a successful attack which had taken place only three days before. However, my warning passed unheeded, the arrangements were concluded between Group and the leader, and I watched the force set out with a misgiving I never felt when I myself was flying.

Hank, Tony and I were standing on the top of the control tower overlooking the aerodrome, when the Baltimore sent out in advance of the striking force came into land. As it turned off the end of the runway into the maze a van went out to fetch the crew and in a few minutes they were with us, bringing the first news of the attack. From their account two facts emerged quickly: the target had been set on fire and an unknown number of the attacking aircraft had been shot down. The Baltimore crew, who had been fully occupied in taking photographs, were unable to satisfy our demands for details, but we expected a fuller account from the Beaufighters who were already approaching the aerodrome. As they came in, we counted them carefully until those which had set out were seen to have returned safely, and it was apparent that the aircraft believed to have been shot down were Beauforts.

We waited anxiously for the fighter crews to be brought in from the pens, hoping against hope that they would allay the fears which the Baltimore's report had aroused, but they could give us no reassurance. One after another they climbed up the ladder to the top of the control tower to tell us what they had seen, and with every new report the little confidence we had felt faded away before the growing certainty that two, perhaps three, Beauforts had been shot down.

The Beaus had not encountered any opposition at all; no enemy fighters had been seen, nor had a single shot been fired upwards from the convoy as they circled overhead, but the flak below they described as intense, with the tracer weaving a carpet of horizontal phosphorous lines at sea level. Into this barrage the Beauforts had flown, advancing relentlessly toward their target, while the Beaus watched their progress from above with the fascination of detachment. As the attackers reached torpedo-dropping range, the splashes on the surface of the water made by aircraft shot down became indistinguishable from those made by torpedoes entering to start their run, but several patches of white foam were still visible as the merchant vessel burst suddenly into flames.

Reports from the fighters were conflicting in detail, but all agreed that the flak had been unusually concentrated, an unknown number of Beauforts had been shot down and that the target most definitely had been hit. With heavy hearts we waited for the surviving Beauforts to come in, counting first one, then another and finally a third as they appeared as specks in the sky, approached the aerodrome and landed. While waiting impatiently for the crews to be brought in from dispersal we scanned the eastern horizon, assuring ourselves without conviction that at any moment one of the missing aircraft would come into sight. But hope was killed dead by the evidence which the Beaufort crews brought back.

Steve, the leader of the second section, described how he had followed Jimmy Hyde in the search along the Greek coast, very per-plexed at his leader's choice of height, for instead of flying at our usual height of approximately fifty feet above the surface, he had climbed gradually to 300 ft. Normally we never left sea level from the time we set course for the target until the attack was completed, partly because our camouflage merged in with the colour of the sea and made our Beauforts difficult to spot from the deck of a ship, partly because detection by radio location was made more difficult by flying low.

Flying high had not been Jimmy's only error, for he had searched too close inshore, with the result that the target, instead of appearing straight ahead, had been first sighted on the seaward side. This position of sighting left the leader with no alternative but to turn and make the long approach from the beam, always avoided because it laid the force open to fire from every ship of the convoy. The escort vessels, no doubt prepared for attack, with guns manned and look-out alert, had not been slow to spot the attacking force, and long before the Beauforts were within torpedo range they were meeting accurate streams of fire, which were particularly lethal from the E-boats.

Steve, experienced and with a DFC to his credit, although suffering agonies of conscience during the search up the coast, had nevertheless followed his leader stoically. But when he found himself still at three hundred feet with the target within sight and firing, fears for the safety of his own section overcame any false sense of loyalty, and he led it down to continue the approach on the water. No decision could have been more timely. The leading section, flying on a steady course and silhouetted against the skyline, must have presented an easy target to the convoy's guns, and before torpedo range was reached every one of its aircraft had been shot down. But Steve's section, flying in low to drop their torpedoes, escaped unscathed from the dangers of a beam attack and left behind them a burning ship.

To piece together a picture of this attack from the fragments of reports was like trying to solve a jigsaw puzzle with some of its pieces missing: the centre of the picture, the line of thought in the leader's mind, was irretrievably lost. Why should Jimmy have flown high? Although no report contained an answer to this question I could, by putting myself in the leader's place, hazard a guess which may not be far from the truth.

In 22 Squadron Jimmy had always been a conscientious operator, carefully searching areas of sea at night when mine-laying, finding one or two targets by day and making determined attacks. On this occasion he had been over anxious to score a success; it was his first operation from Malta as a leader, and no doubt he wished it to result in an attack at least as successful as the last. On that occasion the delay in finding the target had caused me no little anxiety, and this time the convoy again failed to appear until the very last moment; as the search progressed without a sign of the ships, Jimmy, fearing to miss his objective, had thrown caution aside and climbed up in order to extend his field of view and ensure the target did not escape him. It was an action of conscience thus to make certain of a kill, but also an action which should never have been considered by an experienced leader.

It was always the same with daylight torpedo attacks; the stakes were so high and the play so fast that with one slight mistake the game could be lost. A delay in finding the target might lay the force open to interception by enemy fighters, an unfavourable direction of approach might impale every aircraft on the enemy's guns. The sinking of a ship by a handful of aircraft was in itself a feat of skill, but we demanded not only success but that it should be accompanied by small losses. A leader's decisions in the air were critical in achieving the result we desired, but planning on the ground before the operation could do much to simplify his problems. So with a photograph of a burning ship on the table in front of me, I sat down that very evening to think out the next attack.

Four days later this thought turned into action, and we found, attacked and hit another ship. The force of nine Beauforts and six Beaufighters which set out on this attack was similar in composition to those used previously, but on this occasion the aircraft were to be differently employed, and the Beauforts of one section were carrying not torpedoes but a load of four 250 lb bombs.

I wanted a success badly, not for myself but for the squadron. The loss of half the torpedo force in the last attack had been an undoubted blow which had passed without leaving any mark on the crews' spirit, but I knew that a repetition of that loss might leave a scar which would take long to heal. So during the previous days I had been planning not an attack, but a success; failure was unthinkable.

A fact which had emerged clearly and ominously from the experience of the last attack was that in future enemy convoys would be vigilant throughout every minute of the passage down the Greek coast, and it was most unlikely that we should ever take them unawares again. It was apparent, too, that the escort vessels were expecting attack by torpedo aircraft and concentrating their fire low down to meet them. On the last sortie the screaming beer bottles had failed to draw the fire of a single gun, and it had to be admitted that this particular secret weapon was now obsolete.

Not only was the flak likely to become more troublesome, but fighter patrols over our target could not be expected, and I had studied the recent 'covers' of Greek coastal aerodromes with a new interest. However, since the seaboard was mountainous, there were few aerodromes to fear on the northern part of the route, but I noticed that Araxos on the Isthmus of Corinth held no less than fifty Macchi 202s and Navarin, further south, had a smaller number of similar aircraft. Fighters and flak, the old enemies, were ranging up against us, with flak causing the most immediate concern.

I knew that with the chances of taking the target by surprise diminishing with every attack, our pilots would be unable to close to the short range on which success was so dependent unless at least part of the defenders' fire was diverted upwards. Although the screaming beer bottles had proved ineffective, I saw no reason why real bombs should not succeed in drawing the enemy's attention.

While this idea was revolving in my mind, the new AOC sent for me. Air Vice-Marshal Hugh Lloyd, after a year on the island, had been relieved by Air Vice-Marshal Keith Park, well known as the commander of the Fighter Group covering the south-eastern sector, the actual battlefield, during the Battle of Britain. Now for the first time I met the man whom in the following months I came to respect, admire and, dare I say, on occasions inwardly curse.

One such occasion was when, on a very hot afternoon, he took me on a two-hour inspection of the Beauforts being worked on in their pens, discovering in the process my 'trick' of keeping the slow aircraft grounded by minor defects, at which he was highly displeased. Still, geniality was rejoined when he came into tea with me in our Mess, and consumed all that was remaining of my jam from home.

Park was magnificent; behind some personal idiosyncrasies which might give rise to momentary doubts, hid a great man. Hugh Lloyd undoubtedly had his days of greatness at Malta, his sturdy frame standing alone as a bulwark against defeat through the doubts of those dark winter months, but Park came when the night of dogged resistance was dawning on a day of determined attack. Lloyd was the bastion, Park the rapier. The picture I always see of Lloyd shows him standing alone on the highest point of the runway at Luqa, defying the enemy's bombs to move him. Park I see in the Fighter Control room at Headquarters, silently watching the counters, which represented his fighters, climbing up from the Island to ward off the raiders long before they reach their objective. Rarely can two such different personalities have been so right in the right place at the right time. The pendulum swung from defence to offence, and the Command changed.

At this first meeting Air Vice-Marshal Park openly admitted that he knew little about attacking ships, having always specialised in fighter operations, but proceeded to show a very real appreciation of our problem and expressed some concern at the heavy losses of the last attack. After listening to my explanation of that disaster, he was not only willing to try the effect of bombing on the next sortie, but went a step further and agreed to my suggestion that the Beaufighters should adopt a more offensive role and cover us during the attack by firing on the escort vessels with their four cannons. I naturally advocated this arrangement but, being uncertain how the Beaufighters would receive it, suggested that I should talk it over with Ross Shore, the CO of 235 Squadron; if he was agreeable we would try the effect of a cannon attack on our next sortie. With this decision made, the meeting ended, and I left Headquarters very encouraged at the new AOC's open-minded attitude to our problems. I felt that the squadron had a sympathetic counsellor at Headquarters, and it seemed that I, too, had a friend there, for the interview had ended in my promotion to Wing Commander.

As a result of this meeting new tactics had been evolved, and the force which I led was making for a new position of attack in which to try them out. I considered that Cape Geroghambo, although a convenient point for interception, had become altogether too hot and chose this time a point further south, between Zante and Sapienza. Our target again consisted of a single merchant vessel escorted by two destroyers and two E-boats. The PRU pilot, who had last sighted the convoy off Cephalonia, very near the position of the last strike, reported that the escort vessels were weaving nervously, as if expecting attack at any moment, while several Macchi 202s circled overhead. The thought that 'twice bitten' was apparently also an Italian proverb made me smile a little until I realised that we too were perhaps a trifle shy of this third encounter.

I intended making a landfall at the island of Prote, then turning north as usual in order to meet our target from ahead, but an unexpected message from the Baltimore changed this plan. As the outward flight neared its end, some morse buzzed its way through my headphones, and my wireless operator handed John a message reporting a new position of the convoy just beyond the southern point of our search line; without receiving this information we would have turned north and missed our target.

From the very moment this wireless message was received things began to happen so quickly that there was no time for the usual anxiety. With very few minutes to spare before the Greek coastline came in sight, I made John come back to my cockpit and illustrate the new situation on his chart; one glance showed that it was too late to alter course to intercept the convoy from ahead, so I decided to continue to Prote and then turn south to attack from astern.

Hardly had this decision been made when the coastline came up over the horizon, then the tiny island of Prote became visible and we turned south to run down the shipping route. Prote was still within sight when the convoy appeared, oh Heaven! dead ahead.

Again Tony was on my right and Hank on my left, this time leading the bombing section; one of the precautions I had taken against failure was to choose these experienced leaders. Ross Shore, leading the fighter escort, had agreed to try the effect of cannon fire on the destroyers and I was to fire a signal cartridge when I thought his Beaus should climb to start their attack.

A few minutes after sighting, two green Verey lights burnt above my aircraft, and the attack started. I led my section down the landward side of the target, Tony steered a parallel course on the other side, while Hank climbed up with the Beaus in order to bomb in a shallow dive.

The destroyers were not in their usual position on either side of the merchant vessel, but ahead and astern, presumably to increase the effectiveness of their fire against beam targets. Of the E-boats and fighters seen by PRU there was no sign, but I did notice that the convoy was making at least eighteen knots, which was eight knots faster than the reported speed.

Passing abreast of the after destroyer, with my followers in line behind me, I drew level with the merchant vessel without the enemy showing any sign that he had noticed us. Tony's section was just visible skimming over the surface of the water on the other side of the convoy, and it looked as if our two sections might be able to close on the target like the jaws of a nutcracker, without being detected. But just as I turned in, fire poured out from the sides of all three ships simultaneously, and the merchant vessel turned sharply towards my section, upsetting all our calculations. I was manoeuvring to make the best of a bad aiming position, when a Beaufort streaked across the ship in front of me, dropping a stick of bombs which exploded in a line of waterspouts just wide of their mark; I was so absorbed in my own problems that I had completely forgotten the bombing diversion.

Before turning away from the attack I caught a last glimpse of the target heeling over steeply in a sharp turn, a sight which raised doubts in my mind as to whether one of our six torpedoes would reach its mark. But one did; a great column of water shot up on the port side of the turning ship, and we left it stationary, facing the direction from which it had come.

Reforming my section on the seaward side of the target, I saw immediately that the right-hand aircraft was in trouble; white smoke poured out in a long trail behind the starboard engine, and after a few minutes the pilot broke formation and turned back towards the enemy coast. There were also other gaps in both the following sections which made the return flight pass despondently for me, with the thought that three of our Beauforts were again missing.

The loss of Ted Strever, the pilot of my right-hand aircraft, was a severe blow, for he had followed me with some skill on every one of the previous attacks and was about to become a section leader. To add to my discomfort, the wireless failed when we were an hour's flight from the Island, and I was forced to hand over the lead to Hank. It was never worthwhile to risk the force by trusting to navigation alone, even of Creswell's accuracy, for these flights were made to the limit of our safe range and very little petrol was available to cover an error. Hank, his observer receiving the usual wireless bearings, led the depleted force safely home, while I, relieved of the responsibility of leading, pondered deeply on the fate of the missing aircraft.

As usual, the fighter escort, and especially the crew of the Baltimore, which had photographed the result of our attack, described incidents which had escaped my notice. One Beaufighter, seeing Ted Strever's aircraft in difficulties, had circled while it made a forced landing on the water, and last saw the crew climbing safely into the dinghy. The aircraft missing from Tony's section was also accounted for, having been seen to dive inexplicably into the water well out of range of the convoy's guns; but there was no news of Pete Roper, one of the bombing section who had failed to return. However, several of the Beaus had seen Macchi 202s appearing on the scene just as we left, and it seemed likely that Pete, hanging around the target against all orders, had fallen a victim to fighter attack.

The first part of this conjecture was unexpectedly proved true. We were standing on the control tower, cursing Pete's assumed foolhardiness and at the same time still hoping for his safe return, when Fighter Control rang up to say that the radiolocation had picked up a friendly aircraft approaching from the east. All eyes strained towards the eastern horizon, on which a speck gradually appeared; within a few minutes the speck could be identified as a Beaufort: Pete Roper had returned.

In due course Pete's grinning face appeared over the parapet of the control tower, and he was soon describing the scene we had already imagined. After bombing one of the destroyers, he had described several wide circles round the target, hoping to see it actually sink, a hope in which he had been disappointed: the merchant vessel lay stationary and smoking while the destroyers went alongside to give assistance. Pete, engrossed in watching the proceedings of the convoy, had just reached a decision to return for home, when he was rudely disturbed by the rattle of bullets tearing holes through his port wing. There followed several very unpleasant minutes in which three Macchi 202s had chased his jinking aircraft far out to sea before breaking away.

This incident was a lesson not only to Pete but to all the other crews. To wait around the target was attractive, but very dangerous and also unnecessary now that the attack was being covered by a Baltimore, which on this occasion brought back an excellent photograph showing the ship stationary at the end of a semi-circular wake.

With our losses reduced by Pete's return, the result of the attack appeared more satisfactory. I was particularly pleased to have achieved a measure of surprise, for the fact that the convoy had discarded the E-boats and fighter cover seen earlier in the day indicated that attack was no longer expected in a position so far south, a surmise further borne out by the very late start of the gunfire. The bombing and cannon-firing sections had synchronised well with the torpedo attack, the Beaus going in first to rake the vessels with cannon shells while the Beauforts followed closely with their sticks of bombs. To our torpedo aircraft the fast moving target, turning rapidly, had presented no easy target, and although Tony had led his attack brilliantly to coincide with mine, I would not have been surprised if we had failed to score a single hit.

That we had scored only one hit was confirmed by a PRU 'recce' sent out that evening, which reported our target, supported on either side by a destroyer, being towed slowly towards Navarin. I had no reason to complain at this result for it would be many months before that ship left dry dock, but I went to bed that evening a little disappointed. Perhaps it was because I was missing Ted Strever and remembering too clearly the reluctant way he had broken formation and turned back towards the enemy coast, while we continued homeward.

The next day the squadron was released and most of the crews either slept through the midday heat or went to the nearest beach at Sliema to bathe. Tony and I, deciding to go further afield, obtained a route from the Intelligence firm, borrowed bicycles belonging to Porridge and Ponting, and went to a cove called the Blue Grotto. This was a remote and enchanting little harbour at the foot of the steep cliffs on the south coast; native boats, picturesquely shaped and painted in bright colours, were reflected in the clear water and the stone cottages of the little fishing colony clustered around the foot of the cliff. To avoid the many coloured jellyfish which infested the harbour, we swam out to a solitary rock projecting from deeper water, where we spent the afternoon alternately swimming and sun-bathing. We watched, fascinated, the deep sea fishes winding in and out of rocks on the seabed ten fathoms below, while the sun quickly turned the water to salt on our backs, then plunged again and again into the cool water, which seemed to remember no other time but peace. This was an afternoon spent in another world and when at its end we made our way back to the aerodrome, I felt completely rested and free from care.

Leaving Ponting's bicycle outside Intelligence Office, I picked up a few stones, threw them on to the roof and went in, intending to tell the firm how much we had enjoyed the bathing place they had recommended. I knew Malta well enough to expect something of moment to have occurred in our absence; a ship found at sea or an order to attack the next morning would not have surprised me, but the sight which met my eyes was beyond the mundane realms of my conjecture: four grinning ghosts were haunting the office, the shades of Strever and his crew. A second of speechless doubt passed, then the ghosts came to life and I found myself listening to a story such as I never thought could exist outside fiction.

During the attack Ted's aircraft had been hit in the port wing. At first the damage had appeared slight, but soon the port engine was showing unmistakable signs of imminent failure, and Ted, with no hope of completing the three hundred mile return flight, was left with no alternative but to turn back in an attempt to reach the Greek coast. In this he failed, being forced to alight on the sea some five miles from land, where he and his crew had remained floating in the dinghy for several hours before being picked up by an Italian flying boat. They were then flown to a seaplane base, and after being questioned by some Italian Intelligence Officers were made surprisingly comfortable in the Mess, where they were warmly entertained. The description of the food and wine consumed that evening drew involuntary sighs from several rather hungry Malta defenders. Apparently the Italians, although friendly, had volunteered very little information, but I was interested to hear that not only were our aircraft mistaken for Blenheims, but our last attack was believed to have come from Egypt. From my point of view the evening's entertainment reached a climax when a message was delivered to the captured crew from no less a personage than an Italian Admiral, congratulating us on the execution of the attack! The playing of comic opera was, it appeared, still an Italian accomplishment.

The next morning the prisoners had been re-embarked in a flying boat which was to take them to Taranto for further interrogation. This aircraft was curiously under-staffed; in the cockpit two pilots shared the flying and navigation, supported by a Flight Engineer, while a single soldier guarded the four prisoners in the cabin.

Entertainment in Greece was one matter, the approaching internment in a prison camp in Italy quite another. Ted Strever was six feet tall and built in proportion, his wireless operator was of similar size and the rest of the crew capable of looking after their interests; but the guard had a gun of some sort. However, this unfortunate Italian soldier had, it appeared, never flown before and soon fell a victim to air sickness, turning olive green beneath his southern tan and becoming very unhappy. The captives exchanged meaningful glances, Ted hit the Italian very hard and the gun changed hands. The plot of the comedy unfolded a step further when it was immediately found to be unloaded. With this omission rectified, further steps were taken which led towards the cockpit, and soon the pilot felt the gun's barrel pressed firmly against the back of his neck. All had not then proceeded quite smoothly, and the disagreeable situation which developed resulted in the necessity of knocking out the second pilot. For a short time afterwards Ted himself took over the controls, while his navigator tried to ascertain their position, but eventually the atmosphere became more amicable and the Italian pilot agreed to relieve Ted of the difficulties of coping with a strange collection of foreign instruments.

By this time the navigator had found his position to be in the Gulf of Taranto, and the pilot was persuaded to turn round and start the long flight southward down the two hundred mile stretch of Italian coastline. The crew, unthinking in the heat of action, became understandably nervous as the venture settled down to cold-blooded execution; not one of them relished the possibility of recapture and a reception which would certainly be less cordial than before. Anxiety was further increased by a complete ignorance of what demands might be made of them in the way of recognition signals, but after nerves had been frayed almost to breaking point it became apparent that the Italian markings on the aircraft were sufficient; Junkers 88s and ME109s passed within sight without showing any signs of suspicion, and the most southerly point of Sicily was reached with no more serious injury than several cases of near heart failure which had occurred when a 'friendly' Italian aircraft for a few minutes joined formation with the flying boat!

But the unknown dangers of the flight within sight of enemy territory seemed over-estimated when they came to be compared with the known perils of the approach to Malta, and relief at leaving behind the Sicilian coast turned to reasonable apprehension as the Island drew near. The most anxious moment of the whole flight occurred within sight of friendly land, when half a dozen Spitfires sighted the unescorted flying boat and dived to the attack. The pilot had been flying low in case of this very emergency, and on Ted's orders landed promptly on the smooth sea, while white handkerchiefs were waved frantically in surrender. A horrible moment passed while the crew waited helplessly for the chatter of machine guns to break out above the roar of the diving aircraft, but the Spitfire leader held his fire and disaster was averted. A launch sent out to capture what was thought to be a hostile aircraft brought Ted home triumphant with a captured flying boat in tow and three prisoners.

We listened, spellbound, to this amazing story, hardly knowing whether to believe it or not; but it was, we were assured, true; it had really happened. Here before our eyes were Strever and his crew, in Kalafrana Bay an Italian three-engined flying boat lay at anchor; the incredible was fact. For many days afterwards the Island buzzed with the story, and the squadron's joy knew no bounds; that night we entertained the returned captives in the Mess, the next day I sent them on a week's leave. This spectacular event was a fitting ending to a week of successful attacks, to an afternoon of swimming with the deep sea fishes. Optimism coloured the letter which I wrote that evening; it said that the first stepping stones had been firmly laid and that the path would be complete before Christmas.

CHAPTER XII

A CONVOY COMES

AUGUST came, and with it the unwelcome Sirocco, which blew the heat of the African sand northwards over the sea, bringing further discomfort to the beleaguered island; for although the defenders might make sorties from the walls and cross the wide moat to raid the enemy, Malta still remained a besieged fortress waiting to be relieved.

The blockade which the enemy attempted to enforce was strict but not quite complete. Transport aircraft, mostly American Lockheeds and Douglases, brought in cargoes under cover of night from Gibraltar and Egypt, taking away passengers, usually civilians who were being evacuated from the island. But this service, which escaped attention from the enemy by cunning use of the hours of darkness, had an unfortunate drawback: the transport aircraft needed refuelling for the return flight, and the most valuable cargo they could possibly bring hardly compensated for the petrol taken away in exchange. So although a dozen loads at a time would not have been too many for the dire needs of the Island, the service had to be restricted to the running of one, or at the most two aircraft each night.

An aircraft load represented a microscopic drop in the ocean of want, but bringing supplies in by air constituted the only reliable means of reinforcement, and was carried on steadily. The transports landed about midnight, unloaded their cargo, which usually consisted of Spitfire spares, and after taking on board just sufficient petrol to reach their destination, left again within the hour, the service operating with the matter of fact regularity of any peacetime airline.

A less regular, but heavier, reinforcement was carried out by the Navy, whose activities in this sphere were cloaked in such secrecy that it was impossible to judge their effectiveness. Submarines were rumoured to reach the Island at intervals with cargoes consisting largely of petrol, and fast minelayers, the *Welchman* and the *Manxman* made occasional furtive appearances in Valletta, outwitting the enemy in their passage from Gibraltar by speed and the choice of a bold route.

But as July came to an end it became increasingly evident that Malta, in spite of all these efforts at reinforcement, was slowly being starved, not only of food, but of ammunition and petrol. Sorties might be made and the blockade run, but the siege was not yet raised nor was relief within sight; the Island was still surrounded and fighting now with her back to the last wall of hope.

As the hand of rationing gripped the scanty stocks more firmly, the hungry islanders watched with admiration forces of Spitfires continuing to climb to meet the raiders; after counting the fighters safely home they would turn to each other with smiles of encouragement, their thoughts dwelling not on some remote future when bombs would no longer fall nor guns bark at night, but on the day which must surely be near at hand, when supplies would be sent. In the shops, in the streets and in the fields of the Island, the word convoy was whispered not only with understandable longing, but with a strange confidence. Devout Catholic parents prayed in the ruined churches before scarred altars while their children cried in the misery of want; airmen at work on the aerodrome speculated non-committally on the uncertain future while aircrews in the Mess grumbled, good naturedly, at the poor quality of the bread. A murmur of hope went up from Malta in those anxious days which was heard in the outside world; the prayers were answered.

Hope was to some extent substantiated by an activity which had been proceeding steadily ever since the failure of the last attempt at reinforcement: the building of more pens and the laying of new taxying tracks by Maltese labour. This extension of the aerodromes to accommodate a larger force of aircraft pointed in only one direction, towards more petrol and the convoy which must bring it. But real evidence of an early attempt to break the blockade was not supplied until the first week of August, when a PRU Spitfire sighted an enemy convoy sailing south from the Adriatic; three merchant vessels with an escort of nine destroyers were on their way to Africa. But Group decided not to send us out against this tempting and formidable target, explaining that our force was being reserved for some unspecified task. Only one operation could be more important than the sinking of Rommel's supplies; it was at once clear that our force would be used to protect a Malta convoy.

The date of the operation remained a closely kept secret, and it was not until a few days before the ships were due to arrive that details were announced at a meeting held in the Station Commander's Office, to which the COs of the five squadrons based at Luqa were called. This meeting was similar to the larger conference I had attended at Group Headquarters in Alexandria on the eve of the last convoy operation, just a month before. As on that occasion a lengthy operation order was read out, and as the plan became revealed section by section, I saw that all the lessons learnt in the last unsuccessful operation were to be applied in a great effort to secure the safe arrival of ships at Malta.

This time only one convoy was to make the attempt, sailing from England through the Straits of Gibraltar, for with Rommel at the gates of Alexandria it was impossible to consider using the Eastern route. Although this single convoy was to comprise thirteen merchant vessels and a tanker, it was not the size of the convoy but of its escort which drew involuntary gasps of pleasure and surprise from the listening squadron commanders. No less than twenty-five naval vessels were to protect the merchant ships, a force which included battleships, cruisers, destroyers and four aircraft carriers, whose squadrons would provide air cover.

When the air forces to be assembled at Malta to meet the convoy were enumerated, they were revealed to be no less strong than the naval force; so many aircraft of all kinds were to be sent from England and Egypt that every pen on the three aerodromes would be occupied. A complete Beaufighter squadron, No 252, was coming out from England to help 217 Squadron in providing the ships with long-range fighter cover; 69 Squadron was to receive more aircraft to help with the greatly increased reconnaissance work which the operation would entail; Spitfires were already on their way in the aircraft carrier *Eagle*, accompanying the convoy, and more Beauforts were to be sent from Egypt to strengthen our force.

Yet it did not seem to me that too strong a force could possibly be assembled, for their task was a formidable one in the face of very heavy opposition. Five Italian battleships lay in harbour at Taranto, thirty aerodromes in Sardinia, Sicily and Pantelleria flanked the convoy's route. When the situation was considered and the odds reckoned, the running of a convoy to Malta still appeared a most hazardous undertaking.

At dawn on the first day of the operation the convoy and its escort would have passed through the Straits of Gibraltar into the Mediterranean, making only twelve knots, an uncomfortably low speed dictated by the slowest merchant vessel. During the greater part of this day, submarines were the chief menace, since the force was not due to come within range of enemy aircraft until late afternoon, when squadrons based in Sardinia might make an attack. In these last hours of daylight the ships would be protected by fighter patrols flown off the carriers and by a screen of anti-aircraft fire thrown up by the escorting vessels.

During the night the heavier escort vessels were to turn back, leaving a few destroyers to proceed with the merchant ships under cover of darkness, in which they were considered safe until dawn on the next day; then the convoy would be faced with the unavoidably hazardous last section of the passage, which necessitated steaming for long hours within easy striking distance of aircraft from Sardinia and Sicily and passing almost under the very cliffs of Pantelleria.

All through this last day, when the convoy was lightly escorted and most vulnerable, fighter cover would be sent out from Malta and protection against enemy naval units given by our torpedo aircraft waiting at readiness on the aerodrome at Luqa. The merchant ships and their escorting destroyers, after fighting their way through nine hours of daylight, were due to arrive in harbour at four o'clock in the afternoon. The day promised a violent battle at sea and in the air; on its result depended whether the evening would see Malta relieved.

Although the torpedo squadrons made no attack, the first days of August, when the Island was preparing to receive the convoy, were the most exacting of all those I spent at Malta. The hot south wind blew continually, the Island suffocated in the heat of Africa dampened by its passage over sea, and the illness which I had felt in the desert returned; but there could be no rest from the work of preparation which continued endlessly, day and night.

As the islanders exchanged rumours of the coming attempt to raise the blockade, our crews speculated with the same interest, but rather less enthusiasm, on the outcome of a torpedo attack on battleships. Although no Italian naval unit larger than a destroyer had been at sea since the last convoy operation, there was no reason to suppose that a strong Italian fleet would not attempt to engage the coming convoy, most probably on the last section of its passage when the heavy escort had left. Strong forces were required to prevent such a fleet from reaching its objectives, and the strongest possible torpedo force ever assembled at Malta had to be prepared for this difficult task.

217 Squadron, which had absorbed the second flight of 86 Squadron on its arrival from England at the end of June, was further strengthened by the arrival from Egypt of every available aircraft and crew of 39 Squadron, until no less than thirty-six Beauforts stood loaded in

their pens on the aerodrome. With a hundred and fifty pilots, observers and gunners and three dozen aircraft to organise, my days were completely filled, and while crews spent the afternoons bathing or resting from the heat, I worked in Intelligence Office or conferred with the staff at Group, considering how the enemy would dispose his ships and how best our force could be employed against them. The responsibility was heavy, and the knowledge that the force which I was to lead might stand alone between the convoy and destruction allowed me no rest until the plan of attack was made and the organisation complete.

After some deliberation it was decided to divide the Beauforts into two completely separate forces, partly because the full number made too large a formation to manoeuvre efficiently, partly because the enemy might, as on the last occasion, send out two independent fleets against which we would have to make separate attacks.

The first strike, consisting of fifteen Beauforts manned by the most experienced crews, was to be accompanied not only by the usual escort of Beaufighters, but also by a complete flight of Baltimores, sent grudgingly from the hard-pressed front in Egypt especially to supply a bombing diversion to our torpedo attack. This picked force, the first line of the convoy's defence, was to be sent out against the most menacing target, leaving a second strike behind on the aerodrome ready to take on another target or make a second attack in the event of the first strike failing.

The forces were at hand, a plan for their operation made, and after several long days spent in organising work on the aircraft and giving instructions to the crews, preparations were at last complete, and I waited in confidence for the enemy to make the first move. Meanwhile a closer watch than ever was kept on the enemy's ports and aerodromes. Taranto was covered at dawn and dusk, the Sicilian aerodromes photographed daily, and I listened carefully to the reports of pilots returning from these flights, hoping to gain a clue as to the enemy's intentions.

A week before the convoy was due an increasing number of aircraft was observed on several enemy aerodromes and a large force of Savoia Marchettis, the Italian torpedo carriers, was seen to have arrived at Cagliari in Sardinia. Three days later a larger concentration of aircraft than usual was reported on every Sicilian aerodrome; a reconnaissance made on the following day showed the same aerodromes filled to capacity with aircraft, among them Junkers 88s and ME109s, evidence of German reinforcement. It was only too clear that the enemy had been forewarned of the coming attempt to run the blockade, possibly by a chance sighting of the great convoy in the Atlantic by a reconnaissance aircraft, and that he was going to make a determined attempt to prevent it.

However, I was not so much interested in the aerodromes as in the harbours, where there was surprisingly little evidence of activity. The five battleships in Taranto appeared ready for sea but showed no signs of sailing; two cruisers, recently in Palermo, were seen to have arrived in harbour at Cagliari, moved no doubt to guard the western approach to Malta, and a large force of destroyers lay at anchor in Navarin. But this situation, which remained unchanged throughout the week preceding the arrival of the convoy, was usual and without any special significance. While every aerodrome cover produced stronger evidence that the enemy intended challenging the convoy with air attack, harbour reconnaissance failed to reveal any corresponding sign of action by the Italian fleet. With our strong force standing ready on the aerodrome, we waited, perplexed and suspicious; it seemed that the enemy was not going to offer battle, but at the very last minute it seemed as if he would.

On the day before the convoy was due to enter the Mediterranean, suspicions were aroused by a movement in Taranto; a PRU pilot, returning from a routine cover of the port at dawn, reported a tanker and several smaller vessels alongside one of the battleships. A second reconnaissance, sent out to report developments, returned with the news that a battleship, followed by destroyers, was being towed towards the entrance of the harbour.

The moment which I had so often awaited seemed now to be at hand. In England my squadron had on many occasions moved at short notice from its base to some remote coastal aerodrome, where it had waited anxiously for the report that an enemy battleship, seen stirring in harbour, was making for open sea to menace our Atlantic convoys; it was a report which had never come. While our tiny force stood loaded in Scotland with torpedoes and ready to strike on the aerodrome at Wick, I had spent anxious hours in Operations Room waiting for news that the *Bismarck* was at sea; at St Eval, in Cornwall, our twelve Beauforts had spent many long weeks, waiting vainly for the *Scharnhorst* and *Gneisenau* to leave Brest.

The role of torpedo squadrons was never enviable; their crews were often kept in suspense by the hourly possibility of a call which seemed more likely to result in death than in glory; while other squadrons might operate daily without sustaining casualties, the torpedo squadrons were immobilised for weeks on end by some target which would not come out to fight, yet the attack for which they waited might annihilate the squadron. The feelings of the crews could hardly be other than confused by the very nature of their task; anticipation married curiously with dread combined to produce a reckless pursuit of danger in an effort to end at all costs the unbearable suspense.

These memories were my experience, and the spur; if I now worked through the night in the planning of operations, stood firm in my demands to Group, and went out myself at the head of the force, it was because I remembered that year of fighting in England; I knew that waiting must be rewarded by success.

With the crews of the first strike assembled in the crew room, Creswell at hand with chart and pencil, I waited confidently for the return of a third reconnaissance aircraft from Taranto. Memories of past failures were obscured in a shining vision of success, dread was banished by anticipation. It seemed certain that an Italian fleet would attempt to sail into the Western Mediterranean there to await battle with the convoy and its escort; I knew we could prevent it.

But once again the prized target eluded us. Returning shortly after midday, the third reconnaissance revealed little change in the usual position at Taranto; a battleship had been moved from one side of the harbour to the other, and several destroyers had left on a northerly course, but there was no sign of further activity. The enemy, no doubt aware of the strength of the convoy's escort, was not choosing to come out and fight, but, employing a trick with which I was familiar, had moved a ship in harbour hoping by this action to lure our force into a trap of waiting fighters. This ruse failed, our crews dispersed; the vision of a sinking battleship vanished in disappointment and perhaps relief, for in spite of the strength of our force the attack could be expected to claim at least a third of the torpedo aircraft.

While we might wait in vain, apparently destined to be denied action, other squadrons were being operated to their limit. During the preceding days, the Island had been receiving more attention than usual from enemy bombers. Previously the enemy had been showing decreasing enthusiasm for raids, either day or night, doubtless on account of our fighters' tenacity and their very offensive employment by the new AOC; but now an attempt was being made to knock out the force of aircraft which was standing on the aerodromes waiting for the convoy to come within range of its protection. The result of a German stiffening to the Italian squadrons was felt in an increased determination of the raiders, and the Spitfires fought some of their fiercest battles in these few days when it was so essential to prevent the destruction of aircraft on the ground which were intended to hold the air over the convoy. The sirens wailed, fighters climbed up over the sea to engage the raiders, and it is to their credit, and also a tribute to the efficiency of the pens, that scarcely a single aircraft was destroyed on the ground by bombing.

These preliminary engagements were little more than skirmishes compared with the real battle which began in earnest on the day of the convoy's arrival. On the previous evening the expected reinforcement of Spitfires had arrived, their pilots bringing the first news of the convoy's progress; it was not encouraging. All had gone well up to the moment of their departure, when a disaster had occurred. The last fighter had hardly left the flying deck when a salvo of torpedoes fired from a submarine, struck the *Eagle*, which heeled over and sank while the Spitfires were still circling overhead. If this was an attempt by the enemy to prevent the much-needed fighters from reaching Malta, it failed by only a few minutes, and the Spitfires destined to fight in the air on the next day narrowly escaped consignment to the bottom of the sea. In spite of this lucky escape, the loss of a carrier occurring just as the convoy was coming within range of air attack from Sardinia seemed an ill omen for its future safety.

That evening the ships were still too far away to come under the wing of Malta's fighters, but 252 Squadron made the dangerous flight westwards past the Island of Pantelleria to strike a first blow at the enemy's torpedo aircraft assembled at Cagliari. This attack, timed for dusk and led by the squadron commander, was brilliantly executed. The aerodrome defences were taken unawares, and whole lines of dispersed aircraft set on fire by the Beaufighters' cannon shells were seen burning fiercely as the attacking aircraft turned to make the two hundred mile flight back to Malta in darkness.

On their return shortly after midnight it transpired that the Beaufighters had not only made a successful attack, but incidentally witnessed an event which the enemy might have expected to pass undetected; two cruisers had been seen in the half light of dusk leaving Cagliari harbour on a southerly course. It seemed probable that this small force would wait until the heavy escort turned back during the night, and then engage the lightly defended convoy at dawn on the next morning.

This unexpected report of the enemy at sea had me hurrying from my bed to Intelligence Office, there to examine the situation and await developments. Although the possibility of having to make an attack in the western approaches to Malta had not been overlooked, we had hoped that the necessity for such an unenviable task would not arise. The flight westward was one of considerable danger to a large force of twin-engined aircraft,since it entailed flying for at least an hour within range of the enemy's single seaters in Sicily and on Pantelleria, and even if the force succeeded in running this gauntlet undetected on the outward flight, it was unlikely that the enemy would fail to intercept it while returning from the attack. To avoid the great difficulties of such an operation we had decided, whatever the cost, to engage our targets east of Malta and in fact we would have preferred to attack outside the harbour mouth of Taranto rather than in open sea west of Pantelleria. But the fleet, which we had regarded as our target, remained perversely in harbour, and now at this last moment these two cruisers, powerful enough to decimate the convoy, threatened to compel us to make the dreaded flight westward.

An hour before dawn the first strike assembled once more, and waited for the return of a Wellington which had been sent out to shadow our targets during the night. But the cruisers appeared to be in no hurry to join battle; the Wellington, returning from its reconnaissance shortly after daybreak, reported them circling Maritimo, an island off the west coast of Sicily, doubtless waiting for news of the heavy escort's withdrawal before steaming south to engage the convoy. But the reluctant enemy miscalculated; the strong escort remaining with its charge until the very last hours of darkness detached a small but adequate force to deal with this threat. As a result of the subsequent engagement, the PRU Spitfire sent out at dawn to locate the cruisers returned not with the expected report of their descent into the convoy route, but with news that they were limping slowly for harbour. While the convoy, free from this threat of a naval engagement, steamed on towards its destination, our waiting torpedo force— deprived of its last chance to strike—dispersed, and the crews who might have been such active participants were relegated to the role of spectators of the battles which followed.

It was always thus in torpedo squadrons. During the long hours of waiting we might make innumerable flights westward, fight endless engagements with scores of single seaters, sink our targets in the face of great opposition, and die a thousand deaths before our safe return; yet these were only flights of imagination, of which there are no records. John Creswell might easily rub the track-line from his chart to leave no mark, but to me every moment of that flight which was never made remains indelibly fixed in my memory.

The torpedo force might be denied action, but the ships knew no rest from incessant attack, and the convoy which had steamed intact into the darkening eastern sky emerged from the cover of darkness already showing signs of distress. During the night air attack had been heavy, but a submarine penetrating the defences had wrought greater havoc, scoring torpedo hits both on escort vessels and merchant ships. Sorely depleted at the end of a night of heavy fighting, and shorn of its strong escort, the convoy steamed out into the open to defy the strongest opposition on the last section of its passage.

But the ships which had been spared the shells of the Italian Navy could not escape the fury of the enemy air force. Liberators and Wellingtons bombed Sicilian and Sardinian aerodromes during the night; a picked force of Spitfires raked aircraft dispersed on Pantelleria with cannon fire at sunrise, and throughout every daylight hour wave after wave of fighters rolled out from Malta's aerodromes to fight over a hostile sea for the safety of the convoy. But this battle was fought against overwhelming odds, and in spite of all Malta's efforts more losses were added hour by hour of that long day to the considerable damage inflicted on the convoy during the night.

I was no more than a spectator on this momentous day, watching enviously the fighters as they came in section by section to land and refuel, taking off again to join formation over the aerodrome and fly away westward to the battlefield. In their short intervals on the ground these pilots described the great difficulties of intercepting the strong forces of enemy bombers and torpedo carriers which came out end- lessly from Sicilian aerodromes to attack the ships. I experienced their loneliness as they patrolled high over the convoy, understood their feeling of sickness at the sight of fresh flames licking at the pall of smoke hanging over the stricken ships, and shared their inspiration from the defenders' well-ordered fire which still poured out accurately to meet every new attack. But in spite of splashes of heroic colours, the scene they painted was red with destruction; burning aircraft crashed into the water among sinking ships.

Of the fourteen gallant ships which had sailed into the Mediter- ranean on the previous day, three merchant vessels reached Malta that evening, followed the next day by a fourth, and finally by the tanker *Ohio* supported on either side by a destroyer, after an epic struggle, largely on its own. Spectators thronging the hills surrounding the harbour watched the first battered survivor enter Valletta in deathly silence; suddenly the stillness was broken by a cheer, which was echoed and re-echoed from hill to hill, until the voice of the whole island could be heard raised in admiration and thanks.

I, too, standing on the heights of Luqa, watched the procession of scarred ships entering harbour. Disappointed, perhaps relieved, I looked back over the three long days and nights, and still saw clearly the vision of an enemy fleet steaming down the Italian coast, and the fifty aircraft I was to lead flying through its barrage to aim torpedoes, fire cannon and drop bombs, leaving behind them some great battle-ship reeling under the blows of their attack. Yet our force had done its work, and still remained complete. Although the island had scarcely been relieved, although the sleepless nights and days spent in waiting had been in vain, and although the future was no more certain than before, the Sirocco, which blew hotly from the south, did not seem to be altogether an ill wind.

CHAPTER XIII

OTHERS LEAD WELL

MALTA possessed a curious resilience, a quality which was never more in evidence than during the weeks which followed the attempt at reinforcement. It might have seemed that with only five ships safely in harbour at the end of three days' hard fighting, the convoy operation had been at the best a magnificent failure, and that Malta, by throwing all her dwindling resources into this one great effort to break the bonds of captivity, had made her last bid in the unequal game and must now face a lingering defeat. So might the situation have appeared to a baffled and impatient enemy tired of hurling bombs incessantly at the indestructible rock and weary of sending squadrons to batter against the impregnable wall of Spitfires, and who must have despaired of reducing the fortress which stood so firmly in the way of victory.

But Malta was resilient; the enemy's indiscriminate bombing destroyed little more substantial than stone and mortar, and left intact the spirit of the island standing defiant among the splendid ruins of its former achievement, ready to build anew. Behind the wall of fighters which sprang up from the rock to replace the ruined medieval defences stood this defiant spirit; under its influence the thin line of Spitfires stiffened as the opposition attacked more fiercely; at its behest the ships which failed to reach harbour were relentlessly avenged. Without waiting to take stock of a situation which might hardly bear examination, Malta, foiled in her bid for freedom, proceeded to embark upon a policy of action which could not have been more offensive had the convoy operation resulted in an unqualified success.

Yet such a decision was not illogical; although the attempt at reinforcement had resulted in the majority of the ships failing to reach their destination, the operation could not be judged solely on this result. Behind this apparent failure lay hidden a significant success, for the fighter battle, fought for the safety of the ships at first above the aerodromes of the island and later over the waters of the western approaches, had been by no means lost. On the last day of the operation our Spitfires, in spite of the fact that they were operating in most unenviable circumstances, outnumbered by their adversaries and far from their own base, had fought with such tenacity that the initial determination shown by the enemy had decreased noticeably as the day passed, until finally he had ceased his attacks on the ships several hours before they reached harbour, and subsequently made no attempt to prevent their unloading.

So it happened that at the end of that momentous day the Island was not downcast at defeat, but jubilant at victory. Petrol stocks were partly replenished and aircraft stood on the three aerodromes in greater strength than ever before; if food was still to be scarce and discomfort still to be suffered, those hardships suddenly appeared inconsiderable compared with the examples of sacrifice visible on all sides during the convoy operation. The defiant spirit continued to face the enemy; as long as Malta possessed the strength to strike and Rommel threatened our army in Egypt, she could know no rest.

Appropriately it was not the hard-worked fighters but the torpedo squadrons which became the first instrument of the new offensive policy. The surviving ships of the convoy had not spent a day in harbour before our force was in the air on its way to attack a single merchant vessel escorted by two destroyers, which had been sighted steaming on a southerly course between the islands of Pantelleria and Lampedusa, hardly fifty miles from Malta.

The enemy's most curious decisions could often be traced to a complete misconception of the mentality of his adversaries; certainly the only explanation of this ship daring to steam so close to danger was that he believed Malta to have been reduced to impotence by the previous day's fighting. No assumption could have been further from the truth; the Island, roused by success and indignant at the losses sustained by the relieving force, was thirsting for blood, and none welcomed this opportunity to avenge those losses more than our crews, who had been such helpless spectators of the convoy's agony.

When I first took over command of the squadron, I had resolved always to lead myself, a resolution which had been strengthened by the disastrous consequences of allowing Jimmy to take my place. But gradually I had come to realise that a restriction of the leadership to one person was neither practical nor desirable. The work of organisation and planning on which the success of a sortie was so dependent was claiming more and more of my time, and the possibility that I myself might be lost in an attack, or sent to another post, could not be overlooked. Three months was the normal tour of operation at Malta, and the tantalising thought that I might conceivably be sent home at the end of that time was never quite absent from my mind.

These considerations pointed to the necessity of finding another leader, who could occasionally take my place in the air and continue to lead the squadron should I for any reason fall out of line. Yet, although I knew that such a course was desirable, I was so reluctant to release the firm personal grip I seemed to hold on the rope of success, that, had a substitute not been forced on me by circumstances, I would probably have continued to lead every attack until I fell. But now I was ill; a succession of sleepless nights and anxious days spent during the convoy operation in pursuing our faint-hearted targets had left its mark, the hot south wind sapped what little remained of my vitality; to fly would have been unfair both to my crew and my followers.

So it came about that Hank Sharman led this attack. The squadron boasted neither the usual adjutant nor engineer officer, nor the two Flight Commanders with the rank of squadron leader customary in a Beaufort squadron, so it was hardly surprising that I found myself overworked, yet at the same time wished always to lead, for my squadron was both understaffed and inexperienced. However, this promised to be the easiest of attacks; the target being so near not only made it easy to locate, but also permitted the use of Spitfires as escort, and I could not have chosen a more suitable occasion on which to try a new leader. Nor did I feel the least misgiving in the choice of Hank as my substitute; not only did he possess considerable experience, gained in operations from England, but he had followed me on three attacks from Malta, and I placed the fullest confidence in his leadership.

On this occasion I could watch the force take off without experiencing any of those doubts whch had so disturbed my peace of mind when witnessing Jimmy's departure; my only feeling was a tinge of regret that I myself was not leading. In my unaccustomed role of spectator I stood on the control tower, looking on calmly, perhaps a little enviously, as our aircraft came up on to the aerodrome from the maze, tore down the runway and rose into the air. Nine Spitfires, taking off last, climbed up to join the Beauforts and Beaufighters circling overhead, the force wheeled and, diving towards the west, vanished beneath the horizon over which it was due to reappear exactly an hour later.

As usual, the AOC came up to Luqa to witness the return of our aircraft from the attack. Although his natural inclination was towards fighter operations, for which his enthusiasm exceeded that of the most air-struck young pilot imaginable, AVM Park never under-estimated the importance of our less attractive work, and struggling to assume impartiality, always tried on his visits to Luqa to divide his attention equally between the single seater and twin-engined squadrons. But the word Spitfire held a fascination for our AOC which often wrought havoc with his firmest intention. News of every daylight raid would have him hurrying from his office at Headquarters to Fighter Ops Room, where he would watch, as if for the first time, the counters moved unemotionally across the operations table in cold reflection of some titanic struggle taking place high up in the clear blue sky outside. Touring the aerodrome in his car he seemed constitutionally incapable of passing a single Spitfire pen without pausing to admire the aircraft and talk at length with the pilot. He possessed the ageless spirit of the true fighter pilot, and his obvious failure to eschew a lifetime of allegiance to single seaters, which might have been so exasperating to us, had no such effect; this idiosyncrasy, being sincere, was actually endearing. Although the single seaters were operated to the limit of their capacity, and the squadrons which attacked shipping could see nothing more attractive in the future than a steady increase in the already ample hazards of their operations, both followed the AOC with blind devotion wherever he led. It was great leadership.

On this occasion he awaited the result of the attack no less impatiently than I did, for our aircraft were not only being escorted for the first time by his favourite Spitfires, but also trying out some new tactics. On the last sortie the conversion of three of our Beauforts to carry bombs had so weakened the force that although their bombing had been effective, the six torpedo aircraft had only succeeded in scoring a single hit, which had proved insufficient to sink their target.

An unlimited number of aircraft from which to select a force suitable to a particular task was a luxury undreamed of by Malta; we considered ourselves fortunate if nine out of the squadron's twenty Beauforts were available, and in fact we would have been forced to employ even smaller forces but for the prodigious efforts of maintenance made by the airmen who painstakingly rebuilt crashed aircraft, fell upon unrepairable Beauforts for spare parts, and worked endlessly to produce the strong force which contributed so greatly to our safety and success. From every attack several Beauforts would return riddled with bullet holes or damaged by gunfire, issuing a challenge to the ingenuity and patience of our ground crews which they took up with conspicuous success. It was these men who, by working conscientiously on our aircraft throughout the day and often through the night, without leaving the island or seeing an enemy coastline, contributed so greatly to the sinking of our targets.

The AOC, unwilling either to weaken the torpedo force, which at its strongest was only just adequate, or to abandon the bombing diversion used so successfully on the last sortie, had agreed with my proposal that Beaufighters, not Beauforts, should carry the bombs. Consequently a section of Beaufighters, carrying two bombs on racks fitted beneath the wings, had now gone out for the first time to try the effect of bombing the target in a shallow dive during the approach of the torpedo aircraft. With Spitfires keeping watch overhead, one section of Beaus raking the decks of the escort vessels with cannon fire, while another section bombed the target, I might have been inclined to belittle Hank's task of leading in the torpedo aircraft to deliver their attack, had I not known so well the difficulty of securing a hit even in the most favourable conditions.

It was upon the hazards and pitfalls lying in wait for an unwary leader that my mind dwelt as I stood on the control tower beside the AOC, searching the western horizon for the sight of an aircraft. I could no longer prevent doubts as to the outcome of the operation from crossing my mind, and realised to the full a fact I had almost forgotten; that waiting for the return of aircraft from an attack could be a no less exacting task than waiting for news of a target at sea. In both circumstances anxiety, although powerless to influence the news so eagerly awaited, increased so persistently with the passing of time that finally the worst possible news seemed almost preferable to continued suspense. The knowledge that I was responsible both for the success of the attack and the safety of my squadron loomed unpleasantly before me whenever a substitute was flying in my place; it was scarcely to be wondered at that I preferred to lead the attack myself and face dangers which no longer held the fears for me which waiting still possessed.

In spite of my confidence in Hank, I could not suppress memories of the last sortie on which another leader had flown in my place, memories which were unpleasantly revived when, as on that disastrous occasion, the Beauforts again appeared over the horizon flying not in formation but singly, suggesting that the force had been broken up by fighters or gunfire.

Yet my fears of a repetition of the previous disaster were unfounded. While Beaufighters circled the aerodrome and Spitfires came in to land, Beauforts continued to approach one after another from the west, until every aircraft was accounted for. However, it was soon apparent that the force had encountered some opposition, for several Beauforts remained on the aerodrome after landing, an indication that they were too severely damaged to be taxied away to their pens; to one of these aircraft an ambulance was called out across the aerodrome.

It transpired that the damage had been wrought not by fighters, which might have been sent out from Pantelleria to protect the ships, but by flak, which in spite of a well-timed diversion by the Beaufighters, had again been directed on the low-flying torpedo aircraft. Hank, no doubt determined to make a success of his first attempt at leading, had by all accounts ignored the heavy opposition and closed to the shortest possible range before dropping his torpedo. The damage to his aircraft certainly bore witness both to his determination and the accuracy of the gunfire; the starboard engine had been hit, a jagged hole gaped wide in the port wing, and a shell exploding in the cockpit had seriously wounded his observer.

But determination was rewarded; the enemy, who under-estimated our vigilance so grossly that he thought a ship could pass undetected in broad daylight within a hundred miles of the Island, paid the penalty of his foolishness. The merchant vessel, hit by a torpedo which was undoubtedly Hank's, had been left burning fiercely, a state in which it was clearly shown in a magnificent photograph taken from a PRU aircraft covering the attack.

Enthusiasm at this result ran high, particularly among the single-seater pilots, who were rarely able to take part in a torpedo attack and now shared with us the satisfaction of showing the enemy that he was not alone in his ability to sink ships in the western approaches to Malta. We were glad not to have failed when an opportunity to show our strength had occurred at last, while the fighters were overjoyed at having seen with their own eyes one of the ships lost from the convoy they had strived to protect, now fully avenged.

Spitfires in the following weeks carried on the offensive which we had started, and the enemy raiders who had once so easily penetrated the defences found themselves intercepted further and further from their objective. Our fighters, after wresting the ownership of the air over the island from the enemy, contested the sky over the sea which separated Malta from Sicily, and were soon to challenge the enemy over his own territory with offensive sweeps. From the very first of these engagements it was evident that not Malta, but the enemy, was cringing beneath the blows of defeat; the raiders showed an ever increasing reluctance to approach the Island, often choosing to jettison their bombs in the sea and turn for home rather than face the opposition, and when sweeps were started not a single enemy fighter took off from the aerodromes of Sicily to harass the few Spitfires flying boldly overhead. It was hardly six months since the first carrier load of Spitfires had landed on the island, a first ripple of the tiny wave which had succeeded in turning the tide of defeat; small wonder that the word Spitfire exercised a fascination for the AOC... it was magic to all of us.

With the single seaters on the offensive, operating in greater numbers and making longer flights than before, petrol, in spite of some replenishment of stocks from the cargoes of the five surviving ships, was more rigidly controlled than ever. Surplus aircraft had no place on Malta and the strong force which had assembled to protect the convoy from naval attack was quickly dispersed. It was now that occurred the chain of circumstances in which our squadron twice changed its name.

A signal was received ordering No 217 Squadron to proceed to its original destination, Ceylon. This order, originating in London, not only revealed the isolation of Malta from the outside world, but testi-fied to the effectiveness of the improvisation condoned by Head-quarters in Cairo. The No 217 Squadron, to which the signal referred, had long ceased to exist, and only a handful of the original crews who had been detained at Malta in June on their way to Ceylon, remained now to complete the journey. It was true that my squadron was still called 217, but it consisted not only of crews from 39 and 86 Squad-rons, but also of several crews of transit aircraft destined for Egypt.

When Malta protested that if the existing 217 Squadron were taken from the island, no torpedo force at all would remain, authority from the remoteness of the Air Ministry explained somewhat impatiently that 86 Squadron had been sent out expressly to allow 217 to proceed onwards. In reply Malta pointed out that the fate suffered by 217 Squadron had overtaken 86 Squadron, which also had been so reduced in strength that it no longer retained a separate identity. In fact a blissful and perhaps intentional ignorance appeared to prevail not only in HQ Malta but also in HQ at Cairo, particularly in respect of the transit aircraft.

If anyone knew that these transit Beauforts were intended to repel a Japanese sea-borne invasion of India from their Ceylon base at Trincomalee, the matter was tactully never actually mentioned. Yet no authority was ever issued to detain these aircraft and crews, certainly not from the AOC who liked to see a large force take off against the enemy's ships but made no inquiry how it came to be assembled.

It was left to me to retain such Beauforts as I needed, and I interviewed each crew personally on their arrival to discuss their experience. Indeed it could reasonably be said that I ran a sort of private air force at this period of which Air Ministry in London, believing it was reinforcing India, had no knowledge whatever.

This unofficial aspect of our operations gave me the boon of almost complete independence. The command was central; associates, such as the reconnaissance pilots, were contacted personally and my decision accepted as to which targets should be attacked and where.

As a result, there were no misunderstandings, which can be so costly when 30 or more aircraft are involved in an attack. A drawback, though, was that we received no support from other organisations, although this was sometimes sought. On several occasions I asked HQ Egypt to send one of their Liberators, to be over our target at a great height to drop a few bombs timed to coincide with our attack, so providing a diversion. But no Liberator ever came. Similarly, we asked repeatedly to be supplied with VHF radios for the leading aircraft, so that the pilots could communicate verbally before and during an attack—our radios which sent only morse code were useless in such circumstances. But no VHF radios ever appeared, and so much efficiency was lost.

Worse, perhaps, was my position with regard to secret intelligence concerning movement, often in port, of the enemy's ships. Interceptions of the enemy's signals and code breaking did, I believe, supply much useful information to HQ Malta, but it was not allowed to go further, not at least as far as the wing leader, who was not apparently to be entrusted with secret information. Thanks to the efficiency of the photo-reconnaissance, this was perhaps not much missed, but it could, in certain circumstances, have been a real life saver.

Meanwhile we managed, with improvisation much to the fore, not to say inspiration, to solve the difficulties experienced at HQ over the name or rather number of our squadron simply by forming a new 86 Squadron. It was to be composed of 20 aircraft and crews from all those assembled on the island for the convoy operation, the remainder to proceed to Egypt where a new 217 Squadron would be formed for the onward flight to Ceylon.

This order placed me in a dilemma, for Group undoubtedly intended, but did not actually specify, that I should select the most experienced crews for the new squadron, an action which would have resulted in the few crews still surviving from the original 217 Squadron remaining on the island. But these crews, although still fighting as well as on the day they arrived at Malta, were not unnaturally feeling the strain of their hazardous operations, and when they looked for reassurance into the uncertain future could see there no escape from the fate which gradually but relentlessly had overtaken their comrades, who fell one after another out of the line beside them. They both needed and deserved a rest.

So although I knew that I was not only acting contrary to the intentions of Group, but also cutting away my own strongest support, I made the difficult decision to part with these remaining crews of 217 Squadron, my most experienced followers, and sent them to Egypt with those crews of 39 Squadron lent for the convoy operation and now surplus to requirements. Soon afterwards my squadron changed its name once more, and became by a strange stroke '39' Squadron, for the original squadron of that number in Egypt was disbanded. In this way we changed our name twice within the space of a few days.

Tony Leaning, who had reached the end of his tour of operations, also left, leaving a gap in the squadron which was never quite filled, for not only was he a most experienced section leader, my right hand in the air, but on the ground a pillar of strength at my side, relieving me completely of the task of supervising the preparation of our aircraft. His departure broke the last remaining link with the very beginnings of the enterprise. At our first meeting in Alexandria he had been enthusiastic at my suggestion of using Malta as a base for attacks on shipping; in 39 Squadron in Egypt he had been my strongest supporter, and now he was the last survivor of the four crews who had followed me on that memorable night when we crossed the sea from the desert to the Island.

This was for me a sad parting, the loss of a friend and supporter, but Tony had done such fine work that I was glad to see him granted the rest which he had so thoroughly earned. After saying "Goodbye", I stood on the aerodrome and watched the airliner which was taking him to Egypt rise from the end of the flare path and vanish from sight. As I walked back through the night to the room which we had shared, I thought of the time which would surely come when I too would have earned my rest and an airliner would be taking me away from the Island; would it fly east or west?

Although it eventually led me into trouble with the staff at Group Headquarters, I never regretted the decision I made to send the experienced but tired crews on to Egypt. The new crews which I selected from the detachment of 39 Squadron sent to Malta for the convoy operation, made up in enthusiasm all that they lacked in experience. Ever since my departure from Egypt, letters had been reaching me in Malta from the crews I left behind, which told of their inactivity and asked if I could not accept them in my squadron; now these crews were with me, thirsting for the opportunity to carry out the work for which they had been trained. Missing Tony, missing the old team which had followed me so faithfully, I settled down to lead the new squadron, as always solicitous of its safety, demanding its success.

Yet success was more difficult to attain than ever before and the safety of the force more seriously threatened. Ever since the week in which we hit three ships off the Greek coast between Cephalonia and Sapienza, there had been evidence that the enemy would be prepared for attack on this section of the shipping route, and we were forced to look for other localities in which to intercept our targets. It was now becoming almost impossible to take the enemy unawares and complete surprise was a weapon which could no longer be considered as part of our armoury; however he could still be taken at a disadvantage, and this we attempted to do by arranging to intercept our targets in positions far removed from coastal fighter aerodrome. Since the southern part of the Greek coast was within easy range of several aerodromes known to be bases for single seaters, we made no attempt to repeat our successes, and never again attacked on that stretch of coastline. Denied the use of that once happy hunting ground, where enemy ships, if easily covered by fighters, were easy to find and well within our limited range, we looked further afield and in our next attacks struck north and south but never east. To try and repeat a success was a great temptation, but I had seen such attempts fail too often to be caught; I had no wish to learn anew old lessons.

Our first attack after the convoy operation had been made west of Malta, and the next, which took place three days later, was against a ship steaming northwards from the toe of Italy. It was a curious coincidence that after the previous convoy operation, targets had been found in similar circumstances first west and then north of Malta. When I was still in Egypt, the offensive against merchant shipping had opened with the sinking of a target between Pantelleria and Lampedusa, in almost the identical position of Hank's attack, and a few days later I had reached Malta just in time to follow Willie in his attack on a convoy north of Cape Spartavento, exactly where the new target had been sighted.

Events after a convoy operation seemed to follow a definite cycle; a great struggle for the safety of the convoy resulted in the arrival of a few ships; immediately afterwards an enemy ship attempted to cross the sea west of Malta, and a few days later a convoy steamed up the

Italian coast toward the Gulf of Taranto. The sequence of events which had occurred after the arrival of the June convoy was repeated now, a month later, a striking example of that lack of imagination which contributed so largely to the enemy's defeat in North Africa. Although we were continually developing new tactics and changing our positions of attack, the enemy showed a curious reluctance to alter either the routing or the defences of the ships, a weakness of which we gratefully took every possible advantage.

Since this northbound target, two vessels strongly escorted, was both important and formidable, and I was now quite well again, I flew myself on this sortie, hoping to make certain of a kill by employing greater strength than usual, for our force consisted of no less than twelve Beauforts and a similar number of Beaufighters. The reconnaissance pilot who had sighted the convoy told me that the destroyers were disposed in front and on the seaward side of the tanker, information which made me decide to attack from astern and the landward side in order to avoid passing through the strong escort.

After less than two hours' flying we made our landfall as intended at the little seaside town of Siderna Marina, where we turned northwards and flew close inshore just above the surf breaking on the beaches. Exactly the same conditions of low visibility prevailed as on the last occasion we attacked on this coastline, and little could be seen of the land but the dark shape of the hills which rose steeply out of the sea, to vanish in the mists of the interior.

We had hardly completed the turn and begun our sweep northwards before the target loomed out of the mist in exactly the position I had hoped to intercept it. After sighting, I remained flying on a course parallel to the coastline for a few seconds in order to give the Beaufighters time to climb into position for their attack, then turned seawards towards an unsuspecting tanker. The squadron followed, one section after another, and while the destroyers roused by the rattle of cannon fire and the scream of bombs, fired wildly upwards at the diving Beaufighters, twelve torpedoes were launched quietly into the water on the landward side of the tanker where it might have been considered safe from attack.

Yet not a single torpedo found its mark. First in to the attack, I was the first to gain safety; after dropping my torpedo I crossed in front of the tanker, climbed over the destroyers and made for the open sea, where I turned just in time to see the last section of Beauforts dropping their torpedoes. By this time the destroyers were firing fiercely, and shells were exploding not only in the water but on the shore, sending up columns of sand from the beach over which we had just flown unmolested. But amidst the clamour of the fight the tanker showed no signs of discomfort; there was not the slightest indication that she had been hit.

This was a disappointing, perplexing result to a carefully planned attack, a failure for which it was not easy to account. In the discussion which took place in Intelligence Office after our return, all sorts of reasons were put forward to explain our failure, but not one of them really convinced me. I knew that some of the new pilots, lacking in experience, had attacked neither from good positions nor from short range, but this hardly explained why every one of the twelve torpedoes had missed; nor could an explanation be found in the fact that the tanker, which had been reported as making ten knots, was actually almost stationary during the attack, for nearly all of us had noticed that its speed was negligible and aimed accordingly. Although the sea had been calm and the sky hazy, conditions which made it difficult for a pilot to judge his height, the torpedoes I had seen entering the water were accurately dropped, and there was no reason to suppose that our twelve torpedoes had all dived to the bottom of the sea. Altogether our failure was a mystery, strangely comparable with the result of the last attack made on this stretch of coastline, when we had dropped twelve torpedoes at point-blank range without any apparent effect on our targets. On that occasion the depth at which the torpedoes were set to run had been blamed, and once again I thought the fault lay not with us, but with our torpedoes; I believed that the depth setting was incorrect, and that not less than three of our torpedoes had run harmlessly underneath their target.

That no hit had been scored was confirmed beyond any doubt by a reconnaissance made later in the day, which reported the convoy proceeding calmly on its way toward the Gulf of Taranto. At this news the feelings of the squadron combined disappointment with exasperation, for not only had we failed to sink an important target in the easiest possible circumstances, but also sustained a considerable loss. With its escort taken at a disadvantage, the slow-moving tanker had presented a sitting target to our aim, yet we had failed in our task and lost no less than two Beauforts and a Beaufighter. The flak had not really been formidable, but single seaters had been seen over the convoy, and it seemed reasonable to attribute our losses entirely to fighter attack. To me the presence of fighters in this area was an ominous indication that the enemy were taking energetic measures against us for the nearest aerodrome was at Crotone, thirty miles from the scene of the attack, and it was obvious that these single seaters could not have been sent out in answer to a call for help, but formed part of a standing patrol over the ships.

Pete Roper, one of the squadron's most dashing young pilots, leading a section for the first time on this sortie, was one of those who failed to return. By this loss, and the inexplicable failure of the attack, I was swept by a momentary wave of depression, which inclined me to regret my action in parting with the experienced crews and to doubt whether the squadron could ever succeed without them. But this unwonted attack of pessimism quickly passed, to be succeeded by a strong desire for immediate and bloody revenge.

That evening the operation was further discussed at a conference held at Group Headquarters; inevitably it emerged that I had contrived to part with some of the squadron's most useful crews, a fact to which the failure was immediately attributed. My explanations of this action were coldly received, and members of the staff expressed no small displeasure at the wide interpretation I had given my orders which, in their opinion, was responsible for the wastage of a large quantity of Malta's valuable petrol consumed in our unsuccessful sortie.

However, even the loudest recriminations could not recall the cream of the old squadron from Egypt, and when the clamour for my blood died down, I was able to lead the discussion round to considering not past but present problems. The experienced crews might be irretrievably lost, but the tanker still remained afloat and within our range. When last sighted the convoy had been steaming north-east at eight knots; if it continued on its course and maintained this speed throughout the night, as seemed likely, it would appear at dawn on the next day off the heel of Italy, where it would alter course, cross to the Greek coast and start the long journey southward to North Africa.

Since I was unwilling to attack south of Cape Geroghambo, we searched a map of the northern part of this route for a favourable position of attack, and after some deliberation chose the narrow stretch of water between the island of Corfu and the Greek mainland. Although a Beaufort carried just sufficient petrol to reach this position and return to Malta, we had never before attacked so far from our base, and it seemed possible that the enemy might believe himself safe from attack in that area.

In actual fact the chances of taking the convoy unawares, even by stretching the range of our aircraft, were extremely small, and we chose to attack in these restricted waters partly because they were remote from fighter aerodromes, partly because it seemed probable that the destroyers, confined to the narrow channel, might adopt a formation in which we could take them at a disadvantage. But whatever plan we might make, the enemy now held the upper hand. We had wasted the opportunity of any easy kill presented by the slow-moving tanker within easy reach on the Italian coast, and had now to make the best of the unfavourable circumstances which were offered, for the tanker had at all costs to be prevented from reaching its destination, both to deprive Rommel's army of the fuel it carried and re-establish the squadron's reputation, which had never before stood so low.

In whatever position we chose to attack, it was likely that the enemy would be strong, determined and ready to receive us. In these circumstances it was not surprising that the operation appeared both desperate and hazardous; to attempt to stretch the range of our aircraft in order to attack in remote and restricted waters was an ambitious project; it was in fact a gamble, perhaps only justified because it succeeded.

After agreeing upon the position of attack, which was of course subject to the evidence of a dawn reconnaissance, and after giving an assurance to the staff that on this occasion the petrol consumed would not be wasted, I left Headquarters and returned to Luqa, where with the help of the Intelligence firm I settled down to draw up a plan for the attack we were to make on the next morning.

I was inclined to attribute the losses sustained earlier in the day to the slowness of some of our Beauforts, for although the force had included both Mark Is and Mark IIs, the two missing pilots had been flying the slower aircraft. So for the coming sortie I decided to use only Mark IIs, not only because they were faster, but also because their petrol consumption was more reliable. This decision involved sacrificing strength, for Mark IIs were still scarce and the squadron could produce no more than nine; however I sought to balance this deficiency by asking for an increase in the number of long-range fighters to accompany us. Beaufighters were more plentiful, and Group, granting my request, arranged for 252 Squadron, which still remained on the island after the convoy operation, to send six aircraft to join those already detailed to escort us.

To operate in strength on two successive days was almost as great a strain on our resources as making two sorties in a single day, for we had so few reserves that the aircraft which had flown on the first attack had to be hastily prepared for the second sortie. But our airmen, no less anxious than our aircrews to atone for the failure, responded to all our demands, and with work proceeding in most of the squadron's pens I went to bed at midnight, confident that I could do no more to ensure success.

That we should be strong, go fast and straight were requisites I had demanded of Group in return for my guarantee of success, so when the next day I set course for Corfu at the head of a strong force of nine Beauforts and even more Beaufighters, and settled down to cruise at ten knots faster than the usual speed, I relied on Creswell to navigate the force unerringly and enable me to honour my pledge.

And the navigation on which so much depended was again faultless. Unremarkable, except for several minute changes of course made to compensate for some small change in wind-speed or direction estimated by Creswell, the long outward flight neared its end. At the appointed time land came in sight, and the force, which had flown for three hours over sea, made straight for the narrow gap between Corfu and the smaller island of Paxos as if attracted to its landfall by a magnet; we could not have followed the line drawn on the chart more faithfully had it been painted on the surface of the water. My greatest anxiety, that we should waste in searching for the target the petrol needed for the last few miles of the return flight, was removed. Creswell had risen superbly to the occasion; but then he always did.

The fight started before the target was visible. A Junkers 88, which must have been patrolling the stretch of sea between the two islands, saw our force approaching and fired a Verey light, no doubt to warn the convoy of impending attack. After making this signal it turned northwards, but was not allowed to escape and repeat the warning. A section of Beaufighters climbed swiftly to attack, and as we swept on low over the water into the gap between the islands, a burning aircraft dived out of the sky in front of us, leaving behind it a great plume of thick black smoke. We had drawn first blood, but it was evident that as I had feared the enemy was prepared to receive us.

As we passed the most southerly point of Corfu the inner channel was disclosed; there lay our target. The tanker was almost stationary, escorted now by three destroyers, and circled overhead by the strongest force of protecting fighters we had yet encountered. The Beaus rose literally to the occasion, and climbing from the surface of the water, forged ahead to engage the aircraft; while we advanced towards our target low over the calm water of the sheltered channel, the sky above was the scene of a terrific battle in which they fought for our safety.

The destroyers were caught at an even greater disadvantage than I had hoped, but not on account of the narrowness of the channel; instead of forming a front line of defence across the approach to the target, they were huddled close together behind the tanker: the attack which the convoy so clearly expected was from astern, not from ahead.

Although out of position the escort was alert and opened fire as soon as we came in sight, well before we were within reasonable range, but the barrage was not as intimidating as might have been expected from a target prepared to receive attack. Occasionally a succession of miniature waterspouts could be seen rapidly approaching my aircraft, and I rose momentarily in order to hurdle these visible lines of fire, but there was no wall of flak so solid as almost to defy penetration, such as I had known on previous occasions. Much of the convoy's attention and many of its guns must have been directed upwards.

Just as I was approaching torpedo-dropping range, the fire suddenly slackened, the water around the convoy became whipped into a cauldron of foam out of which arose one after another great columns of water; the Beaufighters, timing their attack to a fraction of a second, had dived out of the sun to rake the destroyers with cannon fire and bomb the target.

Recollections come strangely in the heat of action. The ship before me seemed familiar; I conjured up the images of a dozen previous targets, then realised in a flash that for the first time in my experience I was facing a target which I had faced before.

The tanker steamed slowly across my line of sight, the mountains of the mainland towered above it. Columns of water thrown up by the explosions of bombs relapsed one after another, forming great patches of white foam on the surface. Out of the blue sky an enemy aircraft dived to destruction, entering the water so cleanly that it left no trace, while another, blazing fiercely, described a gentle spiral towards the sea, leaving behind a faint trail of grey smoke.

Unrestricted by the network of tracer trajectories usually cast over an attacking aircraft, I was able to close to short range and aim with the deliberation of a practice attack. After dropping I made away northwards, and turning to circle in the narrow channel between Corfu and the mainland, looked back on a scene rarely revealed to a torpedo pilot. The last section of Beauforts were just turning away from their attack when an explosion occurred on the port side of the tanker, throwing up a column of water several hundred feet high; hardly had this explosion died down before it was followed by another, and yet another exactly similar. Three torpedoes, one from each section, had found their target before my eyes.

Wisps of smoke from exploding shells drifted across the blue sky in which the darker trails left by burning aircraft were already beginning to grow faint. Over the calm surface of the sheltered waters strewn with wreckage hurled from the sky and thrown up by explosions spread a great pool of oil, which poured from the side of the stricken tanker. Over the whole scene of destruction towered the mountains of the mainland.

As we turned for home enemy fighters were still hovering over the convoy, as if reluctant to pursue us but unwilling to return to their base, and the destroyers still continued to fire, but somewhat half-heartedly, as if dazed by the rapidity of the attack. Soon the ships vanished from sight behind Corfu, the mountains of Greece disappeared beneath the horizon, and we set out into the open sea on the long homeward flight; only a shining memory of success relieved the monotony of the unchanging view of sea and sky, until at last the Island which we had left six hours before appeared on the horizon in front of us, and our longest, most critical sorties came to an end.

This was, I think, the best executed attack the squadron ever made, for it went so perfectly to plan. Although the forces protecting the tanker were stronger than any we had previously encountered, we succeeded in taking them at a disadvantage, and for the loss of a single Beaufort and Beaufighter achieved our objective, not only crippling the target but also destroying an unknown number of enemy aircraft.

Unfortunately no photograph was available of the actual attack, for the Baltimore, which on this occasion was following the striking force in order to preserve the slender chance of taking the enemy by surprise, had arrived on the scene of the attack rather later than intended; there it was met by one of the Ju88s which we had last seen circling the sinking target, and chased away before it could secure a photograph. However a Spitfire, flying high, covered the area a few hours later and brought back undeniable evidence of our success, an exposure which showed the tanker settling down in a great sheet of oil and the destroyers standing by in the role of helpless spectators.

We were completely satisfied with this result, for a tanker, being divided into several water-tight compartments, was always difficult to sink unless it happened to catch on fire. Had our target been steaming in open sea, it would no doubt have sunk in due course, but with the shore so close it was a foregone conclusion that the enemy would succeed in beaching it. A further reconnaissance made on the next day confirmed this surmise; the tanker was seen to be firmly beached on the mainland not a mile from the scene of the attack, a position in which it was often observed during the following weeks by PRU pilots making routine covers of this area.

That night I attempted to describe in a letter the pursuit of the tanker and its triumphant conclusion, but words failed to convey the elation I felt. The new team had proved itself, the squadron lived again; my indiscretion was forgiven and forgotten. Success could not more swiftly have overtaken failure.

It might have been supposed that the enemy would now take further steps to protect his shipping, and that our task would become more difficult, but strangely that did not immediately happen. Until the end of August there was little chance in the defences of the enemy's ships, and we continued to send forces out against every target which came within our range, meeting with varying degrees of fortune, but never completely failing. In fact our two most successful attacks were made in these last days of August, both of which resulted in the sinking of a target without loss to ourselves.

We attacked behind Corfu on August 21st, and exactly a week later Ken Grant, one of the original pilots of 39 Squadron, led a brilliant attack on our first target to be found in the Central Mediterranean. This sortie came at the end of an eventful week, in which I received two momentous and unexpected signals; the first, from the AOC, congratulated me on the award of a DSO, and the second, from the Air Ministry, asked Headquarters in Cairo if I could be returned to the United Kingdom at the first possible opportunity.

I had entertained reasonable hopes of leaving Malta in the second week of September, when my three months' tour would be at an end, but it had always seemed likely that I would then be sent back to an office in Cairo to complete my term of service abroad. Now I saw for the first time my dream of a return home coming true, and waited anxiously for the reply which Cairo would make to the Air Ministry's request. On the single day which separated the arrival of these exciting pieces of news, the squadron made a sortie. An uneventful attack was made on a target crossing from the Italian to the Greek coast, the squadron scoring a single hit for the loss of one aircraft.

This week, crowded with incident and excitement, ended appropriately with a magnificent feat of leadership; Ken, leading the squadron far into the Central Mediterranean, found and sank a single merchant vessel steaming between Cape Matapan and Benghazi.

This ship originally formed part of a convoy which had been sighted steaming down the east coast of Greece by a reconnaissance sent out from Egypt. Our air force in North Africa was no longer compelled to watch impotently supply ships passing unmolested across the sea to the enemy, for the flow of reinforcement aircraft, both American and British, was now continuous and abundant. Taking advantage of their great range, Liberators flew north from Egypt to attack the convoy with bombs just as it was setting out from the south coast of Greece on its passage across open sea. So successful was this attack that only one merchant vessel and a single destroyer survived to continue on its way, later to be sunk by torpedo aircraft sent out from Malta.

Acting on a report of the Liberators' attack, Malta sent out a reconnaissance aircraft to locate the surviving ships, and the crew, returning just after midday, reported the merchant vessel still escorted by the single destroyer steaming on a south westerly course in open sea, just within our range. While this target was the most lightly defended of any we had attacked, it promised to be the most difficult to locate, for behind it was no guiding coastline on which some point could be recognised to confirm the position of the force at the end of the outward flight, nor could an elaborate search be made to compensate for errors in navigation, for a line drawn on the chart representing the target's track only just touched the arc of a circle drawn at a Beaufort's range. To add to these difficulties the return flight would have to be made in darkness, without any surplus petrol in hand to search for the island.

This sortie cried aloud for an observer of Creswell's stature; his navigation was so supernaturally accurate that I would never have been surprised if a flight had ended with the squadron turned into a herd of camels passing easily through the eye of a needle into a world of perfection. But on this occasion Creswell was not available; he was ill.

The heat of the summer together with the lack of certain foods, particularly of sugar, conspired to undermine our health, and we were all at one time or another laid low by an illness peculiar to the Island, a fever which took hold if its victims, raged unpleasantly for a few days, and then departed as rapidly as it had come, leaving behind no trace. Flies were thought to be the carrier, for cuts and sores took long to heal at Malta; although the doctors applied generous quantities of gentian violet and yellow flavine antiseptic to our facial sores, giving us the appearance of ancient Britons in war paint, and although in an attempt to compensate for the lack of sugar we drank unbelievable quantities of sticky liqueurs and sucked sweets with the delight of children, the fever could never be completely arrested; nearly always there were two or three of our crews suffering from it, and now Creswell in his turn had succumbed.

For me to fly with another observer was out of the question, for without Creswell I would have been lost metaphorically and perhaps literally, so I decided firmly to wait for his return before making another sortie. Hank, whom I would normally have chosen to take my place, had flown on five successive attacks and needed a rest, so I gave Ken the much sought after opportunity to lead. Although only a Flying Officer, he possessed considerable experience, having led several attacks from Egypt, and I knew the squadron would be safe in his hands. However, the success of the sortie was no less dependent on good leadership than on extremely accurate navigation, so when Creswell, who had arisen from his bed of sickness to help supervise the navigational arrangements, expressed a good opinion of Ken's observer, I realised that this was praise indeed, and immediately felt confident that the force would not return empty handed.

Yet this confidence was severely shaken by the discovery of a failure in the reconnaissance arrangements, which was made long after the force had set course for the target and far too late for rectification. The Baltimore, which went out a few minutes in advance of the strike, was used normally as a precautionary measure against the possibility of the force failing to locate the target, and was rarely called upon to play a more active part in an operation than taking photographs during the attack. But on this occasion the success of the sortie was so dependent on the accuracy of a last-minute reconnaissance, that the Baltimore had been sent out half an hour in advance of the striking force expressly to locate the target, and wireless back its latest position. It was on this wireless report that the leader relied for help in finding his target, a needle in the haystack of open sea. Yet from this important of missions the Baltimore returned empty handed; in the great expanse of sea which it had covered in a systematic search, there had been no sign of a ship. Remembering the last instance of a reconnaissance failure, when we had searched fruitlessly a long stretch of the Greek coast, I held out little hope of the force returning success-ful, for even if the target was really on the course originally reported it seemed unlikely that Ken, with his field of view restricted by the necessity of hugging the surface of the water, would succeed where the high-flying, longer-ranged Baltimore had failed.

To my amazement and delight this pessimism proved unfounded. Two hours after sunset the first Beaufighter appeared out of the dark eastern sky followed so rapidly by other aircraft, both Beaufighters and Beauforts, that an endless chain of light was formed around the flare path; every aircraft burned navigation lights, everyone flashed their letter impatiently, requesting permission to land, giving the circuit the appearance of a great roundabout decked with fairy lights. This time their arrival was undisturbed by the enemy. In answer to a letter flashed up in green from the flare path, aircraft detached them-selves one after another from the circling mob and came in to land; the floodlight shone out over the aerodrome at regular intervals, and aircraft landing in quick succession came safely to rest at the end of the runway before vanishing into the darkness of the maze. The whole operation took place with the same precision with which the force had taken off, formed up and set course earlier in the day.

Nor was this precision the only point of similarity between the force's departure and return; after failing to identify all our aircraft from their letters flashed in the darkness, I counted them as they rushed into the floodlight beam, and when the last aircraft had landed it was apparent that not one Beaufort or Beaufighter was missing; the force had returned exactly as it set out.

Since no torpedo was visible beneath the fuselage of the first Beaufort to land, it was at once assumed that an attack had been made, but this assumption was questioned almost immediately by contrary evidence, for several aircraft which landed later still carried their fish, a circumstance which added a flavour of mystery to the operation already rendered somewhat mysterious by the unexplained disappearance of the target.

But the target was found, and an attack had been made. Nearing the end of the outward flight without receiving the expected wireless message, Ken was left with no alternative but to rely entirely on navigation and trust to the accuracy of the original sighting report to find his target. After a seemingly endless flight, made entirely over sea, in which the only evidence of progress was the passing of time indicated by the cockpit clock, his navigator handed him an alteration in course. It was assumed that the force had reached a position identical with the point on the chart where the tracks of the striking force and the target intersected. If the navigation was accurate and the reconnaissance report correct, the target should appear dead ahead after a few minutes' flying on the new course.

I could imagine Ken's anxiety as he completed this turn and started flying on a course which he hoped also to be the target's track. The Baltimore had failed, there were no landmarks by which to correct the navigation, no petrol to spare to search a wider area, and always casting a shadow over these more immediate concerns remained the task of finding the island in darkness before petrol tanks became empty.

Creswell's mantle certainly fell upon Ken's observer that day. The force had hardly settled down on the new course, before a faint wisp of smoke on the eastern horizon betrayed the presence of the target; once more the leader changed course and within a few minutes he was at grips with the elusive target. Execution was swift; just as the last section of Beauforts were coming into position to attack, the merchant vessel completely disintegrated before their astonished eyes, and thus deprived of their target they had brought their torpedoes back to the island to be used on a future occasion.

Ken's achievement, and that of his navigator, was beyond praise; congratulations for the squadron poured in, not only from our friends at Luqa, but from the squadrons at Takali and Hal Far; I felt more proud of this success than any I had achieved as leader. Despite Creswell's many brilliant efforts this feat of navigation ranked highest in the squadron's annals, in fact the whole sortie from start to finish was a model of perfection; none of our previous targets had ever sunk so certainly or so rapidly, yet this result had been achieved completely without loss. A photograph taken after the attack from the turret of one of our aircraft showed no sign of the target remaining on the surface, only a great funnel of black smoke marked the spot where it had sunk.

With the squadron's junior leaders so outstandingly successful, I might have been tempted to retire from active participation in operations, particularly as it appeared likely that I would shortly be going home. Many squadron commanders after gaining experience were content to supply moral leadership, and restricted their activities to the planning and organisation of sorties which were led by their flight commanders. Yet I could not adopt such a role; planning and organisation were to me only the means to an end which I was unwilling to forego: the sinking of our target. As long as I remained at Malta I was determined to fly and fight, a determination in which I was strengthened by the information contained in a signal of which I was shown a copy: Headquarters in Cairo, in reply to the Air Ministry's signal, asked that I might be allowed to remain in Malta since I had just taken over command of No 39 Squadron! This statement, in substance quite true on account of the squadron's recent change in name, conveyed the impression I had just arrived at Malta to take up my duties for the first time!

The indignation with which I read this signal was only equalled by the suspense in which I awaited the reply. Had I not earned my rest? Was my path home incomplete? Did I need one more stepping stone to cross the sea? Instinctively I sought solace in action and seized on the first opportunity to make a sortie. This occurred on the last but one day of August, when another tanker was sighted leaving Taranto, and I led the squadron on the long flight up the Italian coast right into the Gulf to make what proved to be my last and most spectacular attack.

Throughout the previous week reports had been reaching Malta of new developments in the situation on the front in Egypt. After a long period of inactivity the enemy was again on the offensive, probing our positions with armed reconnaissance and employing his air force in considerable strength. However it did not need these reports to suggest that a trial of strength was imminent at El Alamein, for the steps which the enemy now took to protect his ships were eloquent of a new interest in their safety which could only be attributed to a coming offensive in the desert.

The attack behind Corfu appeared to have brought home to the enemy the unpleasant fact that his ships were liable to daylight attack anywhere on that three hundred mile stretch of coastline, for soon afterwards ships were observed negotiating this part of the route under cover of darkness. This innovation was followed by other changes, and it was soon apparent that within the space of a few days the routing of ships to North Africa had been completely revised.

Here at last in this change of route was concrete evidence of the enemy's discomfiture at the sinking of his ships; the proof of success which had been granted to the previous Fleet Air Arm and submarine campaigns in blocking the eastern route, now rewarded our efforts. The enemy, at some inconvenience and with considerable loss of efficiency, contrived to present his ships from appearing within our range in daylight.

The target sunk by Ken Grant's attack was believed to have crept down the Greek coast at night, passed through the Corinth Canal and joined convoy in the Aegean Sea. It was definitely known that other ships were lying in harbour during daylight hours, sailing at dusk and putting in to a convenient anchorage before sunrise; leapfrogging slowly down the Greek coast in this manner they would cross the Suda Bay in Crete, there to await nightfall before attempting the final passage to Benghazi or Tobruk.

But the enemy had become aware of the fatal weakness of his lines of communication too late for these passive measures to be effective. Not only were Liberators available in Egypt, capable of covering the whole Eastern Mediterranean in daylight, but a long-range night-torpedo aircraft was also at hand.

The Wellingtons, which had been modified to carry two torpedoes, adopted the flare dropping tactics used so successfully by Swordfish and Albacores, and were flying regularly into the stretch of water between Crete and North Africa to prove to the enemy that the cover of darkness was no longer an effective protection for his ships. The deficiencies which had made us so vulnerable three months before no longer existed, and the ships which had once so easily crossed the sea were now made to fight on every stage of their passage. On one side of the route stood Malta, on the other stood Egypt; both defied the enemy to pass. Rommel, who had faced our army so confidently at

Gazala, was showing justifiable nervousness at El Alamein, for while his adversaries were daily receiving reinforcements, his transports, particularly tankers, persistently failed to arrive.

The movement of ships now became so unpredictable that we were no longer able to wait until they steamed into positions convenient for interception, but were forced to attack at the first opportunity wherever our target might be found. The game, nearing its conclusion, was being played at a break-neck speed which allowed no time for thoughts of safety, and so it happened that on that last day of August I found myself leading a force northwards, to intercept a target in a position which only a few weeks previously would have been considered suicidal.

This target, a tanker escorted by a single destroyer, had been sighted by a PRU pilot leaving Taranto on a south-easterly course. Although this area was notoriously well defended, we did not dare wait until the target reached a more favourable position of attack for fear it might meanwhile seek shelter in some harbour, so we had taken off immediately after receiving this report, assuring ourselves that our presence would be unexpected in an area not previously visited. This optimism was hardly substantiated by the presence of fighter aero-dromes around the Gulf and strong naval units lying ready in Taranto harbour, but it had been as far as possible supplemented by careful planning. The choice of a position of interception was now denied us, but the freedom to choose, within the limits of our resources, the strength and composition of the attacking force still remained. Ross Shore and I, expecting fighter attack and remembering the success achieved at Corfu in conditions very similar to those we anticipated on this sortie, had decided to use again nine fast Beauforts and as many Beaufighters as his squadron could muster.

Usually, when striking northwards, we flew out to a point some sixty miles due east of Malta, before turning on to a northerly course in order to avoid passing within range of the Sicilian fighter aerodromes and enemy radar, but on this occasion such a detour would have increased the length of the flight beyond our range, and could not be taken. So we were liable to fighter interception not only over the target, but at any point on the outward flight, and although Spitfires sought to divert the attention of the Sicilian fighters by timing a sweep to coincide with our departure, we had to rely on the Beaufighters to protect us on the long flight up the Italian coast. Fortunately the haze peculiar to this stretch of coastline was again in evidence, drawing a curtain across the few miles of sea which separated our aircraft from the mainland, and under this cover Creswell succeeded in bringing the force without incident into the comparatively open waters of the Gulf of Taranto.

Here the haze ceased abruptly, visibility increased to a maximum, and the low-lying promontory which forms the heel of Italy became visible in the distance. Not only was land within sight straight ahead, but also behind us and on the port side, and we crossed the entrance to the Gulf, the Lion's mouth, in an uncomfortable condition of suspense, fearful lest the beast should snap his jaws. But the faint hope, which had been our sole reason for optimism that we might succeed in taking the enemy unawares within sight of his most important harbour was, to our surprise, fully realised.

To have attempted to sweep a stretch of this coastline would have been to ignore the presence of no less than three aerodromes within a few miles of the position in which we expected to attack, so we had decided to abandon our usual tactics and make a straightforward interception. On the chart a single line joined Malta to the target, a line on which Creswell kept the force flying so accurately that when the tanker came in sight some fifteen miles away, it was steaming across our track directly in front of us. Our change of tactics had involved sacrificing the advantages of an attack from ahead, for now we were approaching from the beam with the single destroyer barring our way to the target. After glancing up at the sky to assure myself that no fighters were patrolling overhead, I decided quickly that a short detour was permissible, and repeating a ruse which had often proved successful, I led the torpedo force around in front of the target in order to attack from the shore. While we manoeuvred for position, the Beaus used the delay to climb to a greater height than usual, and succeeded not only in covering our attack but in diverting completely the enemy's attention from our approach.

In an unreal atmosphere of complete and utter calm not yet shattered by the Beaufighters' attack, I flew in from the land towards the target and settled down to take careful, uninterrupted aim. Hardly able to control my finger poised above the release button, I reached the shortest possible range, steadied the aircraft for a final adjustment of aim, then released the most effective torpedo I ever dropped in the Mediterranean. At this very moment the first pair of bombs exploded in the water in front of me, obscuring my target with spray. Unable, on account of the short range of my attack, to turn away before reaching the tanker, I was compelled to climb over it, and in doing so my aircraft became so rocked and buffeted by explosions that I thought it had been hit.

However, I was given no time to reflect on this possibility; a warning from my rear gunner that fighters were coming out from the land absorbed my attention, and for fully ten minutes afterwards everything was forgotten in a desperate struggle to avoid the fire of three single-seaters diving around my tail. Since we had completed the attack and could make for home, the engagement took the form of a running fight in which we had the advantage of being able to draw the fighters away from their base. The Beauforts, weaving violently, relied equally on their avoiding action and turret fire to repel attack, while the Beau-fighters fought gamely to keep the more manoeuvrable single seaters at bay. Although a considerable number of fighters were sent out against us, their small range did not allow them to pursue for long, and as land disappeared from sight they also melted away in the distance.

Gaining the safety of open sea, I reduced speed in order to give the other aircraft an opportunity to join formation, then, breathing more freely, set course for home, unable to ignore significant gaps in the two sections which followed me. I tried to console myself with the thought that some casualties were inevitable in the face of such strong opposition, but this reflection failed to comfort, nor were my spirits raised by a report from my gunner that during the heat of attack he had caught sight of the tanker burning in the distance. I saw to the exclusion of all else that my right-hand section was flying without a leader; the missing aircraft was Hank's.

At Luqa our return was greeted with more enthusiasm than had ever been shown before, for not only did the bold position of attack appeal to the imagination, but a full account of the target's fate had preceded our arrival. The pilot of a PRU Spitfire, while making a routine cover of Taranto, had been amazed to see a column of dense black smoke ascending from the waters of the Gulf almost to the height at which he was flying; investigating further he found the cause to be a great oil fire burning on the surface, all that remained of the tanker.

As if to make our triumph complete, all the missing aircraft returned just as I was trying to explain their loss to the AOC. Hank had found himself in a most unenviable position from which he had been lucky to escape. Owing to a failure in the release gear, he had been unable to drop his torpedo during the attack, and worse still, unable to jettison it when chased by fighters, with the result that he had spent many anxious minutes with fighters on his tail, sweating with exaspera-tion at the loss of the ten extra knots which his lightened Beaufort could have achieved. Not only had speed been sacrificed, but also manoeuvrability, and it was a great tribute to Hank's skill that he managed to bring his aircraft safely home with no more serious damage than a few stray bullet holes, one of which was found to be within six inches of the pilot's head!

If Hank provided the drama, the pilots of the two other aircraft supposed to be missing added the comic relief to the story of this sortie; they had voluntarily declined to drop their torpedoes inspite of the most persistent fighter attack. Seeing the target explode just as they were taking aim, and remembering the favourable comment I had made on a previous occasion when torpedoes had been brought back unexpended, they had decided on their action and given no further thought to the matter. New to the squadron and lacking Hank's experience, these two enthusiasts had yet to learn that ten knots could be the difference between life and death. Of such spirit were my followers.

That evening, while celebrating our success in the Mess, a signal was brought in to me: it was from the Air Ministry to Headquarters in Cairo, and said plainly and firmly that I was to be returned to the United Kingdom "as soon as possible", adding that a relief was being sent out immediately to take over command of 39 Squadron. This news crowned the achievement of the day; August faded into September while we celebrated; under the influence of the high spirits inspired by my good fortune and the two successive sorties in which we had destroyed our targets completely without loss, attacking ships suddenly appeared an easy task; it was suggested that we should in future send out only one section of torpedo aircraft, dispense with our fighter cover and attack ships lying in harbour. But these suggestions, made partly in jest, partly in earnest, reminded me too much of the many rash proposals I had heard put forward on similar occasions in my squadron in England to amuse. In fact I was strangely unmoved by the show of high spirits around me, and although I contrived to appear overjoyed at the good news and carried away by success, that appearance belied my real feelings. At a time when I should have been elated, I felt sad; where I should have been so certain, I was beginning to have doubts.

For in the midst of all the gaiety and rejoicing, I suddenly found myself hating the thought of handing over my squadron to a new-comer; I looked back on the good times we had shared together and wondered if such happiness could ever be matched again. With these thoughts in my mind I escaped from the crowded Mess to Intelligence Office, there to drink cocoa, speculate on the situation in the desert and listen to the night fighters patrolling overhead. Reassured by Ponting, pacified by the calm atmosphere of the office, my doubts vanished momentarily, only to return anew when I sat down at the familiar table to write a letter telling of the good news. Words refused so persistently to tell the story that I was forced to give up the attempt, but I could not so easily dispose of the premonitions which were clouding my mind. Once more I was deeply worried, yet unable to fix the cause of the anxiety; suddenly it came home in a flash. I saw clearly that our recent successes had been too easily gained; the circumstances of these attacks had been almost suspicious, the defences too thin and the enemy too credulous. The situation could not remain in our favour much longer, it was already too good to be true.

CHAPTER XIV

HOME ON THE HORIZON

SEPTEMBER came, and with it the first rains of approaching autumn, giving new life to the vegetation of the Island withered by the hot winds of summer, bringing to many weary exiles memories of their homes. Although rain might provide momentary relief to the soil, the passing of days brought no end to the anticipation in which the Island waited, for the cloud of suspense which hung over the armies in the desert threw its long shadow over Malta. The battle known to be imminent in Egypt had not yet begun.

As the first week of the new months passed slowly and without incident, the premonitions which had so disturbed my peace of mind on the last evening of August were strengthened by reports of ominous preparations taking place in enemy ports. Destroyers from harbours as widely separated as Navarin, Palermo and Naples, were observed to be congregating in Taranto and Brindisi, while merchant vessels known to have been used previously on the North African route were seen to be loading there. The reconnaissance photographs showed columns of tanks, guns and transport making their way down the streets to the harbours; on the wharves alongside which the merchantmen were lying could be distinguished great piles of petrol tins.

I remembered that on two previous occasions strong convoys had been sent to North Africa during the first week of a calendar month. It was one of these monthly convoys that we had at the first attempt failed to find, and afterwards attacked at dusk on July 3rd; another big convoy, which a PRU pilot reported at sea in the first week of August, had escaped attack on account of our preoccupation with the defence of our own ships, which at that time were attempting to run the blockade to Malta.

Now, with the coming of September, there was again every indication that a strong convoy was being prepared in Taranto and Brindisi, and in view of the coming of an offensive in the desert there was every likelihood that the enemy would make a supreme effort to secure its safe arrival in North Africa.

Once more, while ships loaded in enemy ports and destroyers waited to escort them, Malta prepared for the day when they would put to sea. Spitfires and Wellingtons watched the progress of loading by day and night, airmen struggled in the pens to prepare the largest possible force of aircraft, and the staff pouring over reconnaissance reports wrestled with the planning of our most critical attack. With Rommel in Egypt, depending perhaps on the cargoes of these very ships for the strength which might give him final victory, the result of the operation was of more consequence than any we had previously made; the long game, started in North Africa two years before, was nearing its end; this convoy was the enemy's last throw.

In reality the staff had only one decision to make in planning the attack, and that was to decide the position in which the target should be intercepted; the composition of the striking force was a foregone conclusion: every available Beaufort and Beaufighter would be used on this sortie. Unfortunately that imposing designation, which might to the uninitiated conjure up visions of a sky full of aircraft, actually covered the identity of a tiny force hardly adequate for the task set before it. 252 Squadron, whose six aircraft contributed so materially to our success at Corfu, had returned home shortly after that sortie, leaving only 235 Squadron on the Island to provide cover to our attack. Like my squadron, 235 had but twenty aircraft from which to raise a force, and on this occasion we could expect reinforcement neither from Egypt nor from home, for the Desert Air Force was conserving all its resources for the coming battle on land and a squadron from England, even if one were immediately available, could not reach Malta and be ready to operate before the convoy sailed.

Since the opening of the air reinforcement route to the Middle East across Central Africa, transit aircraft had been passing through Malta in steadily decreasing numbers, and we had been forced to rely less and less on this source to supplement the strength of our squadrons. Had the previous flow through Malta been maintained, we could have increased our strength temporarily by detaining aircraft as we had done so often in the past, but during the days preceding the operation not a single Beaufort or Beaufighter passed through, and we were forced to fall back on our own very limited resources. Although the airmen worked at full pressure day and night, it was soon apparent that neither our squadron nor 235 would be able to raise more than twelve serviceable aircraft at the most. To produce even this number was a considerable achievement on the part of the ground crews, for in the last two weeks of August the squadron had made seven attacks, and from every one of these some aircraft had returned damaged by the enemy or requiring a change of engines.

But when I interpreted the phrase "all available Beauforts and Beaufighters" as meaning every serviceable aircraft from our two squadrons, I reckoned without the AOC. Comparing the anticipated strength of the target with the size of the force we could send against it, he saw immediately our inadequacy. Twelve Beauforts and twelve Beaufighters had originally failed against the single tanker escorted by four destroyers off Siderna Marina, yet the same number was to be sent out against a larger and more strongly defended convoy. Although this promised to be one of those rare unavoidable occasions when the "safety of the force" vanished from those factors taken into account in the planning of the operation, leaving the "success of the sortie" standing paramount, the AOC saw the long odds which we would have to face, and made a characteristic, and to me a quite unforgettable gesture: he threw in the night fighters to our support.

At Luqa there was a flight of night operating Beaufighters detached from a squadron in Egypt. It was these aircraft that I heard patrolling overhead at night while I sat writing letters to England; it was their CO whom the AOC now invited to accompany us on the coming sortie. The invitation and its acceptance involved gestures on both sides, for in the event of a catastrophe the AOC would be hard pressed to defend his action in misemploying the night fighters, while their Flight Commander was agreeing to lead into a daylight action pilots who were accustomed to operating always in darkness, and who would actually be flying aircraft painted in the drab colours of a night camouflage. Yet the request was made and accepted; the night fighters agreed not only without hesitation, but with considerable enthusiasm, to accompany us, with the result that the force which awaited the enemy was the stronger by four 'black' Beaufighters, and immeasurably strengthened in spirit by this unexpected support.

With this decision on the composition of the striking force made, there remained only the position of attack to be chosen. Previously the strong convoys had taken a more direct route than the lightly escorted single ships, and instead of hugging the coastline had steamed straight from Taranto to Cape Geroghambo, thence to Cape Matapan and out into open sea, where they had divided, some ships making for Tobruk, others for Benghazi; their cargoes were too valuable to risk in one basket. Although single ships had recently been showing no consistency in their movements, there seemed no reason to believe that the enemy would change either the route or timetable for the coming convoy, both of which had proved successful on at least two previous occasions: we might have succeeded in creating havoc among the single ships, but we had failed in our efforts against the rare large convoys. The enemy was always loathe to alter a well tried plan until forced to do so, and we could not claim to have done that; also the increasing menace of attack from Egypt, of which the enemy could not be unaware, demanded that the final stage of the journey should be completed at night, a consideration which allowed little variation from route or timetable on the first section of the passage. There was, in fact, no reason to suppose that the convoy would not sail on the same route as before. The merchant ships would leave harbour at night, appear off Cape Maria di Leuca at dawn, and steam south under the strongest available escort in an undisguised and determined attempt to reach North Africa before daylight the next morning.

This then was the enemy's plan which we had to frustrate. Within a span of a few weeks we had attacked in the Gulf of Taranto, off Maria di Leuca and behind Corfu; the northern part of the route, like the west coast of Greece before it, was littered with the wreckage of our attacks. Where should we choose now was the question in our minds as we pored over the chart, in search of some stretch of water in which we might take our adversaries at a disadvantage.

After much consultation with the Group Navigation Officer and the Intelligence firm, a position for the interception was decided; it was chosen not as a particular point on the convoy's route but with reference to the timing of the passage: we would attack at the first opportunity. A study of recent covers of the Greek aerodromes influenced this decision, for they revealed a stronger concentration of aircraft than had ever been observed before. As always, it was essential for the force to avoid an engagement with enemy fighters until the last possible moment, and certainly not before it was at least within sight of the target; in view of this requirement it was obvious that we must attack north of Cape Geroghambo to avoid flying within range of the southern aerodromes, on which fighters would be waiting ready for a warning of our approach. The fighter cover patrolling over the target would be sufficient to occupy our attention without stirring up a hornet's nest of Macchi 202s from Araxos or Navarin.

So we decided to attack the convoy as early as possible during the day, when it would be further from the protection of Greek fighters than at any time before nightfall. If a reconnaissance reported the target's position at dawn, we could reach a point on its track three hours later, by which time it would be steaming in comparatively open sea some twenty miles west of the island of Paxos: that then was the position of attack. Although time and not place had determined the point of interception, no more favourable stretch of water could have been chosen, for off Paxos the convoy would be midway between the nearest aerodromes in southern Italy and western Greece, and at the extreme range of single seaters operating from either country.

With fuel tanks filled and armament loaded, the force stood ready on the aerodromes; the return of every reconnaissance aircraft covering the ports of departure was awaited with anticipation, reports were carefully examined and the photographs subjected to detailed analysis. While a dozen destroyers waited, the lines of enemy transports shortened and cargoes were gradually transferred from the wharves to four large merchant vessels. When on the morning of September 5th, a Spitfire pilot returning from the first reconnaissance reported that the ships had completed their loading, the news was received with satisfaction but without undue excitement: we had waited before.

That evening a final conference was held at Headquarters to review the arrangements for the next day, when it was almost certain that the convoy would sail. The AOC himself presided, the Senior Air Staff Officer was on his right, and around the table sat the squadron commanders who were to take part in the operation: Ross Shore, Adrian Warburton, who as CO of 69 Squadron bore the heavy responsibility of locating the target, the Flight Commander of the night fighters and myself.

Only a few details remained to be settled, but the sequence of the whole operation was quickly reviewed in the light of the latest reconnaissance and intelligence information. Nothing new emerged until half way through the conference, when the analysis of the evening cover of the two ports was brought in. As on a previous occasion when enemy naval activity was expected, a battleship in Taranto had been moved from the inner harbour out into the basin. Whether this movement was another feint, or signified that the convoy would be escorted by a battleship as well as the many destroyers already waiting were questions which could not be answered until the next day. However, the unwelcome presence of a battleship, although it might have an adverse effect on morale, was of no more than academic interest to the planning of the attack; no alteration to our tactics would be required, but the already sufficient difficulties of our task would be increased immeasurably. It was disturbing information.

Whatever escort the convoy might have, the merchant ships were the targets; while the Beaufighters created their usual diversion, the

Beauforts would attempt to ignore the opposition and reach torpedo-dropping range. Almost certainly the four merchant vessels would be found steaming close together, probably in 'two columns', circled overhead by an unknown number of fighters, and surrounded by a strong screen of escort vessels, a force which might now include one or more of the unwilling Taranto battleships.

Normally it was considered necessary to launch at least nine torpedoes against one ship in order to be certain of a hit, but on this occasion it had been decided that the Beauforts should divide into two separate forces of six during the attack, each force taking a separate target. With this arrangement the chances of scoring a hit on one ship were not greatly diminished, while the possibility of hitting two targets remained; it was the best possible compromise in view of the small force at our disposal.

No departure from the usual tactics would be necessary; to our pilots the actual attack would be as straightforward as it would be hazardous; but the finding of this important target was a heavy responsibility for the leader. As always the success of the whole operation would be dependent on the accuracy of the preliminary reconnaissance, to which special attention had already been given.

In the early hours of the morning Adrian Warburton himself was to take off in darkness in a photographic Spitfire, fly on a northerly course towards Naples, and then turn eastwards into the Ionian sea, which he should reach at dawn. We meant, literally, to attack at the first opportunity, hence the night take-off; we were intent on securing surprise, hence the Spitfire's initial northerly track. If the enemy picked up a northbound aircraft on the radio location system, its purpose would not be apparent, for by the time it changed to an easterly course, it would have reached a height beyond radio location range. Although the enemy never showed any signs that he was aware of the activities of our high-flying Spitfires, no precaution could be too great for this operation. Warburton was to ascertain the position of the convoy, assess accurately its course and speed and then make straight for home; our force would take off as soon as this information was received and set course for the target, preceded by one Baltimore in its usual role, and followed by another which was to photograph the strike. It was not thought that the Baltimore flying ahead of the striking force would be permitted to hover around this particular target, waiting for our arrival.

No loophole could be found in these arrangements, and with the AOC appearing completely satisfied, it looked as if the conference was about to break up when the Senior Air Staff Officer handed him a note. During the whispered conversation which followed between the two, we sat around in an awkward silence, uncomfortable and expectant. The thought was passing through the mind of each squadron commander, that the note contained information that the convoy would be escorted by half a dozen battleships, but we found that it was on an altogether different subject that the message had been written.

The whispers ceased, the Staff Officer sat back in his chair, and the AOC made a note on a pad in front of him. Then he looked up, and his eyes looked straight at me.

"Who will be leading your squadron?" he asked, as if it were the most natural question in the world. Taken aback, I hesitated, astounded, and before I could summon a reply he continued: "I have information that your relief will be here tonight; my orders are to send you home as soon after his arrival as possible. One of your Flight Commanders must lead this attack".

To say that these words left me speechless would be to state only a fraction of the truth. My tongue might not move, but my head was spinning: contrary thoughts chased each other round my mind, and no words came; no "Yes", no "Sir". Sensing my emotion, the AOC considerately came to the rescue and said kindly, in an effort to ease my conscience: "Your work is just beginning; at the Air Ministry you will be able to do much more than you have achieved here". The words had a familiar sound, recalling other Headquarters, stifling offices and a desire to escape: I had heard them before.

In a haze of confusion, the four other squadron commanders who would be flying on the next day with their eyes upon me, and the AOC waiting for a reply, I stifled the protest I knew to be useless and perhaps not quite whole-hearted, and suggested in a voice I could not recognise that Hank should lead. The AOC assented, the conference broke up, and I escaped from Headquarters to walk in a bewildered state of mind between the ruined houses of Valletta, trying to collect my thoughts, just as I had done three months before. It was all over; my squadron was to fly away from me; it was over and I was going home. The signal had been received, the AOC himself had said that my relief was on his way, and still it was unbelievable: I was going home.

When Warburton landed at nine o'clock in the morning, the squadron's twelve Beauforts were already lined up on the down wind end of the runway, their engines switched off and the crews standing in a cluster nearby, talking nervously on any subject but the coming operation. The Spitfires were now so successful in intercepting enemy raiders, that it was no longer necessary to wait until the last moment before taxying aircraft out from the protection of the pens. Hank and his observer were with me on the contol tower, the Senior Air Staff Officer drove up just as the Spitfire landed, and together we watched Warburton climb out of his aircraft, stretch himself and then get into the transport waiting to bring him in from the aerodrome.

At the foot of the ladder he looked up and shook his head, a gesture which set our minds at rest: there was no battleship in the convoy. In other respects his report was exactly as expected. Two merchant vessels and six destroyers were steaming south from Brindisi, two other merchant ships escorted by five destroyers were on a south-easterly course from Taranto. The two separate forces which had been observed in harbour were at sea; they would meet off the heel of Italy, proceed south in company until nightfall, when they would separate once more, one to Tobruk, the other to Benghazi. At 30,000 feet, the height from which he had surveyed this scene, Warburton had been unable to estimate the strength of aircraft over the two convoys, but that there were aircraft far beneath him in considerable force he was certain.

Hank asked questions, his observer joined on his chart the rendez-vous off Maria di Leuca with Cape Geroghambo, marked off the line in time intervals, then packed chart, divider and pencil into his bag and descended the ladder. Hank and I followed, and together we drove over the aerodrome to the cluster of crews waiting near the line of aircraft. As he got out of the van Hank grinned and showed two up-turned thumbs, the crews exchanged smiles and conversation became less restrained: no, there were no battleships. The destroyer escort, stronger than we had ever met before, suddenly seemed negligible; the task of penetrating their screen, one of the utmost difficulty, no longer appeared formidable. The battleships which would have turned the sea for twenty miles around into a seething foam and set the skyline on fire as far as the eye could see, and which, worst of all, would have presented such an unavoidable obstruction—obscuring the merchantmen as no number of destroyers could—were not to be present. The operation shed its black cloak and took on an almost festive appearance.

Since I had already briefed the crews, it was only necessary to give some last-minute advice. I recalled how five aircraft had attacked an Italian battle fleet and afterwards landed safely, how the bark was often bigger than the bite; I wished them "good luck" and they disper-sed to the waiting aircraft. The familiar roar of engines starting and warming up would have prevented any conversation between Hank and I as we walked together across the dry aerodrome grass to his aircraft at the head of the line, but neither of us attempted to make a remark. Hank climbed into the cockpit, and as he buckled on his parachute and adjusted the harness I stood on the wing beside him, the propellers whirling as the engines warmed, my hair blown back in their slipstream. It was not until he waved the chocks away from under the wheels in preparation to taxiing out, that a word was spoken.

"Good luck," I said, and made my way along the wing and down the ladder of the aircraft I had grown to love as my only possession, to the grass of the aerodrome, the firm ground which my feet had so often found welcome at the end of an arduous flight. But this time the flight was not at its end but just beginning. Hank's aircraft, which had been mine, taxied slowly out.

And the squadron took off. 'N for nuts' which used to be Tony's aircraft and had made a dozen sorties, Marshal, a Canadian, great hearted fighter but indifferent pilot, forcing his aircraft prematurely into the air, and young Stuart leading a section for the first time; the crews whom I had led and the aircraft on which I had lavished such care, all passed too quickly the point where I stood, accelerating up the runway and rising into the air. And I was not alone there on the aerodrome; beside me were those missing pilots who always came to urge on the survivors whenever they took off to engage the enemy, not a lengthening funeral column in the mourning of despair, but a cheerful band who smiled encouragement. The Beaufighters thundered down the runway, and a ghostly cheer greeted the night fighters as they took off last, their dark shapes incongruous against the daylight sky. Forming up on a great sweep of the Island, the force dived towards the East and vanished over the horizon to make the three hundred mile flight to the target. My squadron flew away.

Dismissing my driver without daring to turn my head, I walked alone out into the middle of the aerodrome, to the highest point of that tiny island which stood in the middle of a great sea. I should have been hardened to the demands of war, but it seemed that I was just as vulnerable as I had been a year, or even two years, before. I never experienced personal fear, but I knew too well the fate which lay in store for those who operated against ships. Steady operations might prevail for weeks, perhaps months, in which casualties although heavy would always be compensated by results. Then some unforeseen disaster would occur, like the inexplicable plague which punctuates history; a battleship would be found where a destroyer was expected, or a large force of enemy fighters would intercept an unsuspecting squadron far from its objective. There was always continual uncertainty about the odds a squadron might suddenly be compelled to face, but it was certain that at least once in his tour of operation, a torpedo pilot would be asked to fly through fire. The situation was accepted, we joked about it, circumstances made it inevitable. For attacks on shipping were still only a small part of the Air Force's effort considered as a whole; bombing, fighting and the anti-submarine campaign were still claiming the greater part of the output of aircraft from British and American factories. Although anti-shipping operations were of more importance in the Mediterranean than any other theatre of war, they were nevertheless a sideline, lying outside the three major offensives with which the RAF was mainly concerned, and no more aircraft could be spared for this small-scale offensive than were absolutely necessary. So while torpedo squadrons in England, the Middle East and India might be of sufficient strength to carry out routine operations, they were always liable to be caught up in a situation developing suddenly which was beyond their capabilities.

We all knew that there would come a time of plenty, when wings might fly out a hundred aircraft strong to attack ships, but meanwhile the torpedo squadrons, waiting patiently for that time to come, formed a thin line hardly capable of withstanding the weight of attack which the enemy might send against it. Desperate sorties were sometimes necessary to save the day, and a squadron which had been carrying out steady operations might suddenly be called upon to sacrifice its aircraft and crews in one splendid endeavour. I had experienced several such incidents, and it was only owing to my good luck that I had survived them, but I could still shudder for those who had still to undergo the ordeal. The opposition which my squadron was facing that day was strong; I knew the dangers too well, I feared for its safety.

Yet the attack did not result in the massacre into which it might so easily have developed. Of the twelve Beauforts which set out only two failed to return, of the sixteen Beaufighters another two were missing, but amazingly the flight of night fighters, whose pilots were flying in unaccustomed daylight in aircraft easily silhouetted in the enemy's sights, sustained no loss. Every single Beaufort that returned was hit; one ship was sunk; Hank was missing.

There had been a haze hanging low over the water when the force sighted land at Cape Geroghambo and turned north-west to meets its target. Haze was unusual on this coastline, where previously we had always found the visibility as good as possible, and in these unfavourable conditions the leader might easily have failed to find the target in a wide stretch of open sea. In fact the Baltimore flying out in advance of the force actually flew on a track from Geroghambo to

Maria di Leuca without finding a trace of those fifteen ships. But the leader's navigation, based on Warburton's report, was deadly accurate and inspite of the failure of the precautionary reconnaissance, the squadron succeeded in keeping its most important appointment.

As it emerged from the haze, the target must have looked almost inspiring in its strength; around the four merchantmen huddled close together in a square steamed the eleven destroyers, ringing the target with a seemingly endless chain in which there appeared to be no gaps. Overhead was one squadron of Macchi single seaters, another of long-range fighters, Junkers 88s, and several flying boats patrolling the waters ahead of the convoy looking for submarines. That the enemy considered the air over these ships important was apparent; it was held by German aircraft almost certainly flown by German pilots.

The ferocity of the air battle can be accurately estimated from one single fact: Adrian Warburton, most brilliant and among the most decorated of pilots, who was flying the photographic Baltimore accompanying the striking force, and incidentally making his second long flight that day on account of his unwillingness to miss an epic sortie, was unable to give his observer a chance to obtain a photograph worth developing. If Warburton was prevented from flying on a steady course for the necessary second, the enemy must have been formidable indeed.

In spite of gallant efforts on the part of the Beaufighters, enemy single seaters could not be prevented from intercepting the Beauforts just as sections were spreading into attacking formation, and not a few pilots found as they approached the target that they were weaving not only to avoid gunfire, but in order to shake Macchis off their tails. One aircraft which returned had been hit simultaneously by shrapnel and machine-gun bullets. Yet in the usual inexplicable manner the destroyer screen was penetrated and pilots came as if miraculously face to face with their targets; torpedoes were aimed and dropped in conditions which defy description and aircraft returned for their crews to tell the tale.

About the fate of the two missing Beauforts there was something mysterious: both were flying normally when last seen. Hank's aircraft had been recognised from the letter on its side making away northward with a great gash in the rudder, but apparently still under control, while one of the pilots who returned safely had flown in formation with the other missing aircraft for fully twenty minutes after the attack. It had flown normally on a steady course due south, a ghost aircraft in which there had been no sign of life from any of the crew, and the pilot of the following aircraft, who had hoped to lead it back to the

Island with perhaps the observer at the controls, reluctantly left it to pursue its inexplicable course southwards. What happened to these two aircraft which made away from the target one north and the other south when the correct course to Malta was westerly, and which flew straight and level at our usual fifty feet above the water, a height which does not permit the slightest inaccuracy at the controls, we never knew: their mystery remained unsolved.

And the aerodrome was strewn with damaged Beauforts. Hit in the undercarriage, unable to use flaps and with control restricted, one after another they staggered in, came drunkenly to rest and then limped or were dragged off the runway on to the grass. Wounded were carried from one aircraft, a dead gunner lifted from the turret of another. Crews who had been unaffected by half a dozen previous sorties became either incomprehensibly adjectival or merely mono-syllabic in their efforts to describe the attack.

Reports were so vague that it was not known definitely until the next day that one of the targets had been hit; a reconnaissance pilot sent out to cover the area returned with the report of a ship, which he recognised as part of the convoy, beached on the mainland not far from the scene of the attack. This was the best news we could possibly hope for, indeed we had been awaiting the reconnaissance with some misgiving, fearing that it might result in a negative report. But one ship out of the four which had left Italy failed to reach North Africa; Rommel's reinforcements: troops, transport or equipment were reduced by a quarter. It seemed worthwhile.

It was amazing that the squadron had escaped so lightly. How often had we lost more than two aircraft from a force half the strength against a target incomparably less formidable. It was just ill fortune, my own rare bad luck, that once again a leader who was flying in my place should have failed to return. The AOC's kind words, my posting signal and the letters asking when I would come home all went for nothing, now that Hank was missing.

I left Malta on September 12th; during the week which intervened between the attack off Paxos and my departure no target appeared within range; movements of enemy ships became normal again and the squadron was given a well deserved respite from the continual waiting at readiness to fly out against some target, big or small. My relief, arriving in time to witness the last stages of organisation of the last attack, had watched the briefing, been present at the receipt of the final reconnaissance report, and had stood beside me as I greeted the returning crews; from the experiences of that one day he had gained more knowledge of operations from Malta than many weeks of the less critical sorties could have given him. Sitting beside me in the office through many hours of that last week he came to know the crews whom I had led and who were now to follow him; he learnt of their occasional weaknesses and of their outstanding strength; he came to know how strongly the staff at Group would stand behind his decisions; he learnt that there was no limit to the help which Ross Shore and his Beaufighters would give. He questioned, as I had done before him the reconnaissance pilots returning from their flights; the Intelligence firm did all for him that they done for me, and he was taken under their wing. Every aid was summoned to prepare him for the time when he would fly out into the hard school of experience.

By the end of the week I had tied all the ends of administration, set my successor on the track along which I had flown, and, not least important, sent in my last recommendations for crews to be decorated. To leave only verbal reports on their prowess in the hope they would be believed would have been to insult my followers and invite incredulity from my successor; even a carefully considered chain of written paragraphs hardly conveyed their worth. Already Ted Strever and his crew had been decorated for their escape from Greece in the captured enemy flying boat. John Creswell, commissioned in the meantime, received the well deserved awards of a DFC and DFM; and Tony Leaning had received a DFC after his departure for Egypt, but many who might have received awards had failed to stay the course and become missing just as their recommendation might have been made.

The squadron's achievements were anonymous, for it was seldom known which torpedo dropped by nine or more attacking pilots hit the target, and normally distinction could only be earned by leadership. The few torpedo squadrons had no published list of top scorers like Fighter Command, nor could their crews ever claim to have completed a high sounding number of sorties like their counterparts flying heavy bombers, for few Beaufort crews made more than six operational flights from Malta. In this dead-end, decorations could hardly possess a significance; it was the sinking of ships and the ability to remain alive to sink just one more ship which occupied our minds. On our khaki shirts were worn no medal ribbons, no wings and often no badges of rank: we just fought on in Malta.

But the last attack deserved some recognition, however transitory, not only for feats of leadership but for the efforts of other pilots, not only for pilots but for other members of the aircrews. The list was long; Hank's name headed it. If he were a prisoner of war, forlorn hope, I asked that he should be rewarded with a DFC. Beauforts in their time have flown out against many imposing targets, ranging from the mighty battleships of two maritime powers to the lethal flak-ship escorted Frisian Island convoys, but never in my experience was an attack so finely led as that from which Hank did not return. Yet in operations from England he had achieved little success in a number of sorties; perhaps the spirit of the Island had been standing beside him on the operations from Malta in which he did so well. I think it must have stood in those summer months beside us all.

On the night I left the Island I was nervous as I had never been before an operational flight, and this nervousness was increased by an uncertainty as to whether the airliner would arrive or not. In the after-noon weather conditions were reported to be unsuitable, later the report was contradicted and a welcome message came that the aircraft had left Gibraltar in time to arrive before midnight. The passage home was never certain; on several occasions pilots who had completed their three months' tour of duty in fighter squadrons had been seen in the Mess, conspicuous in their blue uniforms, on as many as five evenings in succession, waiting for an aircraft which failed to arrive, usually on account of bad weather. I could now appreciate the restlessness which Willie had felt before his departure; with the moment of leaving so near and so assured, it seemed as if it would never come.

In the sanctuary of the Intelligence Office I sat talking to Ponting until a message was received that an aircraft approaching from the west had been picked up by radio location, at which point I went over to the Mess to face what I had been postponing until the last moment, to say "goodbye" to the squadron's crews. None of the favourite Crème de Menthe remained now, but drinks such as they were circu-lated, healths were drunk and old occasions recalled. But beneath the facade of gaiety was a great sadness, for I was a deserter and they were being left. As long minutes passed conversation proceeded more awk-wardly; some were talking with their minds far away, others could not concentrate on what was being said; everyone was listening. When at last the faint sound of an approaching aircraft could be heard, a silence broke out, and it was not until the sound had risen to the roar of engines passing overhead on the circuit that everyone began to talk again, simultaneously, about trivialities. The pilot, conspicuous in the blue uniform among so many in khaki, looked nervously at his watch, laughed, drank again and shook hands, and saying a last goodbye to John Creswell left for the aerodrome, hurriedly. It was not strange that I could look on this scene with such detachment, for the pilot in blue was not me.

A Lockheed '14', similar to the Lodestar in which I had flown as passenger from Malta to Egypt, took me to Gibraltar. Rising from the end of the runway at Luqa it turned westward and climbed gradually over the mountains of Tunisia, the steady note of the twin engines replacing silence by their very monotony. When daylight, approaching from behind, overtook us, we were flying over broken cloud, through which the surface of the sea could occasionally be distinguished appearing to me strangely far below. As the sun rose the tops of these clouds became tinted by its first rays, making them appear like a great herd of pink elephants standing in a pond of some fictitious world, for in the distance to the north the high mountains of Spain were silhouetted against the horizon in colours of green and silver like an illustration to a fairy tale. With the passing of time the gaps between the clouds became less frequent, until finally the sea disappeared from sight completely, and we found ourselves flying over a cloudy ocean, white and soft as newly fallen snow. Suddenly the pilot descended into the cloud layer and flew under its cover between sky and sea, just as a submarine sails between the surface and ocean bed. Then without warning the aircraft emerged not a hundred feet above the waves breaking on a beach, the Rock appeared ahead and the first part of the journey home was over.

Because the weather in the Bay of Biscay was unsuitable for the onward flight, I stayed the night at Gibraltar. At the Rock Hotel I wallowed in an endless hot bath, slept through the morning on the softest of beds, marvelled at the food at lunch and tea, and was incredulous again at dinner. That evening, while music played and couples danced, lights shone out brazenly over the town; compared with Malta the Rock was at peace. As night fell I stood on the terrace outside the hotel watching the lights of Algeciras dance across the bay in front of me, and listening to music being played faintly in the background. It still did not seem possible that I was really on my way home; I seemed to be in another world in which England was a remote planet and Malta a million miles away. As I looked out into the darkness across the water, a crescent moon rose and hung above the mountains of Spain to remind me of other times and old wishes; was it any use wishing now? I wondered; could a wish bring me back my life?

For I had died the death I never dreaded in Malta. I was there that day at the head of the force which set out to face the opposition I knew too well; I flew out from the Island which I had come to love at the controls of my own faithful Beaufort, I flew out never to return. The guns, the fighters and the ever-waiting sea which had claimed Hank, claimed me.

You must have known that I would die in Malta; you must know that it was a ghost which made the journey home, a ghost which was haunted not by the past but by the dark shadow of an unknown future.